Early American Theatre from the Revolution to Thomas Jefferson

Into the Hands of the People

Theater has often served as a touchstone for moments of political change or national definition and as a way of exploring cultural and ethnic identity. Heather Nathans examines the growth and influence of the theater in the development of the young American Republic, from the Revolution through to the election of Thomas Jefferson in 1800. Theater was a dangerous profession in the post-Revolutionary period – for actors, for audience members, and for playwrights. In this book, Nathans discusses the challenges faced by the artists who produced the theater and the people who participated in it. From William Dunlap, author of *André* and the "Father of American Drama," to Susanna Rowson, creator of *Slaves in Algiers*, and one of the first successful female authors on the American stage, she traces the controversy that surrounded the birth of a uniquely American drama.

Unlike many works on the early American theater, this book explores the lives and motives of the people working behind the scenes to establish a new national drama. Some of the most famous figures in American history, from George Washington to Sam Adams, from John Hancock to Alexander Hamilton, battled over the creation of the American theater. The book traces their motives and strategies – suggesting that for many of these men, the question of whether or not Americans should go to the playhouse meant the difference between the success and failure of the Revolutionary mission.

HEATHER S. NATHANS is a member of the faculty and Director of Graduate Studies in the Department of Theater at the University of Maryland, College Park. She is also currently a Non-Resident Fellow at the W.E.B. Du Bois Institute for Afro-American Research at Harvard University. Her articles on the early national theater have appeared in the *Pennsylvania History Journal*, *The New England Theatre Journal*, and *The Journal of American Drama and Theatre*.

General editor

Don B. Wilmeth, *Brown University*

Advisory board

C. W. E. Bigsby, *University of East Anglia*
Errol Hill, *Dartmouth College*
C. Lee Jenner, *Independent critic and dramaturge*
Bruce A. McConachie, *University of Pittsburgh*
Brenda Murphy, *University of Connecticut*
Laurence Senelick, *Tufts University*

The American theatre and its literature are attracting, after long neglect, the crucial attention of historians, theoreticians and critics of the arts. Long a field for isolated research yet too frequently marginalized in the academy, the American theatre has always been a sensitive gauge of social pressures and public issues. Investigations into its myriad of shapes and manifestations are relevant to students of drama, theatre, literature, cultural experience, and political development.

The primary intent of this series is to set up a forum of important and original scholarship in and criticism of American theatre and drama in a cultural and social context. Inclusive by design, the series accommodates leading work in areas ranging from the study of drama as literature to theatre histories, theoretical explorations, production histories and readings of more popular or para-theatrical forms. While maintaining a specific emphasis on theatre in the United States, the series welcomes work grounded broadly in cultural studies and narratives with interdisciplinary reach. Cambridge Studies in American Theatre and Drama thus provides a crossroads where historical, theoretical, literary, and biographical approaches meet and combine, promoting imaginative research in theatre and drama from a variety of new perspectives.

Books in the Series

1. Samuel Hay, *African American Theatre*
2. Marc Robinson, *The Other American Drama*
3. Amy Green, *The Revisionist Stage: American Directors Re-Invent the Classics*
4. Jared Brown, *The Theatre in America during the Revolution*
5. Susan Harris Smith, *American Drama: The Bastard Art*
6. Mark Fearnow, *The American Stage and the Great Depression*
7. Rosemarie K. Bank, *Theatre Culture in America, 1825–1860*
8. Dale Cockrell, *Demons of Disorder: Early Blackface Minstrels and Their World*

Early American Theatre from the Revolution to Thomas Jefferson

Into the Hands of the People

HEATHER S. NATHANS

University of Maryland

CAMBRIDGE
UNIVERSITY PRESS

PUBLISHED BY THE PRESS SYNDICATE OF THE UNIVERSITY OF CAMBRIDGE
The Pitt Building, Trumpington Street, Cambridge CB2 1RP, United Kingdom

CAMBRIDGE UNIVERSITY PRESS
The Edinburgh Building, Cambridge, CB2 2RU, UK
40 West 20th Street, New York, NY 10011–4211, USA
477 Williamstown Road, Port Melbourne, VIC 3207, Australia
Ruiz de Alarcón 13, 28014 Madrid, Spain
Dock House, The Waterfront, Cape Town 8001, South Africa

http://www.cambridge.org

First published 2003

Printed in the United Kingdom at the University Press, Cambridge

Typeface Adobe Caslon 10.5/13 pt.   *System* LATEX 2$_\varepsilon$ [TB]

A catalogue record for this book is available from the British Library

ISBN 0 521 82508 3 hardback

Contents

Illustrations

Tables

Acknowledgments

Throughout my research and writing process, I have been fortunate to enjoy the support of friends, colleagues, and mentors, whose caring and guidance have helped to shape my work.

Between 1997 and 1998, I was privileged to hold research fellowships at the Massachusetts Historical Society, the McNeil Center for Early American Studies, and the American Antiquarian Society. In 2000, I held a Gilder-Lehrman Foundation Fellowship at the New-York Historical Society. The generous support of each of these institutions made my research time both pleasant and productive. In particular, I am indebted to Peter Drummey, Len Travers, and Conrad Edick Wright of the Massachusetts Historical Society, John B. Hench of the American Antiquarian Society, and Joseph Ditta of the New-York Historical Society, who all offered guidance and many helpful suggestions for my research. I am also especially grateful to the staff members at the Massachusetts Historical Society and the American Antiquarian Society who often pointed out shortcuts that saved me hours of searching.

During my year at the McNeil Center, I benefited enormously from the sage counsel of its director, Richard Dunn, and my colleagues who gave many insightful comments on my work. I owe a special thanks to Seth Cotlar, Albrecht Koschnik, and William Pencak.

I have had the very great good luck to encounter two outstanding archivists whose interest in my work and whose willingness to share their time and training led me to two of the key discoveries in my research: William J. Mahannah, of the Law Library of Congress, and Christine McKay of The Bank of New York Archives. Ms. McKay was particularly generous with her time, sifting through material on my behalf and guiding me through it. I owe her a great debt for devoting one entire day to me during my final research trip to New York – even prowling the city streets with me in search of the original lots for the Park Theatre!

My professional colleagues and mentors have been unstinting with their support. I owe thanks to Barbara Grossman and Laurence Senelick in the Tufts University Department of Drama and Dance, Stuart Hecht of the Boston College Theatre Department, and to Catherine Schuler, Frank Hildy, and Daniel Wagner of the University of Maryland Department of Theatre. I am also grateful to the University of Maryland for a summer 2001 Graduate Research Board Grant which enabled me to complete my writing.

I am deeply indebted to Professor John L. Brooke of the History Department at Ohio State University. His own work and his careful mentorship of me while I was his dissertation student at Tufts (and beyond) have taught me a great deal about the kind of scholar and educator I hope to become.

I would also like to extend a special thanks to Don B. Wilmeth and Victoria Cooper, as well as the two anonymous readers who commented on my manuscript. The readers offered insightful comments and criticisms which have helped to shape the final product. Nor could I have wished for more thoughtful guidance in my work than I have received from Cambridge. I also owe sincere thanks to my copy-editor, Joanne Hill, who helped to make the entire editing process a very pleasant and productive one.

In addition to the colleagues and advisors who directly shaped my research, I owe special gratitude to the friends and family who supported me throughout the process. I would like to thank Amanda Nelson, Jennifer Stiles, Kathy Weinstein, Brett Crawford, Renee and Victor Serio, Lisa Harvey, and Jeannine Dolan. They all demonstrated a surprising willingness to hear me lecture about my topic at the slightest provocation.

My husband, Garvan Giltinan, cheerfully submitted to endless readings aloud of various chapters and interminable disquisitions on the creation of national banks and the early American theater. His patience and generosity mean everything to me.

To my father, Sydney Nathans, my brother, Stephen Nathans, and my mother, Elizabeth Studley Nathans, I owe my enthusiasm for the pursuit of history, my earliest training as a writer and thinker, and my passion for research. I could not have completed this work without them.

Introduction

In 1832 the "father of american drama," william dunlap,[1] defined the theater as a "powerful engine" that should be given "into the hands of the people," for the transformation of the American nation. Understanding the properties of this theatrical "engine" requires an analysis of the forces that brought it into being and those groups who disputed its ownership. *Early American Theatre from the Revolution to Thomas Jefferson: Into the Hands of the People* explores the process of nation-building as it was played out via the construction of theaters in what were arguably the most prominent urban centers of the early Republic: Boston, New York, and Philadelphia. *Early American Theatre from the Revolution to Thomas Jefferson* illuminates the social, political, and financial forces that shaped the early national theater, studying the connection between the development of city landscapes, elite neighborhoods, and elaborate playhouses built by men who believed that the theater would cement their cultural authority in the new nation.

Though the struggle to establish a post-Revolutionary theater may seem tangential to the process of nation-building, beneath the "democracy of glee" which supposedly reigned in the theater and the young Republic lurked a deep sense of unease about the political and cultural development of the new nation. In this work, I suggest that the early American theater emerged as a cultural product of conflicting ideas of nationalism – shaped by "the hands of the people" into a uniquely American mold.

My approach to the topic is somewhat unusual. I have focused my study on Boston, Philadelphia, and New York, excluding the southern states where theater encountered comparatively little opposition either prior to or after the Revolution. I have also excluded cities such as Baltimore and Newport, whose theaters were primarily off-shoots of the ones established in other major urban centers. My choice of Boston, New York, and Philadelphia was, in large part, guided by evidence I found which suggested that these three cities envisioned themselves as part of a powerful – if competitive – triumvirate. Certainly they were the most economically powerful, and, one might contend, the most intellectually and culturally advanced cities in the new nation. Over and over again, in the popular press and the private correspondence of the period, citizens compared the accomplishments of one city to the other – whether it was Boston to Philadelphia, or Philadelphia to New York. They maintained a keen sense of competitiveness with each other, and saw their progress of civic and cultural development as a means of "one-upping" their neighbors. This competition grew especially fierce at times – for example, when the nation's capital moved from New York to Philadelphia, or when Boston opened its new playhouse within the same two-week period as Philadelphia. Yet these three cities were linked by more than a superficial wish to outvie each other in their new theaters. They deliberately modeled their civic and cultural ventures upon those of their neighbors, invoking their rhetoric, employing their political strategies, mimicking their patterns of association. For example, it is not coincidence that the Boston and New York Tontines evolved during approximately the same period, or that the New York tontiners were able to learn from the mistakes and failures of their Boston neighbors. Nor is it a coincidence that Boston's pro-theater faction applied to Philadelphian Samuel Breck for an account of how the Dramatic Association in that city overturned its anti-theater law.

Ties of blood and business also formed strong bonds among these three communities, as families intermarried and as business partners formed an extended network of associates that sustained (or occasionally menaced) the post-war economy. Their names recur in intriguing patterns on boards of land development companies, stock companies, and banks. These three groups of Boston, Philadelphia, and New York cohorts quickly became interdependent, and when the national economy took a downturn in the late 1790s and land speculation and stock bubbles burst, it impacted all three groups – and the theaters they had created.

Perhaps most importantly, the communities that form the focus of this study seem to have identified a similar "use" for the theater: to cement their cultural authority in the new nation. Shorn of patriotic rhetoric, the motives of each group focus on obtaining and sustaining power in the new nation. Thus the outrage of the Boston Tontine Association at the ungrateful audience who failed to appreciate their theater. Thus the furor in New York over who should have the right to stage plays in the new nation, and whose political agenda should dominate. And thus, the ongoing dispute in Philadelphia about the "anti-democratic" structure of its luxurious playhouse.

Additionally, by focusing on Boston, Philadelphia, and New York, I undertake a detailed examination of the trends that shaped the early American theater. Such a study allows me to situate theater in its social and political context. For example, the hotly contested Boston theater arose amidst bitter debates over not only the propriety of theatrical entertainments, but the establishment of the Boston Tontine Association and a wealthy urban neighborhood known as the Tontine Crescent. The Philadelphia theater was menaced by efforts of Pennsylvania conservatives to impose ruinous taxes – a strategy aimed not only at the theater, but at the much hated Bank of North America which had financed it. The New York theater had its origins in the animosity between Tammany Society Democratic-Republicans and old-style Federalists who resented the appropriation of their elite entertainments.[2]

A reader may well wonder at the exclusion of the southern theaters from this circuit. I would suggest that both pre- and post-war patterns of political, cultural, and economic development in the southern states differed markedly from those of the Mid-Atlantic regions. While the southern states of the early Republic imagined themselves as part of the same national community as their fellow citizens to the north, they faced widely different challenges in the *formation* of their post-war communities. The different economic base (including the growing reliance on slavery), the close pre-war ties to the culture and church of Great Britain, as well as the more diffuse political structure of the South make an intriguingly different model for the development of an imagined American community in the playhouse, and one that will bear investigation in further research. Susanne K. Sherman's *Comedies Useful: Southern Theatre History, 1775–1812* offers an excellent overview and wonderfully detailed accounts of theatrical entertainments in South Carolina, Virginia, Maryland, North Carolina, and Georgia during the early national period. Sherman's study is an excellent source for scholars pursuing a study of the southern theater. Her work provides new insights into the trials of sustaining theatrical activities in regions still struggling to establish themselves in the early post-war period.[3] By the mid-nineteenth century, however, the South presents a better basis for cultural, political, and social comparison to the Mid-Atlantic and New England regions, as William and Jane Pease suggest in *The Web of Progress: Private Values and Public Styles in Boston and Charleston, 1828–1843*.[4]

I have confined the bulk of my study to the period between the Revolution and Jefferson's election in 1800. Jefferson's election wrought a substantial change in the American theater, marking the transition to a more "democratic" drama, and undermining the cultural hegemony established by the theaters' founders after the Revolution. My interest lies in the transitional period between the war and Jefferson's election, when the nation was still in the process of defining its political, financial, and cultural goals.

In this search, I am enormously indebted to theater historians Don Wilmeth and Christopher Bigsby, Jeffrey H. Richards, Joseph Roach, Jared Brown, Barry Witham, and Bruce McConachie, who, over the past decade, have begun the exciting task of re-examining the American theater in the broader context of the formation of American national identity. Together with the aid of such other American theater luminaries as Tice L. Miller, Gary A. Richardson, Mary C. Henderson (among others), Don Wilmeth and Christopher Bigsby have compiled the impressive and award-winning *Cambridge History of American Theatre*, which offers a broad overview of American theater history, encompassing topics as diverse as playhouses, performance styles, and popular entertainment. Jeffrey H. Richards, author of *Theatre Enough: American Culture and the Metaphor of the World Stage*, and *Mercy Otis Warren*, and editor of the anthology *Early American Drama*, has explored the connections between politics and the playhouse in the development of early American theater. Jared Brown's *Theatre in America During the Revolution* links the phenomenon of British military theatricals to the perception of the post-Revolutionary theater. Barry Witham has edited a documentary history, *Theatre in the Colonies and United States, 1750–1915*, which offers a wide-ranging collection of documents, reviews, and engravings, and covers every topic from theater management to antitheatrical protests. Editors J. Ellen Gainor and Jeffrey H. Mason draw connections between the nascent American theater and national identity in *Performing America: Cultural Nationalism in American Theater*. In addition to these recent works, over the past five years articles in journals ranging from *Theatre Survey* to *The New England Theatre Journal* to *The Journal of American Drama and Theatre* have re-examined the drama of the early national period, generally focusing on the difficulty in establishing a successful post-Revolutionary theater.

My work necessarily owes much to those who have come before, yet I argue that the struggle to establish an early national theater must be seen as part of the complicated process of what historian Richard Buel has termed "securing the Revolution," of stabilizing a country still deeply divided over financial and political issues. Such an examination requires an exploration across disciplinary lines, into the field of early American history.

I situate my research in the framework erected by political and cultural historians such as Gordon Wood, Gary Nash, Ann Fairfax Withington, Richard L. Bushman, Michael Warner, and David Waldstreicher, all of whom have sought to ground the birth of the new nation in the social, political, and economic conditions of its formation. In particular, Withington's *Toward A More Perfect Union: Virtue and the Formation of American Republics*, Bushman's *The Refinement of America: Persons, Houses, Cities*, and Waldstreicher's *In the Midst of Perpetual Fetes: The Making of American Nationalism, 1776–1820*, explore the process through which British cultural traditions were appropriated and transformed into something uniquely American. Since Americans inherited the theatrical traditions of the "Old World," their work has been vital in framing my discussion of the post-Revolutionary response to the theater, and the efforts of its founders to "Americanize" it, while simultaneously aping British models. Rosemarie Bank, David Grimsted, and Bruce McConachie have all produced impressive interpretations of the development of nineteenth-century American theater. Their works offer a synthesis of cultural, social, and economic history. Yet, up to this point, no one has applied these methods to a study of theater in the early national period. I hope that *Early American Theatre from the Revolution to Thomas Jefferson* will offer the reader the detailed historical background and analytical framework necessary to understand the development of the early national theater.

Many traditional studies of the post-Revolutionary theater emphasize literary criticism or performance analysis, neglecting the crucial social, political, and financial context for theatrical activity. Others dismiss the early national period as a time of little significant theatrical entertainment, suggesting that a real "American" theater did not emerge until the early nineteenth century. Contemporary cultural historians have not yet incorporated theater into their studies of the early national period, focusing instead on the "theatricality" of public demonstrations and displays, without questioning the possible connections to events taking shape in the playhouse.

My work focuses on the broader agendas of those men who believed the theater's existence was vital to the construction of a civilized society, and who thought that the development of theatrical entertainments in the new nation would both demonstrate America's cultural status to the watching nations of Europe, and establish what they labeled a "school of Republican virtue" to disseminate political ideology to the theater-going public.

I explore the challenges that these men faced in creating a sense of community among an otherwise disparate population – one fractured along lines of class and political divisions. The struggle to establish an early national theater can be seen as part of the complicated process of "securing the Revolution," of stabilizing a country still deeply divided over financial and political issues.

Chapter 1 offers an overview of the pre-Revolutionary perception of theater in Boston, New York, and Philadelphia. The battle waged between pro- and anti-theater factions began almost with the founding of the colonies, and lasted up until the time of the Revolution, when the Continental Congress imposed a ban on all "extravagance and dissipation," including theatrical entertainments. Examining the history of colonial attitudes towards the theater may shed light on its tenuous post-war status, and may suggest the ways in which theatrical entertainments were inextricably intertwined with certain groups' political and social agendas. Prior to the Revolution, resistance to theatrical activities had been largely a subject for debate between factions which opposed the theater on religious grounds and elite groups which supported theater as a tangible link with British culture. As the eighteenth century progressed, and the populations of Pennsylvania, Massachusetts, and New York grew increasingly diverse, pro- and anti-theater debates reflected growing schisms among colonial communities. As it would later in the post-war period, the theater often became linked to an elitist agenda of financial and political reform, and thus theater-going became identified with partisan politics and factionalism. As the break with Britain approached, resistance to theater was increasingly identified with concepts of "republican virtue." Examining the pre-war history of the theater in Boston, Philadelphia, and New York may illuminate the process through which anti-theatrical sentiment, originally grounded in religious bias, gradually became embedded in the struggle to sever all political, financial, and cultural ties with Great Britain.

In chapter 2, I explore the battle to bring an "American" theater to post-Revolutionary Boston, Philadelphia, and New York. I suggest that the struggle exemplified the transition of social and political authority in the early Republic. Power shifted from the "Old Revolutionaries," resistant to the rise of factions and corporations, to a new post-war elite, intent on launching a system of banks, corporations, and cultural institutions that would place them on the world stage. The first years of the Republic witnessed a struggle to determine whose national and cultural vision of America would prevail, and by what means.

In this chapter, I also investigate the rise of America's early banks and stock corporations, suggesting that the same men who pursued sweeping financial reforms (amassing considerable personal wealth in the process) mounted a challenge to the established leaders of American society. Through a complex network of financial and personal connections, these men waged a successful campaign to re-establish theatrical entertainments in the new nation. By dint of persuasion, cajoling, subtle blackmail, and sometimes outright lawbreaking, they overturned or sidestepped wartime anti-theatrical legislation.

Though the development of stock companies and banks may seem to have little connection with the creation of theaters, I argue that *without* the aid of their privately sponsored companies and banks, the rising post-war elite would not have had the requisite authority to impose their cultural agenda on an often resistant population. For example, the stockholders of the Bank of North America and several of the land development companies in Pennsylvania were among the primary supporters of the post-Revolutionary theater. They used their economic and political influence to manipulate groups who opposed the theater, issuing oblique (and sometimes direct) threats to the parties that resisted them. In one instance, they threatened the Quakers' political faction, promising to block the passage of laws that would improve the treatment of Quakers, if the Quakers continued in their campaign against the theater. Their threats appear to have worked, as the Quaker outcry subsequently diminished. In Boston, the shareholders of the Boston Tontine Association were lampooned by one angry newspaper editor as the "Tontine Gentry," and their attempts to use the profits from their life insurance company to build a new theater and new elite neighborhood came under fire from both the public and the state government. New York's financial speculators, most notably William Duer, brought the state to the brink of ruin through their unbridled and often unprincipled transactions. Indeed, between 1792 and 1793, they created a financial crisis that imperiled New York's ability to build a new post-war playhouse.

Chapter 3 chronicles the early successes of the Boston and Philadelphia theaters, as well as the early failures. While New York struggled to regain financial stability in the wake of the 1793 crash, and "made do" with Lewis Hallam's shopworn entertainments in the John Street Theatre, Boston and Philadelphia entered a new age of American entertainments. By 1794, the combination of money, influence, and determination had prevailed, and both Boston and Philadelphia opened new and luxurious playhouses. The founders anticipated a "democracy of glee" in their first season. Every aspect

of the theaters had been carefully planned to ensure that they would become monuments to their founders' cultural sophistication. In this chapter,
I discuss the first season of the Boston and Philadelphia theaters, as well
as the high hopes that their founders entertained for them. I also discuss
the John Street Theatre's efforts to keep pace with its more lavish competitors, suggesting that without the financial and intellectual investment
of New York's reigning elite, its theatrical entertainments remained adrift –
an ineffectual cultural or political tool for its post-war audiences.

The rhetoric that surrounded the creation of the Boston and Philadelphia
theaters points to an intriguing problem that faced the theaters' founders.
On the one hand, they wanted to build theaters that would be uniquely
"American," that would serve as "schools of Republican virtue." The
prologue to Royall Tyler's *The Contrast*, the best-known play of the early
national period, asks, "Why should our thoughts to distant countries roam/
When each refinement may be found at home?" The theaters' founders
claimed that their theaters would inculcate truly democratic principles in
their audiences, and that their theaters would remain untainted by
European vice. Yet, even while they expressed their disdain for the "corrupt"
British theater, they hastened to ape British styles of architecture and
design in their playhouses, importing scenery, curtains, even chandeliers
from England. Moreover, they felt a keen sense of competition not only
with each other, but with European theaters as well. Even as they struggled
to define their playhouses as "American," they wanted to ensure that they
would match or surpass the best that London had to offer.

This tension between the desire to create homespun arts and the yearn-
ing for European splendor and parade permeated the playhouse and its
audience. Some clamored for patriotic productions, while others demanded
the latest plays from England. Wealthy patrons grew annoyed when denied
private, locked boxes like the fashionable ladies of Europe, while middle-
class patrons objected to being segregated from the "well born" in their
expensive seats. The Philadelphia newspaper *Aurora* praised the Boston
theater for its production of *Gustavus Vasa*, a well-known, pro-democratic
play, while the Boston theater founders chastised their manager for failing
to produce commercially viable material. In chapter 3, I explore both the
expectations and disappointments that the theaters' founders faced in their
first season, suggesting that the confusion they encountered was a reflection
of the nation's own ambivalence about its emerging identity and its ongoing
relationship with the "mother country." I also explore the founders' new
dilemma: the invasion of party politics and class rivalry into the playhouse.

I examine the impact of theater riots on the founders' vision – and the way in which their "democracy of glee" fell under the onslaught of partisan demonstrations. Indeed, for many, the theater became the ideal site to display party loyalty, and the popular press took up the cry. Reports of uprisings in the theater spread up and down the country; often citizens of one city would respond to reports of violence in another – either with a show of support in their own playhouse, or with a public demonstration of approval for the beleaguered theater managers caught in the middle of the struggle.

For example, in one particularly violent incident, members of the Boston audience assaulted the orchestra for refusing to play a particular patriotic song, hurling pieces of broken glass into the pit. The riot made the papers in both New York and Philadelphia, and drew a wide range of responses. In other cases, riots were deliberately planned to embarrass political figures who would be attending the theater. I argue that such incidents demonstrated to both founders and audiences how far they were from "securing the Revolution," and how unstable America's post-war identity remained. As scenes of political disharmony were enacted among the playhouse audience, it became increasingly difficult for the theaters' founders to maintain the fiction of a "school of Republican virtue."

Chapter 4 juxtaposes the political instability of the playhouse with the growing class awareness in the new nation. In this chapter, I suggest that as artisans and small merchants sought access to opportunity, they fundamentally transformed the shape of American theater. In particular, the struggle to create a viable American cultural product became an issue that penetrated every social class. The mechanics and artisans vaunted the gifts of their playwrights, John Murdock and John Daly Burk, while the merchant elite touted the talents of their "American Garrick," William Charles White. Not only did the class schisms produce new (and competing) styles of drama, they produced competing spaces as well. The Boston mechanics, snubbed by the Tontine Gentry, invested in their own playhouse, the Haymarket, and the Philadelphia mechanics, excluded from the city's elite entertainments, transferred their loyalty to more "democratic" entertainments, including the circus.

Chapters 3 and 4 focus primarily on the founding of the Boston and Philadelphia theaters, suggesting that they grew simultaneously with a new, post-Revolutionary elite, and that they emerged as an effort to mold the cultural identity of the new nation. My approach for chapter 5, the chapter on the New York theater, will be somewhat different. Much has been written of the city's early national theater, including the first-hand accounts of

both the theater's premiere actor, John Hodgkinson, and one of the nation's foremost managers and playwrights, William Dunlap.[5] Additionally,
George Odell's *Annals of the New York Stage* and Joseph Ireland's *Records of
the New York Stage* offer a comprehensive discussion of season offerings and
company history.[6] Thus I will not attempt to duplicate their accounts of the
city's theater, or to provide a year-by-year chronology of its development.
Instead, I will focus on one of the most puzzling aspects of New York's
post-Revolutionary theater: its origin. In the summer of 1794, a group of
men (whose identities and affiliations have remained largely unknown and
un-investigated), announced that they were taking subscriptions for a new
theater. *Four years later*, they opened the Park Street playhouse. Little to
nothing has heretofore been known of the identities of these men, why they
decided, after more than a decade of enjoying plays at the John Street house,
that they needed their own theater, or the reason for the long delay between
the announcement of their plans and the opening of their new playhouse.
Chapter 5 will focus on the tensions that produced a rupture in the John
Street Theatre, the network of social and economic alliances that backed
the prospect of a new theater, and the struggle that its founders encountered in their efforts to transform a cultural project into a viable financial
venture.

Having built their lavish playhouses, the founders turned to the question
of what should go *in* them. Initially, the theaters were populated with British
managers, actors, and scripts. But increasingly, American audiences demanded plays and performers that would reflect their own "native genius."[7]
Though mine is not a study of eighteenth-century dramatic literature, in
each chapter I try to trace the development of professional theater and drama
in the early national period, as those developments relate specifically to the
theaters or historical moment in question. The best-known dramatists of
the period, Mercy Otis Warren, Susanna Rowson, William Dunlap, Judith
Sargent Murray, and Royall Tyler, have all received much scholarly attention. In my study, I focus on the less well-known "native geniuses" such as
John Murdock and William Charles White whose successes and failures,
I argue, reveal much about the development of our early national drama.
Each of their respective careers illuminates the challenges native authors
and performers faced in establishing themselves among their European
rivals. Through their work I explore the development of a nascent American cultural aesthetic. I also trace the efforts of the Federal Street, Chestnut
Street, and Park Theatre managers to accommodate American audiences
by cutting or altering popular British scripts (excising references to the

aristocracy). For example, Thomas Wignell, manager of Philadelphia's Chestnut Street Theatre, showed a particular gift for "Americanizing" British plays to suit popular taste. Theater manager John Hodgkinson, on the other hand, made his alterations so clumsily that Boston newspapers ridiculed his transparent attempts to curry favor with American playgoers. I suggest that the alterations, and the audience's response to the changes, can offer insight into the changeable political climate of the early Republic.

By the end of the eighteenth century, Boston, Philadelphia, and New York had created playhouses that transformed their civic and cultural landscapes. Unfortunately for the theaters' founders, the end of the century also brought times of increasing economic distress and many of the founders lost the hard-won fortunes that had catapulted them into positions of power only a few years before. Chapter 6 traces the economic and political crises of the end of the century, linking the worsening political divisions and exploding stock "bubbles" to the troubled conditions in the playhouse. I suggest that by the end of John Adams's presidency, the theater reflected the divided state of the nation. In Boston, a rival artisan theater had emerged to challenge the elite one on Federal Street. In Philadelphia and New York, the theaters faced competition from traveling circuses that provided more novel diversions. Only Washington's death – an event commemorated in the New York, Boston, and Philadelphia theaters – reunited the nation in the imagined community of the playhouse. His death marked the end of an era in the early national theater, and left theater patrons and proprietors struggling to answer what role the theater would play in the new century.

While the founders' "democracy of glee" ultimately assumed quite a different shape from what they initially envisioned, nevertheless, by the end of the eighteenth century, they had firmly established the place of theater in America. In this final chapter, I chronicle the "downfall" of the theaters' first supporters, suggesting that in their place rose a new generation of theater-goers, primed to take the powerful engine "into the hands of the people."

The reality of America's early national theater was far different from Dunlap's utopian vision of a democratic refuge for the drama. Throughout the early national period, opposing factions disputed the legitimacy of theatrical entertainments, and not even the theater's most ardent advocates could agree in whose hands final authority over theatrical activities should rest. The theater's supporters and detractors alike recognized it as a powerful tool for influencing thought and for disseminating visions of American national identity. But could it do so objectively? Democratically? Could a theater, run by an elite group of wealthy urban men (as most of the early national theaters were), fairly and accurately represent its audience? Or would it use its position to exercise undue influence on an innocent public?

At the heart of the pro- and anti-theater debates of the post-war era lay complex questions about the formation of American nationalism, and about who should most properly guide the fledgling nation in its cultural, political, and economic progress. To understand the "powerful engine" of the early national theater, we must understand the factions that brought it into being, as well as those that disputed its ownership. My task is two-fold: to suggest the ways in which post-Revolutionary social, political, and economic factors influenced the rise of the American theater; and to examine the theatrical product that these forces produced.

I

Extravagance and dissipation: opposition and support for the colonial theater

Post-war disputes over the theater in Boston, New York, and Philadelphia reflected larger political, cultural, and financial debates playing out in the new nation, but the theater debates did not spring into being full-blown with the Treaty of Paris. On the contrary, controversy over the appropriateness of theatrical activity had plagued the colonies – Massachusetts and Pennsylvania in particular – for more than a century prior to the Revolution.[1] Examining the nature of the pre-Revolutionary theater debates, as well as the ways in which the theater issue was transformed by the Revolution, may illuminate the nature of the post-war struggle, and help to explain how the simple act of attending a theatrical performance could become a highly significant social and political statement.

The battle waged between pro-and anti-theater factions began almost with the founding of the colonies, and lasted up until the time of the Revolution. Though it is not within the scope of this study to offer a minute examination of the century-long history of theatrical controversy in Massachusetts, New York, and Pennsylvania, an overview of the important events in each case, and of how these events reflected larger trends in colonial society, may shed light on the post-war situation, and may suggest the ways in which theatrical entertainments were inextricably intertwined with certain groups' political and social agendas. It is important to note that though the names and faces may change from the pre- to the post-war period, certain strategies and justifications for supporting or opposing the theater were developed before the Revolution, and re-surfaced in the post-war period.

Prior to the war, resistance to theatrical activities had been largely a subject for debate between factions who objected to the theater for religious reasons, and elite groups, who supported the theater as a link with "civilized" British culture. To members of religious sects, such as the

New England Puritans, the Pennsylvania Quakers, and the New York Presbyterians, the theater threatened to subvert their plans for establishing ideal societies. To members of the pre-war elite in Boston, New York, and Philadelphia, theatrical entertainments were a necessary status symbol, signifying their importance not only within the colony, but as part of the larger Atlantic world. As the eighteenth century progressed, and the populations of Pennsylvania, New York, and Massachusetts became increasingly diverse (not only in religious faith, but in social and economic spheres as well), pro- and anti-theater debates reflected growing schisms among the colonial communities. As in the post-war period, colonial theatrical entertainments often became linked to an elitist agenda of financial and political reform, and therefore theater-going became identified with partisan politics and factionalism. As the break with Britain approached, resistance to theater was increasingly identified with religious morality, and with concepts of "republican virtue." Examining the pre-war history of anti-theatrical opposition may illustrate the process through which anti-theatrical sentiment, originally grounded in religious bias, gradually became enmeshed in the struggle to sever all political, financial, and cultural ties with Great Britain.

A "torrent of debauchery": anti-theatricalism in colonial Pennsylvania[2]

While America was still under the dominion of Great Britain, a total theatrical ban was almost impossible to effect, as the Quakers found to their sorrow. William Penn had included an anti-theater law in his original 1682 Frame of Government for the Pennsylvania Colony, which declared playgoing "an offense against God [which incited] people to Rudeness, Cruelty, Looseness, and Irreligion."[3] As a colony of the British Empire, however, Pennsylvania could not pass legislation into law without the crown's approval. Because the British government tolerated theatrical entertainments, they refused to countenance Pennsylvania's anti-theater stance. The crown overturned William Penn's initial effort and repeatedly rebuffed all Quaker attempts to ban theatrical entertainments. (Attempts in 1700, 1706, and 1711 were all overruled by the crown or Pennsylvania proprietary governors.) Ironically, these laws were proposed and overturned before "even a glimmer of theatrical activity had appeared"[4] in Pennsylvania, and before the establishment of a wealthy, resident, non-Quaker elite that could have demanded or financed professional theatrical entertainments.

Though the Quakers had a strong religious motivation in trying to prevent the establishment of theatrical activities within the colony, the anti-theatrical issue in Pennsylvania was shaped by other considerations as well. Quakers had dominated the colony in its early days, both politically and socially. However, by the 1720s, as the colony continued to grow, prosper, and diversify, other local factions moved into power, challenging the Quakers' traditional authority. For example, in 1723, the Quakers appealed unsuccessfully to the city's Anglican mayor, James Logan, to force the removal of a band of strolling players that had recently come to Philadelphia.[5] Logan was no friend to the Quakers, having described them in 1704 as "unfit for Government by themselves and not much better with others."[6] Logan's response to the Quakers' demands in 1723 reflected both his contempt for them as a society, and his unwillingness to challenge the pillars of British culture in America: "There is an expectation that I (as Mayor) should exert the authority to suppress their acting. But as the Governor himself resorts thither [to theatrical entertainments], I can by no means think it advisable to embroil myself."[7] It is hardly surprising that Logan would choose to support the royal government over a meddlesome and often quarrelsome sectarian group whose power seemed on the wane. As Gary Nash has noted, the Quakers' inability to marshal successful resistance to Logan's and the governor's politics suggests that by the 1720s "the social and religious leaders of Quaker society were powerless to extend their control into the secular sphere."[8] That secular sphere included a growing number of non-Quaker Pennsylvanians, who were rapidly replacing much of the traditional Quaker leadership.[9] By 1756, the Quakers had largely withdrawn from politics, leaving the field open to the Anglicans and Presbyterians who dominated the Pennsylvania General Assembly.

Yet, as the Quakers relinquished their political authority, they increased what might be termed a "grass roots" opposition to theatrical entertainments. For the first time, they actively cultivated allies outside their sect. In 1759 David Douglass, manager of the Hallam-Douglass Company, announced plans for a new theater in Society Hill.[10] The Quakers joined with German Lutherans, Presbyterians, and Baptists to protest the new theater. According to Harrold Shiffler, more than 200,000 members of these four religious communities signed anti-theatrical petitions for the governor.[11] There were two significant transformations in the Quakers' tactics with the 1759 petition that distinguished it from their earlier, unsuccessful efforts. The first was their decision to forge connections with outside sects in order to achieve their goals. The second was their choice to couch the terms of the petition in patriotic as well as religious terms, citing the exigencies of the French and Indian War (1754–1763) as reason to "render the Entertainments of the Stage peculiarly Improper at this time."[12]

Though the Quaker victory of 1759 was short-lived (the law, which had been passed on January 1, 1760, was repealed on September 2, 1760), it nevertheless taught the Quakers two important lessons: to accommodate the needs of other sects and factions in order to achieve their own goals, and to appeal to patriotic as well as religious sentiment. Only six years later, in 1766, when Douglass proposed building a second and even larger theater, the Quakers quickly mobilized all sympathetic religious leaders, and presented a petition "signed by upwards of Six Hundred of the Freemen of the Several Religious Societies of Philadelphia."[13]

Despite the best efforts of the Quakers and their associates, however, theatrical performances came to Philadelphia, growing from the unsteady trickle begun in 1723 with rope dancing, puppet shows, and magic lanterns, to a more respectable flow in 1749–1750, with the arrival of the Murray-Kean Company. These entertainments were attended by members of the royal government and by the growing Philadelphia Anglican elite. A new elite group had come to power in the late 1750s, as the Quakers were completing their withdrawal from colonial politics. This Anglican-dominated group of merchants and businessmen "had accumulated tremendous wealth through mercantile activity and buying and selling land."[14] Though there were many wealthy men among the Quaker population, the Anglican elite were more willing to invest their money in the trappings of wealth, including fine houses, carriages, and displays of cultural sophistication, such as playgoing and dancing assemblies. As Stephen Brobeck has noted, "members of the non-Quaker elite were considered by most Philadelphians to possess a great deal of social status,"[15] status derived in part from high visibility and from participation in various social and voluntary organizations. Membership in groups such as the Philadelphia Dancing Assembly, St. John's Masonic Lodge, and the Mount Reagle Fishing Company offered the non-Quaker elite the opportunity to socialize and form alliances within a relatively small and well-regulated social sphere.[16] The Dancing Assembly, which also played a significant social role *after* the Revolution, was one of the most important and prominent elite organizations in Philadelphia. Founded in 1748, the Assembly aped the habits of the British gentry, since "following the British model, one important attainment of any colonial gentleman or lady was grace of manner, evidenced in good part by skills in dancing."[17] The Assembly's members were drawn from "a group of gentlemen who led the city's political, professional, and mercantile life."[18] Participating families included the Willingses, Binghams, Mifflins, Shippens, and Plumsteads (owners of the site used as a theater in 1749). The Dancing Assembly offered the elite "opportunities for social intercourse and display," and these men subsequently became Philadelphia's leaders of commerce and culture. Such activities "became crucial to the establishment of power, to the attainment of rise in class stature, and to the facilitation of political and commercial business."[19]

But the new elite were not content with homegrown cultural and social diversions. As Richard Bushman observes, in colonial America, "stamped on every form of genteel culture was the mark of its origin in Europe and more specifically in aristocratic English society."[20] William Dunlap explicitly connected the rise of Philadelphia's pre-war elite with the successful introduction of English theatrical entertainments into Philadelphia. He described the Anglican elite as the "men who changed the city of Penn from its drab-colored austerity to the bland and polished amenity of the many-colored receptacle of literature and fine arts," suggesting that the gentry promoted British theater within the colony because having been "accustomed to the representations of the dramatists in their native land, [they] longed to renew the associations of their youth."[21] This gentry approached the Hallam-Douglass Company first in 1754 to encourage them to visit Philadelphia. That one season of twenty-four plays housed in Plumstead's warehouse whetted their appetites for a more permanent and luxurious playhouse, and a real theatrical season.[22]

With the royal government's support and the Anglican elite's eager patronage, David Douglass (new leader of the company after the death of Lewis Hallam, Sr.) built two theaters in the Quaker City. The first was the small Theatre on Society Hill that aroused the Quakers' wrath. Built in 1759, and used for only one season, it was insufficient for the needs of its patrons; the second was the larger Southwark Theatre, which opened in 1766 and remained Philadelphia's primary playhouse for the next twenty-eight years. The Southwark Theatre cost approximately £600, and at an impressive fifty feet wide and ninety-five feet long was the largest theater in the colonies.[23] Divided into pit, boxes, and gallery, the building resembled, in basic structure if not luxurious appointments, the playhouses of London. Though the exterior and interior fixtures of the building were plain, Douglass lavished money on expensive costumes and elaborate scenery imported from London. For example, in 1766 Douglass commissioned from England "a most excellent set of scenes done by Mr. Doll [Nicholas Thomas Dall], principal scene painter at Covent Garden House." As Brooks McNamara observes, "By the period of the John Street [New York] and the Southwark, Douglass had acquired enough equipment to accommodate his audiences with a fair degree of spectacle." If the Southwark Theatre was not an *exact* replica of those in Britain, it "could at least approximate some of the less difficult trickwork employed at Covent Garden and Drury Lane."[24] On stage audiences could see old favorites like *George Barnwell*, or the latest imports from London, like *Love in a Village* (1762).[25]

Although the theater had gained a foothold in Philadelphia society by the 1760s, it remained a volatile issue. A 1767 review of *Love in a Village*, which appeared in the *Pennsylvania Gazette*, offered a subtle commentary on the status of theater in the Philadelphia community. The writer praised the work, as a "pleasing" play, performed "beyond expectation," but at the same time he cautioned the Hallam-Douglass Company about the need for special sensitivity in performing for a society still divided over the merits of theatrical entertainments. The author, a "Gentleman Contributor," warned the actors that "one indecent, unguarded, ill-judged expression, will do them inconceivable mischief in this country." He suggested that the theater's supporters were relying on the actors not to disprove the beneficial properties of theatrical entertainments: "If they are prudent in their choice of plays, the rational entertainment must and will succeed, agreeable to the highest wishes of those who are concerned in it."[26] Though the author's gentle warning may seem to refer solely to Quaker and Presbyterian opposition to the theater, it is possible that his caution extends beyond the moral to the political.

By the late 1760s, the Hallam-Douglass Company could offer the Philadelphia elite fashionable entertainments which resembled those they might have seen at "home" in England. Yet just as the theater seemed to gain a permanent foothold in colonial society, its future was thrown into doubt by events outside the playhouse. By the mid-1760s, political tensions were increasing between the colonists and the English government. A series of bitter struggles over the Stamp Act, the Sugar Act, and the Townshend Act were causing the colonists to question the nature of their dependency on Britain.

As part of that process, the theater came under fire as an expensive British luxury that sapped American resources and kept people from focusing on the growing political crisis between the colonies and the mother country. As Peter Davis points out, by the 1760s "[t]heatre, like all other British commodities, had become politicized."[27] Thus the reviewer who cautioned the Hallam-Douglass Company to beware of how they presented material in "this country" may have been aware of the potential of plays to rouse anti-British sentiment at a time of economic difficulty and political uncertainty. Indeed, only a few weeks after the review of *Love in a Village*, the House submitted a petition to Governor John Penn, which protested the theater as "too expensive, hurtful of business, and destructive of frugality." It is interesting to note that in this instance the House was acting in cooperation with a group of Quaker and Presbyterian ministers who had submitted an anti-theater petition on February 17, 1767. Though the governor ignored the petition, it is important to recognize the local government's willingness to support a renewed effort to ban theatrical entertainments in a time of political crisis.[28]

In addition to the tension between Britain and the colonies, there was a growing split within Pennsylvania society in the 1760s and 1770s. As war approached, Pennsylvania society divided between the urban non-Quaker elite, who promoted British-style entertainments, operated private banks (rather than land banks),[29] and largely controlled the Pennsylvania Assembly; and the Quaker elite, who, with a growing body of citizens (primarily rural-based Scots-Irish Presbyterians from western Pennsylvania), resented and feared the behavior of the urban elite.[30] The war completed this division, as it brought men from the western part of the state into positions of power, and allowed them to temporarily impose their political and cultural agenda on the state in its time of crisis. Part of these changes included anti-theatrical legislation created in 1779 under the new State Constitution. These changes did not long survive the post-war years, but by that time the nature and configuration of Pennsylvania society had been permanently altered.

"A danger to the souls of Men": Boston against the theater

In his *Record of the Boston Stage*, William Warland Clapp, Jr., devotes only one-and-a-half pages to Boston's 106-year-long opposition to the theater, with the explanation that its detractors "in their ignorance deemed the theatre the abode of a species of devil."[31] While it is undeniable that Massachusetts's pre-Revolutionary experience with the theater and anti-theatricalism was much more limited than that of its sister city to the south, it is nevertheless important to examine instances of early anti-theatrical activity in the colony as a means of understanding the composition of the post-war debate.

In 1687, Increase Mather denounced the theater as a "danger to the souls of Men."[32] Mather's angry edict came in response to the efforts of tavern owner John Wing to set up a temporary, and certainly amateur (as there were no professional companies in America during this period), theater site within his tavern. Mather's reaction, while extreme in its apprehension of the evils of stage plays, was not out of line with general Puritan sentiments on the theater. As Jean-Christophe Agnew suggests, for the Puritans theater displayed the precariousness of social identity, by exposing human actions as a series of enacted or pretended behaviors, and therefore as behaviors open to suspicion.[33] For the Puritans, who believed that a man's character would be known by the "outward signs" of his behavior, this was a dangerous concept. But perhaps more significant for the future of Boston's theatrical debates, and for interpreting the resistance to the establishment of any kind of theatrical culture in Boston prior to the war, was the connection between the Puritan distrust of the theater, and their distrust of the growing Massachusetts merchant population. According to Agnew, the New England mind linked the hypocrisy of the stage with that of developing commercial markets, the inference being that what an actor could dissemble on the stage, a merchant could dissemble in the city square, selling bad grain for good and extorting high fees for shoddy merchandise. Agnew comments, "The very historical circumstances that had hardened the hearts of New England settlers against an outcast theater rendered them only grudgingly tolerant of the players' more enterprising neighbors: the commercial middlemen."[34]

New England had been founded on what Peter Dobkin Hall calls the "corporate idea." For the Puritans, the ideal society functioned as a unified body, operating with the understanding that "there is no body which does not consist of parts, and that which knits these parts together gives the body its perfection . . . (because) they mutually participate with each other."[35] Thus Puritan New England leaders feared invasion of a marketplace mentality, which emphasized the individual and which potentially divided the Puritan "corporate body."

Part of the early eighteenth-century anxiety concerning the marketplace in Boston arose from its unregulated structure. Boston had made its first attempts to open a public, centralized market in 1696, but it lasted only a few years. When the issue re-surfaced in the 1730s, a strong group of merchants emerged to defend the need for a centralized system.[36] This group of merchants was, as Gary Nash notes, linked by marriage, "closely allied to Governor Jonathan Belcher,"[37] and formed part of a new, secular elite

(meaning that they did not derive their status solely from church membership). They used their influence to establish a centralized market system,
and to try to re-establish a currency system backed by specie. As Robert
E. Wright has observed, most merchant transactions of the colonial period
were a complicated series of exchanged "notes" or bills of credit, promising
payment, and facilitating the transaction of goods and services not only
in the colonies, but across the Atlantic. Notes (presumed to be backed by
specie) could be treated as cash or even offered in payment.[38] Merchants
objected to the use of paper money (issued by the Commonwealth, and unbacked by specie, or gold reserves), in part because it impeded their ability
to do business outside state lines, in other words, to participate fully in the
Atlantic system of trade. But by backing the regulated market system and
the use of specie, they alienated a large portion of the lower middle classes,
who supported paper money and viewed centralized markets as a boon to
the few and a hazard to the many. The merchants' efforts in the marketplace
had been part of a larger plan to extend the authority of the royal governor's
party, to set parameters on the Massachusetts town meeting system, and to
control the spread of paper currency within the Commonwealth.[39] Though
the merchants failed in their 1730s efforts (their victories were quickly undermined by an opposition that favored land bank systems, a de-centralized
market, and the paper currency system), the issues of the 1730s marked a
division between a growing merchant elite and a rural- and artisan-based
opposition.[40]

This division made itself felt in other ways as well. Though the Boston
merchants were ultimately unsuccessful in their efforts to regulate the
colony's marketplace, they used their financial influence to establish New
England's first institutions of "polite" society. Dancing schools and assemblies sprang up in a colony notorious for its opposition to such entertainments. A letter to the *Boston Gazette* in 1732 predicted great peril for the
spiritual well-being of the colony if the merchant elite were allowed to
continue in their schemes for pleasure: "In vain will our Ministers preach
Charity, Moderation, and Humility to an Audience, whose thoughts are in-
gaged [*sic*] in Scenes of Splendour and Magnificence, and whose Time and
Money are consumed in Dress and Dancing."[41] In their quest for gentility,
Boston's early merchant elite defied the basic tenets of the Puritan faith,
and (unwisely) flaunted their wealth and leisure at a time when their fellow
colonists were struggling with crop failures, food shortages, and economic
crises. Small wonder then that such leisure activities as dancing (and the
theater) quickly became identified with the most undesirable and wasteful

of economic policies. Though restrictions against trade and the market could be only imperfectly enforced, the issue of permitting theatrical entertainments could be settled with some finality, since, as the founders of the colony agreed, theatrical entertainments were not necessary to sustain life.

For sixty-three years, the edicts of Mather and the efforts of local government kept theatrical activities out of the colony (although several dancing schools and assemblies were established in the interim). But Mather's invective could not keep the theater at bay indefinitely. In 1750, two amateur English performers enlisted the aid of a group of Bostonians to mount a production of Otway's *The Orphan* in the Coffee House on State Street.[42] This incident, coupled with the arrival of the professional Murray-Kean acting company in Quaker Philadelphia, encouraged the General Court to pass a law prohibiting all theatrical activities. The law imposed a heavy £20 fine on any person who sponsored or participated in a theatrical performance, and a £5 fine on any individual present in the audience. The justification for the act read as follows:

> For preventing and avoiding the many great mischiefs which arise from public stage plays, interludes, and other theatrical entertainments, which not only occasion great and unnecessary expense, and discourage industry and frugality, but likewise tend generally to increase immorality, impiety, and a contempt of religion.[43]

The wording of the 1750 anti-theater ban is particularly significant. On the surface, it seems a fairly standard protest against the extravagance of theatrical activities. In fact, as Davis has observed, it is a carefully crafted statement, aimed at the British Board of Trade, and is therefore a more political document than it first appears. In his discussion of Puritan mercantilism and anti-theatrical legislation in colonial America, Davis comments that all colonial legislation in Massachusetts had to be vetted by the British Board of Trade, a body founded in 1696 to "devise a means of fostering manufactures that were useful and profitable, and to determine how new manufactures might be introduced," and to "oversee the administration and profitability of the plantations."[44] Though ostensibly designed to monitor trade, the Board eventually became the *de facto* regulator of the "social, political, and religious welfare of the colonies."[45] Therefore, as Davis argues, the colonists quickly learned to couch any appeals for new legislation in terms which seemed to address the mission of the Board. This reasoning suggests an explanation for the description of theater as an activity which "discourages industry and frugality." Colonial legislators framed their anti-theatrical legislation in these terms both to win the Board's approval and to circumvent the power of pro-theater factions within the colony (a group which included both the royal governor and the merchant elite). Using the Board of Trade's own language in their appeals was, they discovered, "the trick to avoiding eventual revocation."[46]

What was the underlying motive in banning theater in Massachusetts in the 1750s, a decade before the crisis with Great Britain had reached the boiling point? By that time the Great Awakening, a powerful, grass roots religious revival, had swept through the colonies, upsetting traditional religious structures and values. With its vivid emotional impact and leveling preaching style, it left in its wake a people who increasingly questioned the value of religious, political, and social hierarchies. The preachers of the Great Awakening emphasized direct participation for every citizen, and in so doing "greatly undermined the concentration of power and prestige in the elite."[47] The Great Awakening kindled a spirit of agitation, if not outright rebellion, and primed people to participate more directly in the political process.[48]

Additionally, the 1740s had brought a worsening economic crisis to Massachusetts. The general population (as opposed to the merchant elite) had favored the circulation of paper currency, unbacked by specie. One of the reasons the general populace distrusted specie as a means of exchange was that it could be so easily counterfeited. Additionally, the use of foreign, specie-backed currency often complicated financial transactions to the point of chaos.[49] The Massachusetts General Court regularly issued paper currency, backed by land securities, as a means of sustaining economic activity within the colony. However, since that currency possessed little value in the larger Atlantic marketplace, many merchants opposed its use.

In 1741 the Board of Trade ordered the Massachusetts colony to recall its outstanding paper money, and not to issue any further supplies without the Board's approval.[50] While this move benefited the merchants who relied on specie-backed transactions, it crippled those accustomed to dealing in the paper money, and it heightened their resentment against a financially powerful group they felt was taking unfair advantage of the colony.[51]

Though there was little the Massachusetts General Assembly could do to resist the Board's financial decrees, they could subtly reject Britain's attempts to establish dominance over the colonies through their dependence on imported goods. Therefore, by rejecting the theater (although doing so in a language the Board would have found acceptable), the Massachusetts General Court was in fact rejecting one of Britain's imported cultural artifacts. It was a first step towards a complete repudiation of all British imports. It is important to note, however, that in the 1750s the colonies had no inkling that they would eventually declare their independence from Great Britain. They saw their actions as a form of political protest, but one still operating within the system of the British Empire.

In his essay, " 'Baubles of Britain': The American and Consumer Revolutions of the Eighteenth Century," Timothy Breen comments on the extent to which British goods became politicized during the decade preceding the war, noting: "Observances of non-consumption . . . forced ordinary men and women to declare exactly where they stood on the great constitutional issues of the day." Breen contends that the embargoes on British products "thus took on a new symbolic function, and the boycott became a social metaphor of political resistance."[52] Breen's assertion sheds new light on Massachusetts's next spate of anti-theatrical activity, which took place at the height of the Townshend Act controversy in 1767.

Between 1750 and 1767, there had been sporadic attempts to mount some theatrical entertainments in Massachusetts. In late 1760, David Douglass had appealed to the Massachusetts General Assembly for the right to perform, but had been rebuffed. Despite the refusal of the colony to countenance professional productions, it appears that at least a few amateur presentations were permitted (or ignored) during this period. The diary of John Rowe, a wealthy Boston merchant, records not only the fashionable dinners he attended (with men such as John Hancock), but the entertainments he enjoyed as well. On October 26, 1764, he attended a display of scenes of Jerusalem at the White Horse Tavern, which he derided as a "great imposition on the publick." On March 13, 1765, his diary contains the following entry: "Went in the evening over to Gardner's to see the *Orphan* acted, which was miserably performed, about 210 persons there."[53] This entry, though brief, suggests a number of interesting points. In noting that there were 210 people in attendance, Rowe implies that some notice of the performance had been circulated to attract a sizable crowd. Rowe's observation that the play was "miserably performed" may suggest that he was comparing the ineptitude of an amateur company in Boston to his own previous encounters with the professional theater outside Massachusetts. Additionally, Rowe makes no mention of attempts to prevent the performance, or to impose fines on either the performers or the audience members, which suggests a tacit tolerance on the part of the local authorities. Rowe was clearly undisturbed by the impropriety or illegality of witnessing a theatrical performance. It is interesting to note that Rowe's theatrical ventures took place in a tavern. From his descriptions of his social activities during this period, Rowe may have been a member of the tavern-frequenting elite that David Conroy discusses in his *In Public Houses: Drink and the Revolution of Authority in Colonial Massachusetts*. While most taverns were open to a broad range of clients from every social class, Conroy notes that a few specific taverns became the havens of the wealthy merchant elite. These taverns offered not only the best food and drink, but all the trappings of European luxury, including mirrors, clocks, comfortable chairs, plentiful supplies of candles, and elegant china and glassware.[54] These taverns may have also provided a site for the illicit theatrical entertainments Rowe mentions.

But by 1767, the Massachusetts government was no longer willing to ignore illegal theatrical performances. The resurgence of anti-theater sentiment in Boston coincided with the controversy over the disastrous Townshend Duties. Resistance to British economic policies throughout the colonies had been on the rise since the introduction of the Sugar Act in 1764 and the Stamp Act in 1765. Britain's policy of "taxation without representation" sparked an outpouring of anti-British sentiment and demonstrations, some of which were turned against the theater. On May 12, 1766, the Sons of Liberty attacked New York's Chapel Street Theatre during a production of the British favorite, *The Twin Rivals*. According to *Wegman's New York Gazette*, the rioters tore the theater to pieces, "inside and out," and set the building on fire. Terrified spectators leapt out of the windows, and one actor was "whipped" by the rioters.[55]

Though Boston lacked a similar site to inspire such demonstrations, the general populace expressed their contempt for those members of the wealthy elite who supported the British system, or who resisted the non-importation policies. Citizens targeted symbols of British oppression, whether those were individual politicians or British luxury goods, and transformed the streets into a stage upon which they could enact their disapproval.[56]

The 1765 and 1766 crises over the Sugar and Stamp Acts had inspired fairly widespread resistance to British economic policy, but had not yet caused the complete repudiation of British culture. However, the 1767 Townshend Act, a tax on paint, paper, glass, and tea, which would have rendered the royal governors financially independent of local authorities, pushed the colonists of Massachusetts to formally reject British manufactures, as well as British cultural importations like the theater.

On June 6, 1767, the Massachusetts General Court appointed a committee of five men, including future state governor John Hancock, to "bring in a Bill for the more effectually preventing Stage Plays and other Theatrical Entertainments."[57] This incident marks John Hancock's first direct involvement with anti-theatrical legislation, and it represents a shift in the rhetoric of Massachusetts's anti-theater laws, from a Puritan-based disdain for the ungodliness of theater, to a more overt resistance to British interference in American life. Hancock's involvement in this 1767 ban may also help to account for his post-war resistance to theatrical activities. His pre-war experiences conditioned him to identify the theater with symbols of British oppression, such as the Townshend Acts. Therefore he might resent the theater, not as an immoral activity, but as tangible evidence of the persistence of British domination of American culture in the post-war society. Ultimately, the 1767 ban set a pattern for the interplay between the Massachusetts state government and the theater that persisted well into the first two decades of the early national period.

The New York difference

Of the three, Boston, New York, and Philadelphia, New York's pre-Revolutionary social and political structure was, in many ways, the most diverse, yet simultaneously, the closest to Great Britain's. Studies like E. Digby Baltzell's *Puritan Boston and Quaker Philadelphia* have twinned the aims and goals of Boston and Philadelphia, detailing the many similarities in their religious and ideological missions. Other studies, like Rhys Isaacs's *The Transformation of Virginia*, have focused on the development of Virginia's culture, seeing in the colony the potential to produce future leaders like Patrick Henry, George Washington, and Thomas Jefferson.[58] Yet New York, with its odd amalgam of ethnic and religious backgrounds, its yawning gulf between the "haves" and the "have nots," and its unstructured local government, differed in almost every way from the other colonial "experiments" up and down the east coast, and has often proved the exception rather than the rule in its patterns of economic and cultural development.[59] The same is true of its theatrical entertainments.

Initially settled by the Dutch West India Company in 1624, New York began its history as a commercial outpost for the Dutch shipping industry. Envisioned as little more than a glorified trading post, New York (or New Amsterdam as it was then known) grew at a much slower rate than the other colonies. Yet it also gained a reputation as a commercial hub for fur traders and other merchants who wished to move their goods up and down the Hudson River. Having seen the expensive and disastrous failures of Virginia's colonial experiment (the disaster of Jamestown still lingered in popular memory), the founders of the Dutch West India Company wasted little effort in developing the settlement, or in trying to cultivate cash crop plantations. The market of New Amsterdam lured a diverse range of customers and traders, representing a range of races, religions, and nationalities, including Dutch, Walloon, French, English, Portuguese, Swedish, Jewish, Brazilian, and black. No one religious denomination controlled the colony, as Catholics and Protestants mingled with Jews and Anabaptists.

In 1629, Kiliaen van Rensselaer (whose descendant Stephen van Rensselaer would become a shareholder in the Park Theatre) recommended the creation of "patroonships," or vast estates that would be managed by an on-site "patroon," but would profit shareholders back in Holland.[60] While Van Rensselaer's concept spurred some agricultural development in the colony, for the most part it remained a disenfranchised collection of poorly maintained and inadequately governed villages and townships.

Such a disorganized structure naturally invited trouble, not only from within (the colony was notorious for its riotous character), but from without as well. Besieged by Indian raids,[61] to which Governor Peter Stuyvesant responded by the imposition of martial law, the colony seemed on the verge of anarchy and extinction by 1664, when English forces invaded New Amsterdam and claimed it for Great Britain.

Yet New York's troubles were far from over. The Glorious Revolution of 1688 once again threw the region into turmoil. On May 31, 1689 Captain Jacob Leisler marshaled the local militia to march against the royal governor (who was suspected of being a Catholic sympathizer, and thus disloyal to William and Mary). Leisler pushed the governor out of power and established a "protectorship," with himself as head for a period of thirteen months. When a new royal governor arrived to take over the colony, Leisler and his supporters stood trial for treason, and were executed. As Gary Nash has suggested, the Leisler uprising demonstrated the tenuous fractured quality of New York's political and social structure. Nor did the restoration of royal authority heal the breach between the wealthy, privileged merchants who had supported Governor Nicholson, and the malcontents who had backed Leisler's government.[62]

The successive upheavals of King William's War and Queen Anne's War brought further trouble to the colony. Smaller merchants foundered as lines of trade were cut first by Spanish, then by French fleets. Only the wealthiest merchants (or those who would collude with the growing number of pirates off the eastern coast) managed to stay afloat during this period.[63]

The widening gap between the wealthy and poor in New York society, coupled with the political instability in the region, did little to promote the colony's cultural development. Thus while Boston and Philadelphia consolidated their political and social structures, creating clear parameters for how their societies would be governed, New York lagged behind in almost every stage of its development.

However, despite its social backwardness, by 1710 New York had become a focal point of trade for Long Island Sound, the Hudson River Valley, and much of northern New Jersey.[64] The sugar trade played an increasingly important role in the city's prosperity.[65] Additionally, as Jack Greene has noted, by the early eighteenth century the chaos that had characterized the colony's early years had mellowed and evolved into something "more coherent and settled."[66] English customs – ranging from church practices to language to social habits – came to dominate a colony long home to a diverse group of citizens. As Edwin Burrows and Mike Wallace have noted, "every year prominent Dutch families went over to the Church of England."[67] Many of the family networks established during this period – the DeLanceys, the Livingstons, the Schuylers, the Van Rensselaers, and the Verplancks – became the controlling forces in New York's financial, social, and political scene. This gradual process of assimilation fostered the creation of a more unified social, economic, and cultural life for the city as well.[68] Perhaps more importantly, this network of financial and personal ties created a pattern for a post-Revolutionary system of alliances, providing New York with an important framework for the development of political, economic, and cultural relations in the early national period.

By the early decades of the eighteenth century, New York had begun to establish some theatrical venues, including one sponsored by its acting governor, Rip Van Dam, who served from 1731 to 1732. Both Arthur Hornblow's and T. Allston Brown's histories of the theater describe the primitive playhouse, located in a building "near the junction of Pearl Street and Maiden Lane."[69] The improvised theater site which nestled in a building belonging to Mr. Van Dam could seat approximately four hundred patrons, and contained a raised stage platform for the performers.[70] While these early attempts indicate a growing interest in cultivating theatrical entertainments in the colonies, and while the choice of productions like *The Recruiting Officer* suggests a wish on the part of the audience to enjoy popular British fare, New York's earliest efforts at sustained theatrical entertainments had a relatively short life span. Performances appeared sporadically between September, 1732 and February, 1734.[71]

By the 1730s, the city of New York had received its official charter, and boasted a population of approximately 7,000 free white citizens.[72] Though this might have been a substantial enough population to support a modest number of theatrical entertainments under normal circumstances, the 1730s also brought a period of financial hardship to the city, or what Gary Nash has described as "serious economic stagnation."[73] The instability of and strong competition for trade in the British West Indies led the city's wealthiest merchants to forsake the shipping trade in favor of money-lending and speculation.[74] The withdrawal of their sizeable investments and interests had widely felt repercussions throughout New York's working population. Shipbuilding yards closed and trades associated with shipbuilding, from carpenters to brewers, felt the loss. Many artisans who had lost their source of income left the city, so that New York's population actually declined slightly during this period. Though New York never faced as serious an economic depression as either Boston or Philadelphia during the 1730s and 1740s, when combined with the yellow fever outbreaks that continually plagued the city, it was still substantial enough to hinder the development of the colony, and to drive wedges between those segments of the population who had used the time of economic crisis to drive up interest rates and those left unemployed and at the mercy of the city's almshouses and poor laws.[75]

New York's first theatrical endeavors may also have failed to thrive because of the political infighting that engulfed the city shortly after the New Theatre opened in 1732. Its owner, Rip Van Dam, had served as acting governor for the colony for thirteen months before the arrival of Royal Governor William Cosby in 1732. Cosby demanded that Van Dam turn over half of his salary to him as the new governor. Van Dam refused. Cosby brought suit against Van Dam through the provincial court. When the chief justice, Lewis Morris, failed to rule in his favor, Cosby threw him off the bench and appointed a member of one of New York's leading families, James DeLancey, to his position.[76] A "political warfare" ensued – one that consumed New York's reigning elite, as well as its artisans, in a vituperative battle over the rights of the "people" versus the hierarchy of the royal government.[77] Cosby was a boon companion of British "prime" minister Robert Walpole,[78] a devious and unpopular Whig who, many colonists believed, wanted to use politicians like Cosby to "accelerate the subversion of English liberty by exporting ministerial corruption to America."[79] Given the animosity generated by the Van Dam–Morris/Cosby–DeLancey controversy, combined with the economic troubles and declining population, it is perhaps not surprising that interest in theatrical entertainments should have dwindled during this period.

By the end of the decade, the political landscape of New York had shifted as well. The turmoil of the mid-1730s had mobilized the city's artisan and poorer populations, and they had united to overthrow some of the wealthier merchants on the city council. Their actions demonstrated to the city's elite that the mechanics' faction merited serious consideration, and that they would perhaps make better allies than enemies, and so, by the elections of 1739, the tone of the political and economic rhetoric had turned into a more inclusive one that forged at least tentative alliances between artisan and merchant interests. The city also divided between parties that supported the royal governor and his cronies (Cosby and DeLancey), and those that supported the former chief justice and his allies (Morris and Van Dam). Yet these parties comprised men from all walks of life, who realized that "each group held its own interests, but to promote them each could form a pragmatic alliance against a common opponent."[80] Again, this type of interest-based alliance would set a pattern for New York's post-Revolutionary government and continue to complicate its efforts to establish permanent theatrical entertainments.

The 1750s finally brought serious professional theater to the city. On February 26, 1750, the *New York Weekly Post Boy* announced the arrival of a company of comedians, the Murray-Kean Company.[81] Interestingly, the Murray-Kean Company also made use of property that had belonged to Rip Van Dam (who had died some years earlier), housing the theater in an old brewery on Nassau Street.[82] Brooks McNamara suggests that the Murray-Kean Company made some effort to modify the Nassau Street Theatre to make it resemble English-style playhouses. Newspaper advertisements of the period suggest that by 1751 the company had contrived to set up box, pit, and gallery seating areas.[83] As numerous histories of the colonial American theater note, the Murray-Kean Company enjoyed a relatively brief heyday in America. The Hallam Company (later known by a variety of names, including the Hallam-Douglass Company, the American Company, and, after the Revolution, the Old American Company), soon succeeded them in the colonies. Though Hallam initially occupied the improvised Murray-Kean theater on Nassau Street, he complained publicly about its many inadequacies.[84] Hallam's complaints appeared in the papers in early July of 1753. On July 17, 1753, Matthew Clarkson wrote the following letter:

We are to have the diversions of the stage this season. There are several actors from some part of Europe who after much solicitation have at last obtained leave of his Excellency to perform. They talk of building a house for that purpose and have offered themselves to subscribe (£100) for the encouragement of it. This is a malencholy [sic] story among considerate persons that so small a place as this should encourage the toleration of such public diversions. People are dayly [sic] murmuring of the badness of the time as though they were actually concerned for their interest, but their conduct proves a contradiction to it. For men in every profession are as fond of some party of pleasure or other, and as if they had not room enough to spend their mony [sic] that way, they must for all put themselves under greater temptations in going to the playhouse.[85]

Clarkson's letter suggests that plans for the building of a new theater were still under discussion in mid-July of 1753, yet by September of 1753 the *Weekly Post Boy* noted that the players had built a "very fine, large and commodious Theatre in the place where the old One Stood."[86] Such a short time span between a *discussion* of plans to re-build the theater and its re-opening suggests that either the renovations had been fairly superficial, or that citizens and performers alike were spurred by a great eagerness to create a well-appointed theater. Yet Clarkson's letter underscores both the financial instability of the colonies and the "badness of the time," which would make theatrical entertainments a waste of funds better spent elsewhere, and the fact that by the 1750s, much of the anti-theatrical rhetoric that dominated the colonies traced the theater's evil to financial, rather than strictly moral, considerations.

In 1754, less than a year after Lewis Hallam, Sr. renovated and re-opened the Nassau Street Theatre, he sold the property to a "society of German Calvinists who converted the theater into a church."[87] Perhaps Clarkson had been right in his assessment that "considerate persons" would not sustain theatrical entertainments. In any event, New York remained without a permanent playhouse for the next seven years. Then, in 1758, the new manager of the Hallam Company, David Douglass, tried to establish entertainments near the very edge of the city, a place known as Cruger's Wharf. Somewhat surprisingly, given the city's relatively tolerant attitude towards theater in previous instances (certainly more tolerant than Boston and Philadelphia, for example), the city magistrates denied him permission to perform. Their refusal is all the more puzzling because the place that Douglass proposed to set up his theater belonged to the Cruger family, one of the most powerful families in New York society. Moreover, John Cruger, Jr., one of the wealth-iest members of the family, was also the mayor of New York. With the support of the city's mayor, how could Douglass fail to win the support of those elite members of the colony who comprised the bulk of his audience?

Part of Douglass's difficulties may have sprung not from a sudden upsurge of anti-theatrical sentiment, but from a rivalry among two of New York's most powerful families that was slowly tearing the colony in half. John Cruger, Jr. belonged to a faction known as the "DeLanceyites" for their support of the prominent DeLancey family (in particular, the powerful Lieutenant-Governor James DeLancey). The DeLanceys, ardent Whigs, had initially clashed with the colony's other powerful faction, the Livingston family, over the issue of the Cosby/Van Dam controversy in the 1730s. Their rivalry had grown more and more embittered in the intervening years.

Shortly before Douglass and his company returned to New York, a pivotal battle had taken place in the ongoing DeLancey/Livingston war. James DeLancey, backed by a strong pro-Anglican faction, had proposed "a scheme to found a college in New York City under the patronage of the Church of England."[88] The Livingstons and their supporters (many of whom were Presbyterians) feared the establishment of a sectarian school. However, the DeLancey faction carried the day, and King's College (known today as Columbia University) emerged as a DeLanceyite triumph over the "Triumvirate" led by William Livingston and his cronies, William Smith and John Morin Scott.[89] Unfortunately for the DeLanceys, their victory in the King's College battle prompted the Livingston faction to mobilize, with the result that the DeLanceys lost control of the Assembly in 1758.

Thus, the timing of Douglass's failure to re-establish theatrical en-tertainments in a city that had previously been willing to support them becomes suggestive. What better way for a pro-Presbyterian, increasingly anti-royalist faction to exert its authority against a pro-Anglican, pro-crown party than to deny it its luxuries and diversions? By dint of complaint and persuasion, however, the company eventually secured permission to per-form, and gave an abbreviated season from January to February of 1759.[90]

By 1761, Douglass had secured permission to construct a new theater at a more propitious location on Chapel Street. Yet his troubles were far from over. The controversies over the Stamp Act, the Townshend Act, and the Sugar Act that had plagued Boston and Philadelphia wrought equal havoc in New York and drove the final wedge between the DeLancey and Livingston factions. Their split ultimately spilled over into the theater and brought about the destruction of the Chapel Street Theatre on May 11, 1766.[91]

How had New York's theater moved from a mildly contentious issue, rousing brief flashes of interest among both its opponents and supporters, to an enterprise that would become the focus of a "grand rout," with the "inside and outside" of the Chapel Street house "torn to pieces and burnt"?[92] Ultimately, the crisis occasioned by the passage of the Stamp Act mobilized the DeLancey and Livingston parties and transformed their rivalry from "an essentially private and gentlemanly quarrel between a few top leaders among the colony's governing elite into a broad dispute involving at one level a variety of political, economic, and social issues, and at another level the future of the empire itself."[93] Thus the political and cultural legitimacy of the theater as a symbol of Great Britain was cast into doubt as the warring parties vied for control of an increasingly restless populace.

The Livingstons turned their attention towards petitioning the crown for a repeal of the Stamp Act, on rhetorical grounds now familiar to students of American history – the issue of taxation without representation. Yet, as Leopold Launitz-Schurer has noted, the Livingstons failed to mobilize popular sentiment, and had no "fall-back" plans if petitioning the crown failed to produce results.[94] The DeLanceys, on the other hand, used their influence to forge alliances among the middle and lower classes, bringing the threat of mob violence to bear on the supporters of the Stamp Act. Neither group was wholly successful, but the DeLanceys carried the day through sheer bravado and adroit stage-management, which positioned them as the most "active" campaigners against British oppression.[95] Ironically, the DeLanceys also appear to have played a significant role in encouraging the creation of the New York Sons of Liberty, a vigilante group composed largely of artisans and apprentices, who took it upon themselves to force compliance with boycotts of British goods – including the theater. It was, in fact, the Sons of Liberty who destroyed the theater in the immediate aftermath of the announcement that the Stamp Act had been repealed. After the destruction of the Chapel Street Theatre in May of 1766, and in the wake of the colonists' victory over the Stamp Act, Douglass constructed another, hardier playhouse on John Street. The John Street Theatre (as it was known) operated during a period of increasing political instability. Though the Sons of Liberty subsided in their attacks against any pro-British activities or institutions, theatrical entertainments in New York faced opposition from the citizenry who regarded such entertainments as decadent and luxurious in financially troubled times. In 1768, the *New York Weekly Post*

Boy denounced the theater as a "tax" on the people of the city (drawing an implicit connection between the cost of the theater and the hated Stamp Act tax). The *New-York Journal* asked, "What an enormous tax do we burthen ourselves with? It is computed at least £300 a week." The writer added, "Some pretend the money is spent amongst ourselves – deceitful reasoning! Is not foreign finery their chief expence [*sic*], and their dresses [the actors'] imitated by our young folks? – Luxury and extravagance is the bane of the age."[96] The *New-York Journal* also spread the rumor that one theater patron had offered £50 for a private box at the theater, commenting, "It would seem from this that people were grown mad after plays...Rather let it be said that we are distinguished by our benevolence and humanity, than by our luxurious pleasures."[97]

Other critics denounced theater as an enterprise that corrupted manly resolve at a time when the citizens most needed it. As Ann Fairfax Withington has noted, critics drew on classical rhetoric and comparisons to support their anti-theatrical stance: "The theatre had a very considerable share in sinking the Athenians into effeminacy and indolence."[98] Many of these attacks on the New York theater coincided with two perhaps poorly chosen ventures on David Douglass's part. The first was a December 30, 1767 performance for the benefit of debtors in the New York City jail, and the second was a "command" performance for the governor's wife, Lady Moore, on January 1, 1768. Within a week of these performances, a spate of anti-theatrical diatribes flooded the newspapers. Perhaps the idea of a theater raising money for those jailed for debt struck some as inappropriate, while anything done at the "command" of the governor's lady may also have smacked of luxury and idleness (not to mention pro-British sympathies). Douglass and the rest of the company finished a not very profitable season in June of 1768, leaving New York for points south, and not returning to the city until April of 1773.[99]

But by the time Douglass returned to the city, a mini-revolution had taken place in New York. The DeLanceys had enjoyed a period of almost unchecked influence between 1766 and 1769, but their party made a series of fatal errors in 1769 and 1770, and thus, by the end of 1770, they had been relegated to the margins of New York politics.

New York entered a period of serious economic depression in 1769. Non-importation agreements meant that New York merchants had little or no means of earning a living, since they could neither import and sell British goods, nor export American raw materials. The sight of ships rotting at anchor did little to bolster the merchants' sense of allegiance and common cause with their fellow colonies. They complained that other colonies were in fact taking advantage of New York's absence from the marketplace and violating the boycotts with impunity. They demanded that the DeLancey faction (which controlled the government at that point) take steps to re-peal the non-importation agreements. New York's mechanics and laborers, on the other hand, insisted that the colony stand firm in its resistance, and that it enforce serious penalties for non-compliance. The DeLanceys found themselves in an unenviable position, with little hope of being able to gratify both parties.

The Livingston faction quickly took advantage of this situation. In 1769 and early 1770, the DeLanceys had waged an active campaign to re-formulate the colony's election laws to make the Livingstons and their allies ineligible to serve in the government. Their success simultaneously robbed the Liv-ingstons of the chance to win "official" power in the colony, and re-invented them as "a powerful natural center of opposition."[100] The Livingstons made overtures to the Sons of Liberty (the DeLanceys' former allies), promis-ing to take more active steps to enforce the non-importation agreements and to stave off British tyranny. The DeLanceys suddenly found them-selves politically isolated. In failing to act decisively on the issues of the non-importation agreements and New York's struggling economy, and in seeming still to support the royal government, they had lost the loyalty of their followers. To add insult to injury, the DeLanceys also supported a bill to grant support for English soldiers in the colony.

Opponents immediately denounced the DeLanceys as "the Minions of Tyranny and Despotism," claiming that the DeLancey party had "betrayed the liberties of the people."[101] Alexander McDougall, a popular leader and businessman who backed the Livingston party (and who later became the first president of the Bank of New York), penned a broadside entitled *To the Betrayed Inhabitants of the City and Colony of New York*, aimed at the DeLanceys and their supporters, and in 1771 he circulated the *Association of the Sons of Liberty*, uniting the Livingstons with the DeLanceys' former friends and supporters. McDougall and other popular leaders in the city did their best to rouse anti-British sentiment between 1770 and 1774. Though initially successful, it seemed in 1774 as though their mob-inciting methods might backfire when a group of New York's wealthiest and most conservative merchants united to resist the tide of "Cobblers and Tailors" threatening to take over the city.[102]

Ultimately, however, the first meeting of the Continental Congress in October of 1774 put an end to the power of the conservative, loyalist merchants and to theater in the colonies. The Congress, in addition to its ban on theatrical entertainments and other luxuries, instituted economic policies that halted all trade with Great Britain. In 1775, New York's Assembly refused to appoint new representatives to the second gathering of the Continental Congress. In response to their inaction, the city's Committee of Sixty (an extra-legal patriot group) assumed control of the city.[103] New York's elite had only two choices – declare for the side of liberty and join ranks with the Livingstons, McDougalls, and Sons of Liberty, or join the DeLanceys, pledge allegiance to the crown, and count on the king for protection. Either way, it *seemed* that their theatrical "diversions of the stage" were ended for a time.

2

Revolutionary transformations: the struggle to establish a legitimate theater

Pockets of local resistance against the theater and against the elite crystallized into national policy in 1774, with the Continental Congress's wartime ban against theatrical entertainments. In October of 1774, the Congress issued the following proclamation: "We will in our several stations encourage frugality... and discourage every species of extravagance and dissipation [including] exhibition of shows, plays, and other expensive diversions and entertainments."[1] The injunction against theatrical entertainments represented the first "national" stance taken against the theater in America. The edict proscribed theater on both financial and patriotic grounds (rather than religious ones), and effectively superseded individual anti-theatrical prohibitions which had been previously established in individual states. Moreover, the ban attempted to sever *all* cultural connections with Great Britain, the traditional source of America's theatrical amusements.

The Continental Congress's ban of 1774 (re-issued in 1778) appears as a sharp break with Britain's "imagined community" of the playhouse, identifying playgoing as a "violation of colonial political goals."[2] But perhaps more importantly, the Revolutionary War and the actions of the Continental Congress fundamentally changed the nature of anti-theatricalism in America, transforming it from a simple matter of religious preference to one of patriotic duty.

Although, as Ann Fairfax Withington has noted, there is no record of any member of the Continental Congress dissenting from the anti-theater ban,[3] it is clear from the events of the Revolution that the edict had not carried with it a widespread conviction of the evils of theatrical entertainments. George Washington himself was fond of playgoing, and staged productions of favorite pieces, such as *Cato*, to raise the sagging spirits of his army during the hard winter at Valley Forge. Washington might have gotten away with these fairly innocent entertainments, except that the British, bored with their long occupations of Boston, New York, and Philadelphia, had also taken to staging plays. The colonists, wearied by the privations of the war, regarded this as the ultimate insult – that the British should take such a casual approach to the war as to spend more time painting scenery and putting on plays than fighting! Indeed, one Hessian officer stationed in Philadelphia observed that there were enough "assemblies, concerts, comedies, clubs, and the like [to] make us forget there is any war, save that it is a capital joke."[4]

Did the British hope to use their wartime entertainments not merely as a means of passing the time during a dull war, but as a method of winning back American loyalty to British culture? While this seems a particularly naive (and arrogant) assumption on the part of the British, it is possible that they believed that theatrical entertainments and concerts would persuade Americans of the benevolence of British authority. They might also have assumed that they could successfully undermine the "rebels" by satirizing them on stage (as they did repeatedly with George Washington). But whether their motives were boredom during the long and tedious times of occupation, or a sincere wish to bring the colonists back into the British cultural fold, the net result of their actions was a growing and widespread bitterness against theatrical entertainments in those urban sites, Philadelphia and Boston, which had always fostered resistance to the theater, and which had been particularly hard hit by the occupation. Jared Brown has advanced the theory that British wartime military theatricals fostered American appreciation for playgoing. He writes, "It may be reasonably argued that a new and dedicated audience was formed by these productions," suggesting that the British *legitimized* theatrical entertainments in America.[5] While this assertion may apply to New York, it is more problematic in the cases of Boston and Philadelphia, where many of the post-war theater supporters were ex-Revolutionary War officers. There were loyalists who attended the theater, such as Bostonian John Rowe, whose diary records his visits to British military performances of *The Busybody* and *Tamerlane*.[6] But Brown's study of Boston and Philadelphia seems to overlook the increasing American resentment against British theatrical activities, as evidenced in the 1778 renewal of the Continental Congress's anti-theater prohibition:

> Whereas frequenting playhouses and theatrical entertainments has a fatal tendency to divert the minds of the people from a due attention to the means necessary for the defence of their country and the preservation of their liberties:

> Resolved, That any person holding an office under the United States, who shall act, promote, encourage, or attend such plays, shall be deemed unworthy to hold such office, and shall be accordingly dismissed.[7]

Samuel Adams, who remained resistant to theatrical entertainments throughout his long political career, expressed his scorn at the taste for wartime entertainments in a letter to a friend:

> You must know that in humble imitation, as it would seem, of the British Army, some of our officers have condescended to act on the stage, while others and ones of superior rank were pleased to countenance them with their presence. This with some other appearances as disagreeable to the sober inhabitants of this city as to Congress gave occasion for the [anti-theater] Resolution. I am very sorry that by a representation of theatrical performance, which at least appears to be done in contempt of the Laws of Congress, another resolution became necessary.[8]

State governments also took steps to preclude the introduction of theatrical entertainments. In 1779, Pennsylvania's State Constitutionalist party introduced the state's first successful anti-theater legislation. Such actions hardly suggest a nation developing a taste for British theater. General Anthony Wayne mocked the British for their devotion to theater at the expense of military progress. In an angry letter, dated June 28, 1778, he wrote, "Tell those Philadelphia ladies, who attended [General] Howe's assemblies and levees, that the heavenly, sweet pretty red coats... have been humbled on the plains of Monmouth."[9]

Anti-theatrical sentiment underwent a transformation during the Revolution; by the end of the war for many citizens anti-theatricalism had become identified with patriotism and, by extension, republican virtue. What then, would be the fate of the theater in Boston, New York, and Philadelphia once the war was settled? Would America try to establish its own national theater? While some states, including New York, did re-establish theatrical entertainments immediately after the Treaty of Paris, others like Massachusetts and Pennsylvania persisted in their resistance.

Why? In the wake of the Revolution, Massachusetts's and Pennsylvania's wartime regimes assumed responsibility for the supervision of their citizens' moral as well as physical well-being. With the memory of British wartime entertainments fresh in their minds, they adamantly rejected any activities that savored of luxury and elitism, rejecting all theater – "American" or otherwise – as a corrupting force.

But who were the post-war opponents of the theater, and how had they established their authority? The Revolution had brought to power a group of "new men" in Philadelphia and Boston, who had supplanted the pre-war ruling class. Just as the post-war period offered a time of economic opportunity to adroit businessmen, the crisis of revolution provided an opening for politicians and parties who supported the ideals of republican virtue, and who wanted to use their authority to enforce their beliefs.

In 1776 a strong Presbyterian/Scots-Irish faction assumed control of the Pennsylvania legislature. This party "promised to be the party of the future... and afforded the anti-establishment ambiance which attracted the aggressive men who spearheaded the Revolution in Pennsylvania."[10] Drawn from the Philadelphia Committee of Resistance and from members of both the artisan and merchant classes, the Scots-Irish faction comprised roughly 70 percent of the General Assembly by 1778. These men held long-standing grudges against the Quakers, who they believed had failed to provide adequate military defense for the western portion of the state (an area dominated by the Scots-Irish), and against the wealthy Anglican merchant and business elite of Philadelphia who had remained loyal (or at least neutral) towards the crown.

"With the election of a new government in 1776, new men took over Pennsylvania...and by 1777, an almost complete reversal of power had occurred."[11] The creation of a new Pennsylvania State Constitution in 1776 was intended to "clear away every part of the old rubbish...and begin again upon a new foundation."[12] The Scots-Irish/Presbyterian faction set about eliminating its enemies with ruthless efficiency. The Test Acts of 1777 and 1779 demanded that citizens take a loyalty oath, or be barred from political participation in the state in perpetuity. This act, aimed primarily at Quakers (whose religious beliefs precluded oath-taking), effectively shut the Quakers out of state government. The Scots-Irish faction attacked the Anglican elite by "dismantling the Anglican-dominated College of Philadelphia," and replacing it with the Presbyterian-governed University of Pennsylvania.[13] They also passed a 1779 law prohibiting all theatrical entertainments. Why did the Scots-Irish faction resent the Anglicans and Quakers so bitterly? Part of the reason may have been financial. Quakers and Anglicans had traditionally represented the wealthiest segments of the population and had, the State Constitutionalists believed, acquired a disproportionate amount of power in the state government through their wealth.[14]

The question remains: why, with their apparent wealth and influence, were the Quakers and Anglicans unable to defend themselves against these attacks? Brobeck suggests that the Quaker elite had been diminished by deaths among its senior members, and by the failure of the elite to "recruit" new members. The war also proved a dividing factor among the Quaker elite, since those who chose to take arms or to support the American cause were excluded from Quaker society, and those who remained loyal to the crown were persecuted as Tories.[15] The Anglican elite were also tainted with the "Tory" brush. The pre-war cultural institutions that they supported, ranging from the Dancing Assembly, to theatrical entertainments, to the College of Philadelphia, seemed symptomatic of an outlook directly at odds with the cult of republican virtue that the State Constitutionalists hoped to foster.[16]

Though the State Constitutionalists' aims were noble, their methods were brutal and heavy-handed, and could not long survive the Revolutionary crisis. As critic William Hooper noted, the State Constitutionalists had not created a government, so much as they had spawned "a motley mixture of limited monarchy and an execrable democracy – a Beast without a Head."[17] Unfortunately for the State Constitutionalists, the system they created rested on a power base so narrow that it could not withstand the transformations of the post-war years. Nor could their policies permanently suppress the Anglican and Quaker elite, who began re-asserting their authority as soon as the war ended.

Pennsylvania's wartime regime attempted to abolish elitist standards of wealth and deference, elevating men whose backgrounds tied them to rural, western influences, rather than urban society or Atlantic culture. Massachusetts's revolutionary government was in large part directed by members of its elite class, men who were grounded in systems of Atlantic trade, and who represented urban mercantile interests. Pennsylvania's State Constitutionalists labored to silence all opposition to their government, through their various restrictive acts and through the creation of a unicameral legislature. The Massachusetts wartime regime, on the other hand, was a product of ongoing factional opposition, which persisted into the post-war period.

"At the outset of the Revolutionary War, no other former British colony seemed as well prepared as Massachusetts to stand as a strong independent state,"[18] Gregory Nobles has noted. But that stability splintered under the pressure of party wrangling over the nature of how Massachusetts's republican government should be administered. Nobles suggests that the party factionalism in Massachusetts "was a conflict over the nature of republicanism itself... [and] of how the standards of republican government would be defined and by whom."[19] Throughout the Revolution, citizens of Massachusetts struggled with distinctions between "private" and "public" interests. These fears had their origins in pre-war divisions among rural and urban parties, between "Court" and "County" factions, between elite and poor communities, and between eastern and western districts.[20]

While Pennsylvania's State Constitutionalists had proposed a system which ignored the differences among its inhabitants, the Massachusetts State Constitution of 1780 attempted to reconcile the seemingly permanent differences among the people via a system of government that could address all of their interests equally and fairly. John Adams, who was instrumental in creating the 1780 Constitution, realized that a unicameral legislature (like Pennsylvania's) would only promote party divisions, since it would encourage factions within the legislature to compete for control. Adams's design for government offered a tacit acknowledgment that "the people" could not be relied upon to govern themselves in a disinterested fashion. Massachusetts inherited a republican system which resembled the charter system under which it had originally been formed.[21]

The State Constitution of 1780 in many ways enforced, rather than elim-inated, party opposition. The Constitution of 1780 tried to ensure that Massachusetts's republican government would be protected by its laws, rather than being at the mercy of its charismatic leaders; nevertheless, Hancock, a member of the Boston merchant elite, emerged as one of Massachusetts's most powerful wartime leaders. Although biographies of Hancock give varying accounts of his motivations (and his intelligence), Hancock's pre-war role as "agitator" won him a place at the "Revolutionary Center" for many Americans.[22] What is particularly interesting about the choice of Hancock as Revolutionary leader (and later as state governor) is that, with his elite background, his lavish entertainments, and his habits of patronage, he exemplified what many Massachusetts Republicans – such as Mercy Otis Warren – found most dangerous in the old British system.[23] Nevertheless, through his pre-war and wartime activities, Hancock became a self-appointed guardian of republican virtue, and as such, the bitter foe of any activities which threatened to promote the private interests of one Massachusetts faction over another. If the Commonwealth had been will-ing to acknowledge (however subtly) the necessary evil of parties, they also acknowledged the need to restrain those parties or any outside groups from exerting undue influence over the government. For this reason, it is perhaps understandable why the post-war government (under Hancock's aegis) later reacted so strongly against proposed systems of banks and stock companies – companies which included the contradictory language of "private" and "public" in their very constitutions. The 1780 Constitution had pledged the state government to both promote the well-being of its people and to oversee arts, education, and manufacture within the state. Thus *private* companies – whether banks or theater companies – which threatened to impinge on the public welfare were a danger to the always tenuous stability of the Massachusetts system.

New York offers a different model for both wartime occupation and post-war recuperation. The DeLancey party had counted on royal intervention to solve the growing revolutionary crisis. Initially, it seemed that royal help might be forthcoming. British soldiers captured the city of New York in 1776, and occupied it for almost seven years. During that time, loyalists from all the colonies flocked to the city, and at the end of the British occupation more than 28,000 loyalists left New York (a number greater than the city's entire pre-war population).

Much has been written about the fate of occupied New York and of the activities that the British forces pursued there. Brown's *Theatre in America During the Revolution* details the British wartime military theatricals offered there, and provides an insightful look into the operations of a military theater, ranging from season selection, to box office management, to scenic painting. He suggests that the British army's performances helped to establish a sense of "normalcy" among New York's loyalist citizens during the Revolutionary crisis, and that they helped to reinforce ties with British culture. He also makes the more problematic assertion that British wartime entertainments created a new New York audience that would be receptive to American professional theater after the Revolution. In the absence of direct evidence, and given the post-Revolutionary upsurge in *anti*-theatrical sentiment, this seems like a challenging transition, especially when taking into account that at the time the British took control of New York, less than 5,000 of its original 25,000 inhabitants remained, and the population that flooded the city during the war was largely composed of Tory refugees from other colonies, many of whom left New York immediately after the Revolution.[24]

While the goal of the British wartime theatricals may have been to convince the colonists that all was well, that was obviously far from the truth, as the struggle between loyalist and patriot continued to play out in New York's social and political spheres. Janice Potter-MacKinnon has described the American Revolution as a "civil war, in which Americans were deeply divided over fundamental issues."[25] As she notes, between 1774 and 1776, many New York loyalists tried to work alongside the Revolutionary forces and extra-legal committees of correspondence, in the hopes of achieving

some kind of compromise or reconciliation. The capture of the city effectively put an end to such plans. The arrival of British troops in New York
in September, 1776, while it quieted the loyalist/patriot debates in the city
(which had been marked in the months immediately preceding the occupation by an escalation in violence), launched a veritable "civil war," as
pro-British and pro-patriot troops and mobs fought for control of the state.
Pro-patriot Committees of Safety in Albany arrested and persecuted those
suspected of Tory leanings.[26] They often whipped or tarred and feathered
those they believed sympathetic to the British. On the loyalist side, James
DeLancey formed a militia group, known as DeLancey's Cowboys, that
terrorized Westchester County.[27]

Unraveling the network of political alliances that stretched from the
pre-war years through the Revolution is a daunting task. Many loyalists
initially tried to cooperate with Revolutionaries. Additionally, there were a
number of men who, though they initially joined Committees of Safety or
Committees of Correspondence, ultimately declared allegiance to Great
Britain. Thus, what had seemed a relatively simple schism between the
Livingston and DeLancey parties in the decades before the Revolution
developed into a much more complex series of ruptures, reconciliations,
and negotiations. The ambivalent and fluctuating state of New York politics
during the Revolutionary period would have a profound effect on its post-
war structure, impacting every aspect of its development from politics, to
economics, to culture.

During the Revolution, the general prohibition of theatrical entertainments became synonymous with republican virtue, and the theater itself was
linked to negative images of British tyranny and elitist luxury. In Boston
and Philadelphia particularly, theater became an issue which ignited a violent "republican" backlash. In New York, it was a reminder that the city had
harbored loyalist fugitives. How then, could a post-war theater be created?
Its supporters would have to convince the people that theater *could* form
a vital part of the new republic – that in fact a "republican" theater could
exist. However, before they could do so, they would need to re-establish the
power that the revolutionary regimes had taken from them. In each case,
they turned, not to politics, but to the financial opportunities created by the
Revolution as an means of regaining authority. Their theaters would become testimonies to their financial acumen and influence, rather than their
political clout. These playhouses offered their founders – excluded from the
seats of political authority – an alternate site to disseminate their views on
how a republican state should be governed.

"Something like a professional stage" in post-war New York

As I suggested in the Introduction, New York's pre- and post-war development offers an interesting contrast to Boston and Philadelphia, whose social and political structures were derived directly and indirectly from religious and revolutionary ideology. New York, on the other hand, appears as a labyrinthine network of personal associations and family and party vendettas that make it infinitely more challenging to trace a coherent pattern of development.

Thus New York's post-war theater offers an excellent case-study for a city still struggling to re-configure itself in the wake of a long occupation. I will discuss the development of New York's politics and economy at greater length in chapter 5. But a brief overview of the city's theatrical entertainments between 1785 and 1794 (the time of the Boston and Philadelphia theater openings, and the first stirrings of New York's own wish for an elaborate "American" playhouse) may hint at reasons for the theater's inability to establish a comfortable cultural niche in the new nation.

By August of 1785, "something like a professional stage" re-appeared at New York's John Street playhouse.[28] Lewis Hallam returned to New York with what Odell describes as a company of "feeble actors," who presented a series of performances that combined transparent efforts to demonstrate the theater's patriotic fervor (such as a "Monody to the memory of the Chiefs who have fallen in the Cause of American Liberty"), with pantomimes, including "Harlequin Traveler" and "The Genii in the Rock," and comic dances like "La Fricassee."[29] Audiences quickly tired of this fare, as their complaints to local newspapers attest. Yet, though they touted the theater as a potential "school for virtue, elegance, and politeness," neither the citizens of New York nor the John Street managers had formed any concrete plans for making the theater more "American."[30] Aside from the premiere of *The Contrast* in 1787 – the John Street Theatre's great claim to nurturing American "native genius" – the managers relied heavily on a repertoire of old English favorites, including *The School for Scandal*, *The Rivals*, *She Stoops to Conquer*, *The Padlock*, etc.

Personalities have always played a major role in the theater, and the Old American Company, as Hallam's troupe was now called, was no exception. Indeed, much of the difficulty that the Park Theatre proprietors would later encounter in their efforts to establish a playhouse sprang from their conflicts with some of the more recalcitrant members of the old company. It is telling that the founders of both the Boston and the Philadelphia theaters deliberately sought *new* managers for their playhouses. Between 1785 and 1793 the stage at the John Street Theatre witnessed a power struggle between the established members of the Old American Company, Lewis Hallam, Jr. and John Henry, *versus* rising stars Thomas Wignell, who joined the company in 1785, and John Hogkinson, who came over from England in 1792. As Weldon Durham suggests, young stars like Wignell, Mrs. Kenna, and Hodgkinson were trying to promote their own careers, and to secure roles traditionally played by the older members of the company (who were aging out of them). One New York critic had ridiculed Hallam's efforts to sustain the younger roles: "His battered looks, and shrunk carcass look the debilitated rake, but the soul, the animation, and the fire had left the withered body."[31] When, despite this stinging criticism, "the oldsters refused to yield," the younger stars struck out on their own, further weakening the company.[32] Dunlap's diary contains an account of the strife between Wignell and Hallam,[33] and much of John Hodgkinson's later writings attempt to justify his efforts to establish his own independent place in the early national theater.

Durham also suggests that marital conflicts played an important role in the dynamics of the Old American Company. Manager John Henry resisted encouraging actresses who might compete with his wife (also a performer in the company). In 1793 the fifty-three-year-old Lewis Hallam married a Miss Tuke, an actress in the company less than half his age.[34] Hugh Rankin quotes a brutally honest account of the terms of marriage between Hallam and Tuke (who had apparently been co-habiting while Hallam was separated from his first wife, Sarah). According to this source: "'The old wretch [Hallam] has been long under restraint by reason of a wife, from whom he has been parted many years. However, to his great satisfaction no doubt she died about four weeks ago in Virginia.'" The observer added a more personal and scandalous comment: "'The result is that in about a month's time after her death, he married Miss Tuke. Damn the old scrawny boned wretch how I should like to cuckle [cuckold] him.'"[35] Unfortunately for Hallam, his young bride was prone to bouts of heavy drinking and violent temper which alienated both the other members of the company and the audience. As tensions in the company increased, the relationship between Hallam and Henry disintegrated. Henry left the company in 1794.

Not surprisingly, the constant strife within the Old American Company made it difficult for the group to cooperate with outside patrons and propri-etors who hoped to create new theaters that would reflect their own polit-ical and cultural agendas. As newer (and more cooperative) stars emerged, patrons of the Boston and Philadelphia playhouses who had organized to champion the rights of the theater in their cities sought alliances with individuals willing to shape the theater to *their* vision of republican entertainments. Thus, by 1794, Hallam's Old American Company, which had helped to sustain the theater in America during a period when its very existence in the new nation seemed in jeopardy, found itself outdated and old-fashioned in its outlook. Only the competition provided by the Boston and Philadelphia theaters would revitalize the New York theatrical scene, and transform it from a mediocre site of threadbare entertainments to one of the most vital and influential theater centers in the new nation.

A "subject of earnest discussion" in Boston and Philadelphia

In February of 1789, the Dramatic Association of Philadelphia submitted a proposal to the General Assembly of Pennsylvania, requesting a repeal of the state's 1779 anti-theatrical legislation. The petitioners noted:

> The Drama is now a subject of earnest discussion: from a topic of private discussion, it has become the object of legislative decision, and contending parties are formed, on the one hand denying and on the other asserting the propriety of tolerating the stage.[36]

How had the theater become a subject of such broad and heated debate in the years after the war; one which, as the petitioners observed, was not confined to the private sphere, but which had intruded on the public notice and polarized factions within the new nation?

For nearly a decade after the war, theatrical debates raged in Boston, New York, and Philadelphia, as both pro- and anti-theater factions gained and lost ground. Yet by the winter of 1794 New York had resumed its entertainments at the old John Street Theatre, and the citizens of Boston and Philadelphia eagerly awaited the opening of their new playhouses. Henry Jackson of Boston wrote to a friend in Philadelphia, "Tomorrow week we open our new Theatre. I assure you it's one of the most Elegant and beautiful buildings on the Continent. The Theatre Room is a perfect picture and I believe far surpasses the one in *your* city."[37] Opening night at the Boston and Philadelphia theaters promised more than a new evening's diversion; it represented a milestone in the struggle for dominance in post-Revolutionary society.

The battle to bring theater to the City of Brotherly Love and to the crooked and narrow streets of Boston exemplified the transition of social and political authority in the early Republic. Post-war power shifted from the "Old Revolutionaries," resistant to the rise of factions and corporations, and focused on fulfilling the "historic mission" of their states, to a *new* post-war elite, brought to power by the war, and intent on launching a system of banks, corporations, and cultural institutions that would place them on the world stage.[38] The struggle to establish Boston's and Philadelphia's post-war theaters demonstrates the competition among conflicting social elements to establish and legitimize their own cultural spheres. The contest between the old order and the rising post-Revolutionary elite forms the basis for understanding the process by which Boston and Philadelphia established a theatrical culture, and the symbolic significance that it assumed. Benedict Anderson has suggested that the arts can be viewed as a "cultural product of nationalism."[39] But whose nationalism? The first years of the Republic witnessed a struggle to determine whose national and cultural vision of America would prevail, and by what means.

The efforts of Boston's and Philadelphia's new post-Revolutionary elites to establish theatrical entertainments reflected not only their social and intellectual position in the new nation, but their wish to cement their cultural authority. To Boston's and Philadelphia's "well-born,"[40] the playhouse – that School of Republican Virtue – offered a forum to circulate the correct cultural doctrine of the new nation. The "young men of the Revolution" saw themselves as "pushing back the boundaries of darkness," and implementing Lockean principles of Enlightenment thought in their re-education of the American people.[41] To the theater's post-war opponents, which encompassed both religious groups such as the Quakers and political figures such as Samuel Adams of Boston and State Constitutionalist William Finlay of Pennsylvania, the playhouse loomed as a "school of vice" that would encourage people to "forget their political duties."[42]

Given the vehemence of the wartime anti-theatrical sentiment, it may be surprising that attempts were made to establish permanent theatrical entertainments in Philadelphia and Boston before the ink on the peace treaty had dried. Lewis Hallam, Jr., son of the well-known actor/manager, and inheritor of the pre-Revolutionary Hallam-Douglass Company, had spent the war in the West Indies. After the war, he hoped to re-establish his profitable touring circuit in the states (and to expand it). In 1782, Hallam petitioned to re-open the Philadelphia theater, ostensibly to recoup the financial losses that his troupe (tactfully renamed the Old American Company) had sustained during the wartime ban. Between 1782 and 1789, he repeatedly petitioned the General Assembly for the right to re-open the Southwark

Theatre, citing every reason from financial necessity to the importance of playgoing as a "necessary concomitant of our Independence."[43] His efforts only served to revive all the anti-theater sentiment of the war years. The diary of Quaker Christopher Marshall records the struggle between pro- and anti-theater supporters in 1784, one of the many times Hallam tried to re-open the theater. Marshall chronicles the efforts of the Quakers to circulate anti-theater petitions in protest against Hallam's initiative. When the pro-theater measure was defeated, Marshall commented with pleasure: "So the players left disappointed to the great satisfaction of the honest and upright citizens."[44]

Though Hallam claimed that it was "easy to submit"[45] to the Quakers' and government's decrees, he nevertheless continued to campaign for a legal theater, and in the meantime persisted in staging illegal entertainments, thinly disguised as pantomimes, lectures, or concerts.[46] By 1786 the Pennsylvania government (still under the rule of the State Constitutionalists) was sufficiently frustrated with Hallam's disobedience and deceit to pass a new anti-theater law, enlarging the original 1779 edict to include performances billed as "pantomimes."[47] This move came as a blow to the theater's supporters, who tried to argue that theatrical entertainments could have a positive effect on the Commonwealth:

> Witness the factions and animosities that subsist in our own Commonwealth – witness also the dangerous insurrection and rebellion that have enkindled throughout almost every part of the Massachusetts Bay... What does all this anarchy proceed from? From the want of theatres, dances, shows, and other public entertainments. A theater will never be prejudicial to a state unless the tool of party or the vehicle of obscenity and scandal.[48]

In the face of the State Constitutionalists' staunch resistance to allowing any kind of legal theatrical entertainments, the creation of a legitimate postwar theater in Philadelphia seemed unlikely, and indeed, seven years elapsed between Hallam's first petition to Pennsylvania's post-Revolutionary government and the repeal of Pennsylvania's 1779 anti-theatrical legislation.[49] The successful repeal of the anti-theater law in 1789 coincided with the ousting of the radical Constitutionalists by the Anti-Constitutionalist/Federalist party. The Federalist victory paved the way for a decade of social and cultural reform in Pennsylvania.

While Philadelphia seemed on its way towards establishing a legal theater by 1789, no significant attempts were made to create a playhouse in

Boston prior to 1790, and in both states popular resistance to the theater remained strong. Why was it so difficult to convince the citizens of Boston and Philadelphia that the theater was a desirable and necessary recreation? The negative example of British wartime entertainments had inspired a strong anti-theater opposition among devout republicans, who viewed playgoing as incompatible with civic virtue. But more importantly, in the early 1780s the theater's advocates had not yet achieved a financial or political status that would allow them to support the establishment of a theatrical culture. As the decade progressed, they consolidated their power and their fortunes through the establishment of private banks and stock companies. They also accrued the necessary social and political clout to effect change in their communities.[50] With the end of the war, paradoxically, the onus of building an American national identity fell to members of new local elites willing to pit their power against that of an old order who feared the introduction of potentially corrupting institutions into their virtuous republic.

A complex web of financial, social, and political associations linked the theater's supporters in Boston and Philadelphia. The theater's opponents also maintained a system of alliances based on common interests, and they began with one crucial advantage in the early post-war years – possession of what Ronald Formisano has termed the "Revolutionary Center."[51] Centrality and legitimacy in the early Republic were bound up in complex rituals of "ceremony, celebration, and sermon."[52] After the war, political power in Boston and Philadelphia rested with the men who had guided their local revolutionary regimes. These men (among the most vocal, Maier's "Old Revolutionary" Samuel Adams and John Hancock of Massachusetts, and Pennsylvania State Constitutionalist William Finlay) were determined to suppress activities that smacked of British tastes, or that would permit one group of men to acquire substantial economic and social privilege over another.

"I can do everything with money and nothing without":[53] the Pennsylvania Federalists take control

During the first years of the early Republic, Philadelphia experienced "a series of distinct but overlapping and interrelated struggles for power... over whose vision of America would become a reality, whose values would produce the institutions and laws that would govern the new country."[54] The Philadelphia elite (primarily Federalists) transformed the Revolution and post-war years into a time of economic opportunity, building the very institutions that would let them guide the new nation. Amassing substantial fortunes through trade, but more importantly through the creation of bank and stock companies, Philadelphia's wealthy Federalists gained political and economic control of the state by 1788. But the pre-war cultural institutions that they supported – and tried to resurrect after the war – such as the City Dancing Assembly, theatrical entertainments, and the College of Philadelphia, seemed at odds with the "republican virtue" that the State Constitutionalists had hoped to promote.[55] The State Constitutionalists believed that entertainments and speculative ventures corrupted the government and the people. They emphasized equality and direct representation, fearing anything that savored of "private interest" or luxury. However, in their zeal for reform, the Constitutionalists had enacted laws which alienated a significant portion of the Pennsylvania population, including the Quakers and other sectarian communities as well as the Anglican/Federalist elite.[56]

Pennsylvania politics entered a tug-of-war during the first years of the early Republic. Between 1784 and 1788, the struggle between Federalists and State Constitutionalists centered on two main issues: the charter of the Bank of North America and the ratification of the Federal Constitution. Improbable as it may seem, these issues were inextricably linked to Hallam's efforts to re-open the theater in Philadelphia. Prior to the Federalist victory of 1788, no member of the Philadelphia elite initiated any organized action to secure a legal theater for the state (though many may have attended the illegal theatrical activities Hallam offered during this time). But the intense arguments over the Bank and Federal Constitution created a new set of opposing parties who ultimately faced off over the issue of a legal theater. The acrimonious character of the Bank and Constitutional struggles spilled over into the theatrical debates. The State Constitutionalists resisted the theater partly as an expression of partisan solidarity, since they felt that the prospect of a theater undermined the cultural simplicity at the heart of Pennsylvania's democratic experiment. They formed a phalanx of opposition against a group that they believed was trying to subvert the Commonwealth. One 1784 observer noted, "As long as stage plays are prohibited, the present Constitution will stand its vigor, but no longer."[57]

The first blow to the State Constitutionalists' authority came in the struggle over the Bank of North America. The Bank, founded in 1781 to support the Revolutionary Army in a time of crisis, soon appeared to its opponents as a cabal of "conspicuous Federalists,"[58] who controlled 40 percent of its stock.[59] State Constitutionalists (who did not support the Bank or receive any direct benefits from it) called the Bank a danger to public safety, claiming that it placed too much power with "a certain body of monied men."[60] The pro-Bank party consisted of Philadelphia men like Robert Morris, Thomas Willing, and Thomas Fitzsimmons – members of the post-war elite with financial ties to one another and to a common political agenda.[61] The anti-Bank party was led by Constitutionalists such as John Smilie (Fayette County), Robert Whitehill (Cumberland County), and William Finlay (Westmoreland): men who sprang from western Pennsylvanian, Scots-Irish backgrounds and "had welcomed the Revolution as a means of seizing control of state politics from the East."[62]

Why was a bank considered such a danger to the fledgling republican government, since the natural assumption would be that a strong banking system would benefit the state? As Robert E. Wright has suggested, the American Revolution substantially undermined the system of "deference" that had governed colonial society. Wright suggests that this system had regulated not only social exchanges, but financial ones as well, and thus had confined lucrative economic ventures to the hands of a relatively small, well-placed, and interconnected group of merchant elite. The chaos of the Revolution disrupted many of the relationships that had formed the basis of the colonial economy, and the radicals who moved into the "power vacuum" during the war were anxious to prevent the wealthy classes from re-establishing the patterns of association that had excluded the mechanic and yeoman classes for so long.[63]

Indeed, the Revolutionary radicals had good cause for their anxiety. Banks of the eighteenth century operated largely at the whim of their private shareholders and investors. They could engage in both public and private transactions, so that it was often difficult to determine where the personal politics of the bank managers separated from official bank policy.[64] The lack of distinction between "public" and "private" roles and preferences raised anxieties among Pennsylvania's State Constitutionalists, who saw the bank as the potential "weapon" that the Philadelphia Federalists would use to regain control of the state government. Thomas Fitzsimmons, a member of the Bank's Board of Directors, a Federalist, and a future theater supporter, scoffed at these fears. He attacked the State Constitutionalists, suggesting that their motives for opposing the bank were purely selfish: "The most that the country gentlemen can any ways contend for, is that they, living at a distance, and wishing to be accommodated with loans of money...cannot have them."[65] Nevertheless, since the State Constitutionalists retained the majority in the Pennsylvania General Assembly in the mid-1780s, they were able to successfully attack the Bank and its directors.

The anti-Bank party succeeded in revoking the Bank's charter in 1785, a move which united and mobilized Pennsylvania's Federalist faction. During the next three years, the Bank debate played out in the government and in popular pamphlet literature. The State Constitutionalists argued that the circulation of specie should be under the control of the state government, while the Federalists argued that the State Constitutionalists had no right to revoke a charter formed by the Continental Congress, which represented the federal government.[66] Among the most famous accounts of the battle are James Wilson's 1785 *Considerations on the Bank of North America*, Mathew Carey's 1786 *Debates and Proceedings of the General Assembly of Pennsylvania on the Memorials Praying for a Repeal or Suspension of the Law Annulling the Charter of the Bank*, and Thomas Paine's 1786 *Dissertations on Government, the Affairs of the Bank and Paper Money*. Each of these pamphlets accused the State Constitutionalists of ulterior motives in repealing the Bank's charter. Carey suggested that the Bank debate formed part of a larger pattern of abuse of power, since the State Constitutionalists had refused to hear any debate on the subject, nor had they visited the Bank or spoken with its directors, displaying a "pre-determination to condemn."[67] Paine accused the anti-Bank party of undemocratic behavior – of conspiring "to prevent their constituents comprehending the subject."[68]

The anti-Bank party retaliated with similar charges of undemocratic conduct against the Federalists; as representative John Smilie noted, "the gentlemen on the other side of the question, feel interested in it personally . . . whereas we have no private interest to serve on the occasion." Smilie also insinuated that the pro-Bank petitioners had forged names on their petitions, or had used "the influence and terrors of the Bank . . . to procure subscribers." He derided the "aristocratical" pretensions of the Bank's directors, charging that they used their wealth to influence elections.[69]

By 1786, the Bank had become a campaign issue which exposed the personal and ideological animosities in Pennsylvania's post-war society. Looking back over the events of those three years, William Finlay observed, "Repealing the charter, instead of reducing the size of the Bank, had 'changed the majority'."[70] Finlay's words proved prophetic: the Bank victory – won by a narrow margin of thirty-three "yeas" to twenty-eight "nays"[71] – positioned the Pennsylvania Federalists to push for the ratification of the Federal Constitution.

During the ratification crisis and the debates of 1787, the State Constitutionalists resisted the Federal Constitution for many of the same reasons that they had opposed the Bank. Claiming that the Federal Constitution would

create an oligarchy in the new nation, Anti-Federalists tried to rally support
in the western counties traditionally opposed to federal authority (such as
Westmoreland and Bedford).[72] Unfortunately for them, the State Constitutionalists' wartime activities had alienated a sizable portion of the Quaker
population who dominated these regions, and in 1786 they had provoked the
Pennsylvania Presbyterians with their decision to disenfranchise the Scots-
Presbyterian Church in Philadelphia. The Federalist party recruited these
disgruntled Quakers and Presbyterians, as well as large numbers among the
Philadelphia mechanics. They promised to reverse the State Constitutionalists' harmful policies, and, more importantly, to extend them aid from the
Bank of North America.[73] State Constitutionalists protested these tactics,
accusing the "well-born junto" in Philadelphia of "attaching to their party
the weighty interest of Quakers and Tories," as the foundation upon which
to build "their mediated schemes of profit and aggrandizement."[74] Despite
the State Constitutionalists' efforts, the Federalists were able to win a sufficient majority both to pass the Federal Constitution and to assume control
of the Assembly.

Once the Federalists came to power in 1788, they immediately took steps
to reverse the restrictive policies of the State Constitution – including those
dealing with the theater. In November, 1788, a group of the Philadelphia
elite[75] formed a Dramatic Association "for the purpose of obtaining the
establishment of a theatre in Philadelphia under a liberal and properly regulated plan."[76] Self-described as "men of science, friends to virtue, and approved guardians of their country,"[77] the Dramatic Association bombarded
the press with pro-theater material. Much of their writing asserted the value
of theatrical entertainments, but other portions attacked the theater's enemies and questioned their motives. In a "Letter in Favor of the Drama,
part 3," which appeared in the *Pennsylvania Packet* in February, 1789, the
author asserted:

> If I thought the legislature passed the law prohibiting stage plays from a
> persuasion that they were prejudicial to the morals of the people, I would
> have more charity for them, notwithstanding its being contrary to the
> [Federal] Constitution. But it is evident that this was not the case – many
> of the members of that body have invariably opposed everything that was
> proposed for the benefit of Philadelphia.[78]

Lest his readers doubt what he defined as "for the benefit of Philadelphia," the author explicitly cited the Constitutionalists' efforts to revoke the

charters of the College of Philadelphia and the Bank of North America as his negative examples. The Dramatic Association invoked the Federal Constitution to defend the theater by criticizing those who would "deprive a freeman of a natural right [to attend innocent entertainments]."[79] They also criticized the State Constitutionalists' appeal to Quaker and Presbyterian prejudices to oppose the theater. Ironically, the Constitutionalists used much the same tactic to recruit opposition to the theater as the Federalists had to generate support for the Constitution, and the same two groups – Quakers and Presbyterians – were involved. The Federalists who supported the theater noted with annoyance the Quakers' shift in allegiance. Their pro-theater petition of 1789 carried a veiled threat to the Quakers, concerning the repeal of the Test Acts:[80] "Men who have suffered under the lash of persecution, should [not] now wage a virulent war against freedom of thought and action – particularly at the same moment when they are soliciting the legislature to release them from one fetter, should prevail upon this honorable body to rivet a fetter upon others."[81]

Despite the efforts of its opponents, the bill in favor of repealing Pennsylvania's anti-theatrical legislation became law on March 2, 1789, by a vote of thirty-five to twenty-nine.[82] A comparison of roll-call votes on the issues of the Bank, the Federal Constitution, and the theater suggests that resistance to all three initiatives was concentrated in western Pennsylvania, among counties such as Westmoreland, Cumberland, Dauphin, and Mifflin, while support was focused in Philadelphia. Certain counties such as Lancaster demonstrated pro-Federalist leanings, but still opposed the theater (hardly surprising, considering the sizable Quaker population of this area).[83] When the repeal was announced, the theater ran triumphant new advertisements for performances with the heading "BY AUTHORITY."[84] Now all that remained to the Philadelphia junto was to create a theater that would fulfill their expectations.

Public or private? Boston's Tontine Gentry *versus* the old order

Philadelphia's battle to establish legitimate theatrical entertainments in many ways provided the model for Boston's, which took place a few years later and which was of much shorter duration. In July, 1789 General Henry Knox of Philadelphia wrote to his friend Samuel Breck, then living in Boston:

This letter will be handed to you by Mr. John Henry [Lewis Hallam's partner], one of the managers of the American Theatre, and is generally designed for such other open friends as you may think it proper to communicate it to. As the state of Pennsylvania has repealed laws against dramatic performances, Mr. Henry has flattered himself with the idea that the same might be effected in Massachusetts, and he accordingly visits Boston to examine whether his hopes are well-founded in this appeal...My enlightened Townsmen know the full value of such a refined entertainment.[85]

Though Knox's letter suggests that interest in establishing theatrical entertainments may have been bubbling in Boston as early as 1789, and though John Henry petitioned for a repeal of Boston's anti-theatrical legislation in 1790, no group took immediate action to support these efforts. The "open friends" to which Knox referred in his letter lacked the necessary financial and political clout to bring theatrical diversions to a state still reeling from the impact of Shays's Rebellion, and still firmly under the thumb of members of the old order, such as Samuel Adams and Governor John Hancock. Though Hancock and Adams might have disagreed over some points concerning Massachusetts's revolutionary government, they were united in their distaste for any ventures that threatened their social and political dominance. Hancock had been part of the committee in 1767 that renewed Massachusetts's strict anti-theatrical legislation as a protest against the Townshend Duties, and Adams had expressed his scorn for British wartime military theatricals and for those Loyalists who attended them.[86]

In addition to the "Old Revolutionaries" who opposed the theater, there was another party in Boston resistant to the allure of "European" diversions: the proprietors of the Massachusetts Bank. Founded in 1784, the Massachusetts Bank consolidated the authority of many Boston-area merchants who had enjoyed significant influence in the pre-war years. It did not allow access outside its small circle of subscribers, remaining under the firm control of what Peter Dobkin Hall has described as a network of "kin-alliances."[87] In addition to their family and business connections, the Bank's founders also shared participation in organizations such as the American Academy of Arts and Sciences (1780), the Massachusetts Humane Society (1786), the Society for Propagating the Gospel Among the Indians (1787), the Massachusetts Historical Society (1791), and the Massachusetts Society for Promoting Agriculture (1792).[88] Their participation in such "worthy" enterprises suggests that they identified these causes as relevant to the development of the Commonwealth. The Massachusetts Bank founders also supported the intellectual development of the new republic in the form of literary magazines, or what Tamara Thornton has called the "Whig literary tradition...of Addison, Steele, Pope, and Thomson."[89] Interestingly, few of the men involved in these enterprises supported the development of a new theater. They prized "republican" gentility (which valued rural retirement) over "European" manners.

During the mid-1780s, sporadic efforts had been made to establish a new "polite" society in Boston similar to that of Philadelphia and the cultured cities of Europe. Among the diversions proposed were tea parties, card playing, dancing assemblies, and playgoing. These early initiatives were ridiculed by the older, more established groups in the city – both in print and in private. As Richard Bushman has noted, "Gentility seemed to carry within itself the cultural seeds of its own destruction."[90] The 1785 farce *Sans souci, alias, Free and easy, or, An evening's peep into a polite circle* lambasts Boston's social aspirants and the real-life members of Boston's Sans Souci Club,[91] who believed that card playing and theater-going offered more cultural cachet than republican virtue. As the character Little Pert remarks in the play:

> D—m the old musty rules of decency and decorum – national character – Spartan virtues – republican principles... Fashion and etiquette are more agreeable to my ideas of life – this is the independence *I* aim at – the free and easy air which distinguishes the man of fashion...from the republican.[92]

While Little Pert scorns the "musty" principles of republicanism, Madam Importance mourns the leveling effect of democracy, and hopes that the institutions of card playing, assemblies, and theater-going will "be the most effectual means to establish a precedency – we have for a long while been too much at a level." She describes frequent public entertainments as a means of winnowing out those who cannot afford to keep pace.[93]

In a 1785 letter, Samuel Adams noted that a theater under proper regulation might not be harmful, but that a theater directed by supporters of the Tea Assembly/Sans Souci Club definitely would be detrimental to Boston society (since presumably it would perpetuate the same shallow system of values as its sponsors). Writing to her son, republican and sometime playwright Mercy Otis Warren described the Sans Souci Club as "a subscription party consisting principally of the younger gay class of people in the town... their amusements optional, dancing or cards...a ridiculous institution for a country such as this."[94] Warren (named by some as the author of *Sans souci*), the sponsors of the Massachusetts Bank, and "Old Revolutionaries" like Samuel Adams targeted the theater and the trappings of elite society as a danger to republican virtue – and a symptom of sympathy with Tory interests.[95]

The late 1780s also witnessed a growing anxiety on the part of the "Old Revolutionaries" and the patrons of the Massachusetts Bank about the rise of new men with new money. The June, 1789 issue of the *Massachusetts Magazine* denounced local upstarts who used their wealth to cultivate frivolous entertainments in Boston. The "Reformer" railed against "[m]en who in the days of our forefathers would scarcely have been set in comparison with the dogs ... [who are now] received in every polite circle with attention." The "Reformer" added that these "most abandoned characters" had been "lifted by wealth," rather than merit.[96] How could these "new men" hope to penetrate the tightly closed circle of Boston society? By creating their own institutions of finance and culture.

By the early 1790s, this "mushroom gentry"[97] had gained a foothold in Boston society, and Boston's sense of cultural and civic competitiveness with its sister city to the south had emerged. In a 1791 letter to his wife, representative Theodore Sedgewick compared the nation's capital to Boston, noting that:

> They [Philadelphians] seem in their improvements to have got the start of any other place in the continent ... They believe themselves to be the first people in America, as well in manners as in arts ... and are at no pains to disguise their opinion ... In point of polished manners, they are certainly in a grade vastly below the inhabitants of Boston. The species of pride in which the Philadelphians excel perhaps every other people is in decorating their town.[98]

Could Boston afford to fall behind, in either cultural ventures or civic improvements? Apparently not. But transforming Boston into a city that could compete with, or outstrip, Philadelphia required initiative on the part of the "new men" prepared to defy Hancock's political, social, and economic agenda.[99] These men, some representatives in state government, some wealthy merchants and lawyers, and some former army officers, eventually drew together to form the Boston Tontine Association, using private insurance companies and bank ventures to accumulate the necessary capital to finance their plans for Boston's development. The Tontine represented a new type of interest group in Boston. Peter Dobkin Hall observes that during the post-war period "[m]erchant families, both old Bostonians and newer arrivals, began intermarrying, forming political alliances, and engaging in jointly funded corporate enterprises." The effect of this unification "became the means not only for extending their hegemony over larger areas, but also for structuring and mediating their new relations with one another."[100]

Formed in 1791, the Boston Tontine Association's original subscribers included politicians and professional men such as William Tudor, Benjamin Austin, Thomas Dawes, John Codman, Jr., and Jonathan Amory, as well as wealthy merchants, Stephen Higginson, Nathaniel Fellowes, Joseph Russell, Jr., Oliver Wendell, Caleb Davis, Frederick W. Geyer, Ebenezer Storer, and William Phillips.[101] The tontine was a life insurance company, the type of corporation which Pauline Maier called "the instrument of those economic changes that transformed Massachusetts between 1780 and 1860," allowing greater private development of financial and public ventures, ostensibly for the good of the Commonwealth.[102] Narrowly, a tontine is an annuity, shared among a group, but the term can also refer to those who share in the annuity. The members of the Boston Tontine Association proposed "raising a fund by a subscription on lives to pertain to uses private and public."[103] Though the venture sounds like a simple life insurance group, a true tontine functioned along the lines of a private bank – issuing loans and accepting collateral at the discretion of its directors. The Tontiners had amassed roughly two million dollars by the winter of 1792, when they petitioned the State for the right to incorporate. Their request raised anxieties about the direction and regulation of Boston's post-Revolutionary economy, since there appeared no way to monitor the Tontiners' use of their funds. Because of the anxiety that the Tontine proposal generated, it was rejected each time it came before the House.[104] Paul Goodman has suggested that post-Revolutionary social and political divisions frequently "occurred between entrenched groups and others seeking access to opportunity,"[105] and this dynamic may certainly have influenced resistance to the Tontiners' schemes. Part of the opposition to the Tontine stemmed from the concern among leaders like John Hancock and Samuel Adams that the rising elite was overtaking the established social structures of Boston society. As John W. Tyler notes, by the 1790s the market in Massachusetts belonged to a "new generation" that left Samuel Adams and John Hancock behind.[106] Moreover, in a society ostensibly committed to civic virtue and *pro bono publico*, the mere mention of a tontine signaled a growing and unpleasant tide of liberal capitalist practices with dangerous and divisive potential.[107]

At the same time that the Tontiners were forming their association, they were preparing and presenting the first of many petitions to the Assembly for the repeal of Massachusetts's 1750 anti-theatrical legislation. The language of the 1791 petition offered to Boston's selectmen outlines the type of theater that the Tontiners envisioned:

> A theater, where the actions of great and virtuous men are represented, under every possible embellishment which genius and eloquence can give, will not only afford a rational and innocent amusement, but essentially advance the interests of private and political virtue; will have the tendency to polish the manners and habits of society, to disseminate the social affections, and to improve and refine the literary taste of our rising republic.[108]

The petition further claimed that it was "repugnant to the Principles of a Free Government to deprive any of its citizens of a rational entertainment."[109] There is a striking similarity between the text of the Massachusetts and Pennsylvania pro-theater petitions, though this is hardly surprising, given that the Pennsylvania petition had been widely published.

Neither the Tontine proposal nor the theater petition met with success. The theater petition was rejected with the explanation that it was "not expedient at this time" to consider repealing the anti-theater laws.[110] Newspapers and pamphlets raised the cry against the evils of Tontine and the theater. Editor Abraham Bishop of the Boston *Argus* penned a vehement series of articles in which he "exposed" the Tontine as a grossly inflated stock scheme and likened the theater to the plague. He pointed out the links between the men who supported the theater and the Tontine, deriding their "ambitions" for Boston: "Is New England to be infested with Theatres because some of our Tontine Gentry have been Southward and have heard some very pretty plays?" He added, "Do some of our rich men threaten to leave Boston if we will not have a Theatre? Let them go by all means." To Bishop, the Tontine and theater combined to symbolize all that was negative and dangerous in the seemingly unregulated economy of the new republic. "The rich are now playing a game against the poor. Unable to gain enough by Tontine and other plans, they wish to [corrupt] your ideas about property... Why does not the whole truth come out?"[111]

Supporters claimed the Tontine and the theater were patriotic enterprises that would advance the interests of the Commonwealth. The Tontiners promised that their organization would "loan funds to farmers and expand the circulating medium."[112] They also hinted that a rejection of the

Tontine would damage the Massachusetts economy, threatening that the public, "having their genius of enterprize [sic] cramped... [must resort] to foreign aid, for all know the Massachusetts Bank hath not of late been able to supply the calls of the people."[113] One Tontine enthusiast noted that "of all the various monied schemes which have been brought forward, none strike the mind of the philanthropist and republican more than that of the TONTINE [sic] lately established in this State."[114]

The theater's supporters pledged to sponsor "only such Theatrical Exhibitions as are Calculated to promote the Cause of Morality and Virtue, while at the same time conduce to polish the Manners and Habits of Society."[115] Defending the theater in a 1792 speech before the House, representative John Gardiner asserted that "the old things are rapidly doing away; already (within the last twenty years) the face of the political and moral world has changed." Speaking more pointedly to the opponents of the theater within the House, Gardiner noted, "There are some among us, in this House, who presume to take too much upon themselves, and attempt to control and direct, where they have no other right than to advise and attempt to persuade."[116]

Like the supporters of the Philadelphia theater, Boston's pro-theater party believed that they were victims of a conspiracy among members of the Assembly determined to block initiatives that would modernize and improve their society. In an anonymous 1792 publication, *The Rights of the Drama*, the author observed that "in an age of refinement and in a nation of free men," it was extraordinary "that there should exist a single enemy to the manly, rational amusements of the Theater." The author praised the "patriots" William Tudor and Charles Jarvis (both Tontiners), who were laboring to establish a theater in Boston.[117] In his pro-theater pamphlet, "Effects of the Stage on the Manners of the People: and the Propriety of Encouraging and Establishing a Virtuous Theater," Bostonian William Haliburton encouraged the government to support the theater, claiming that men who sponsored the theater would be remembered as "promoters of a design so grand and beneficial... [that] the history of the stage will ever after have a conspicuous place in the History of America."[118] Despite these efforts, state officials (most notably John Hancock, who, as noted earlier, had been a key player in the Commonwealth's 1767 ban against theater) continued from 1790 to 1793 to resist both the establishment of a theater and the advancement of the interests of the Tontine.[119]

Sidetracked by the opposition to the theater and the Tontine, both in the Assembly and in the press, the Tontiners tried another tactic. In 1792,

the Tontiners petitioned to incorporate as the Union Bank[120] whose ros-
ter of investors and capitalization were virtually identical to the Tontine,
including William Tudor, Nathaniel Fellowes, Stephen Higginson, Oliver
Wendell, Caleb Davis, David Greene, Frederick W. Geyer, Joseph Blake,
Charles Jarvis, Samuel Sewall, William Wedgery, and John Gardiner.[121]
Though the Tontiners' purposes in forming the Bank seemed transparent –
letters to newspapers derided the Bank as nothing more than a "stock-
jobbing shop, just to answer the purposes of speculators"[122] – the Bank did
receive the Assembly's permission to incorporate in early 1792, just as the
second Tontine-backed petition in support of the theater was being rejected.
(The Bank may have succeeded where the Tontine failed because the Bank
promised to loan funds to the state government!)

   According to roll-call votes (county by county), most of those who opposed the theater also opposed the Tontine and the Union Bank. Opponents
generally came from districts outside of Boston, and represented rural or
farming interests. The theater's supporters generally came from Suffolk and
Essex County and were affiliated with the Tontine and Bank.[123] The Union
Bank provided a comfortable and legitimate front for the Tontiners, who
continued to operate informally as an association. The Bank could serve
the Tontiners' purposes effectively since, as Naomi Lamoreaux notes,
in the early Republic bank directors "often funneled the bulk of funds under
their control to themselves, their relatives, and others with personal ties to
the board." She also observes that during this period, "there was a growing
confusion as to whether banks were public or private institutions."[124] The
ambiguous nature of the post-war banking system offered the Tontiners the
necessary economic clout to put their plans for a theater into action in spite
of the government's continued opposition.

Refined entertainments? First steps in Boston and Philadelphia

From the pro-theater rhetoric that the theaters' supporters spouted during
the 1780s and early 1790s, it is clear that they anticipated that their theaters would transform the cultural shape of the new nation. But what the
Philadelphia and Boston elite expected from their theaters and what they
got were two very different things. After the repeal of Pennsylvania's anti-
theatrical legislation in 1789, Philadelphians turned their attention to the
Old American Company, expecting that the removal of the last legal road-
block would allow manager Lewis Hallam to proceed with renovations to
the Southwark Theatre and improvements to the company that would make

Philadelphia's theater the best in the country. Similarly, once the Tontiners decided to act in defiance of Massachusetts law and establish their own small 500-seat theater in Board Alley, they expected a theatrical product that would, as their first petition had claimed, "improve and refine the literary taste of our rising republic." Both groups were destined for disappointment.

Philadelphia's Southwark Theatre, built in 1766, in addition to being inconveniently located by increasingly rundown dockside neighborhoods, was "an ugly, ill-contrived affair."[125] Spectators froze in the winter and roasted in the summer. Charles Durang claims that the theater became so hot during the summer season that the city fire engines were brought in so that water could be hosed onto the roof to cool the building.[126] Hallam and Henry, beset by financial difficulties after the war, had lacked the funds to renovate the house. Thus it fell far below the standards of theater patrons like Ann Willing Bingham,[127] who were familiar with the great European playhouses. The company seemed sloppy as well. As I suggested earlier, infighting among the company members seems to have undermined the quality of the performances. Hallam and Henry had promised the Philadelphia Dramatic Association in 1789 that they would replenish the troupe with new talent. Yet by 1791, they had neither repaired the house nor improved the quality of the performers.[128] In a published letter to Hallam and Henry, the members of the Dramatic Association expressed their frustration:

> The friends of the Drama, more particularly the members of the late dramatic association, whose labour and influence procured for you the license for opening a Theater in this city, have become so much dissatisfied with your want of attention to the promises you made them relative to the strengthening of your company by good actors from Europe, that they are determined to evince publicly their resentment of your conduct.[129]

Indeed, they were so annoyed by the poor quality of the players that the "Friends of the Drama" threatened the actors of the Old American Company with cries of "hiss! hiss! off!"[130]

Though Hallam tried to appease the Dramatic Association with promises that he would secure new players, they seemed disinclined to believe him after his previous stalling. Feeling that Hallam's theater reflected little credit on the city of Philadelphia, they began to circulate suggestions for "an association of citizens for the purpose of erecting an independent theater, and encouraging performers who will make greater exertions to please."[131] Hallam had clearly alienated his former supporters. Whether he felt that they wanted too much control over the running of his company in exchange for their continued support is unclear. However, the phrase "performers who will make greater exertions to please" suggests that the Dramatic Association expected that their opinions should guide the theater's policies to some degree.

They got their wish in 1791, when Hallam and the popular Old American Company actor Thomas Wignell had a disagreement about Wignell's role in the management of the troupe. The *New York Daily Advertiser* had called Wignell the "Atlas of the American Theater," claiming that he "carried" the rest of the Hallam Company.[132] Wignell was, therefore, in a strong position to demand concessions from Hallam. When Hallam refused, Wignell left the company to form one of his own, recruiting musician and composer Alexander Reinagle to accompany him. Together they created a proposal for a new theater, appealing to the former members of the Dramatic Association for support. Among their sponsors were such Philadelphia worthies as Robert Morris, the "financier of the Revolution," William Bingham, one of the wealthiest men in the United States, Henry Hill, John Swanwick (Morris's partner/agent), Thomas Fitzsimmons, General Walter Stewart, Thomas Willing, director of the Bank of North America, and Charles Pettit.[133]

Wignell and Reinagle struck at a propitious moment. The Philadelphia junto were in the process of developing new neighborhoods and establishing activities and entertainments that mimicked the European courts and urban centers. By 1790, "a substantial portion of the wealthy had broken away from the city's commercial center," which was concentrated around the public marketplace on Market and Second Streets, "and formed a new, upper-class residential area."[134] This area, known as the New Society Hill, was located between South and Market Streets, above Second and below Seventh Street. Among the residents of this section were Thomas Willing, William Bingham, and Robert Morris.[135] Part of Wignell and Reinagle's plan for the new theater included choosing a new location that would make it more accessible to patrons who had grown tired of wading through the mud to the unfashionable Southwark location. Wignell and Reinagle justified "erecting a new Theater in some Central part of the City," on the grounds that the city's "encreasing Wealth and Importance" demanded that its "places of Amusement should be put to a larger and more suitable scale."[136] The lot chosen for the theater, on the north side of Chestnut Street, and on the west side of Sixth, was not only convenient to the residences of the elite, it was situated near Independence Hall, the national capitol and the State House. What better way to impress upon the minds of foreign visitors the dual strengths of the city – its government and its cultural life? And what better way to legitimate the much-opposed theater than to plant it directly in the sightlines of the government officials who had tried to squash it?

A rumor circulated in the fall of 1791, while plans for the theater were still in progress, which demonstrates the significance of location for the new playhouse: "The place said to be chosen . . . is perhaps more improper than any other in the city . . . The lot in question is . . . near to the center of the city, it lies in and near the public walks . . . the university, the college, the Quakers' academy, the public library, and the courts of justice." The writer, obviously no admirer of the theater, admonished the "Parents, Masters, and mistresses, Legislators, citizens, Matrons, and Virgins" to protest and "avert this impending evil."[137]

Why was the location of the theater so "inappropriate" to the concerned observer? Part of the battle over the theater in the early national period concerned possession of the "Revolutionary Center," as demonstrated by a system of signs and symbols. By situating the theater in a central location, and essentially re-configuring Philadelphia society around their own homes and places of amusement, the post-war elite laid claim to the sites where the ceremonies of nationalism would take place and in which the shape of America's national identity would be determined.

Events in Boston followed a similar pattern, with one important distinction. Like the Philadelphia junto, the Tontiners had been busily accumulating and developing property within the city, creating new neighborhoods modeled on wealthy European urban centers. Like the Philadelphians, they planned their theater to ornament the city. But unlike the Philadelphians, the Tontiners undertook construction of their new theater while it was still illegal.

After their repeated petitions to the Assembly failed, the Tontiners took matters into their own hands. Throughout the late 1780s and early 1790s, the Tontine Associates and a group of "satellite" professionals and merchants involved with them had acquired a sizable portion of the available land in Boston's Ward 10.[138] By the mid-1790s, they owned multiple lots on several streets, including Board Alley and Federal Street, the sites of Boston's first two theaters.

In 1792, the Tontiners built Boston's first theater on land belonging to merchant Joseph Russell. Described by one patron as a "rough-boarded hovel," it was nevertheless enough of a start to encourage the Tontiners.[139] The Board Alley Theatre season opened in August of 1792 and ran throughout the fall with a series of acrobat acts featuring Joseph Harper (formerly

of the Old American Company) and the Placide Family. During the fall of
1792, patrons enjoyed such entertainments as:

A Favorite PANTOMIME Entertainment – called
Harlequin Skeleton
With Machinery
Where will be introduced, LA DANCE DE LA
FRICASSEE
DANCING on the
SLACK WIRE
Mons. Placide will balance a Peacock's Feather in different ways[140]

Some letters to the newspapers objected that "the tightrope applied to the
legs is not so effectual to refine the *morals* of the people as the old fashioned
way of applying it to the *neck*."[141] And those who had read Gardiner's impas-
sioned defense of the theater might have wondered how gazing at someone
balancing a peacock feather would "polish the Manners and Habits of
Society." But for all its faults, the Board Alley Theatre was in many ways an
experiment to gauge the public's appetite for entertainment, and to test the
government's willingness to uphold the law. The appearance of advertisements for "opera glasses" in November 1792 suggests that Boston audiences
had begun to enjoy theatrical entertainments on a fairly regular basis,[142] as
does the notation found at the bottom of playbills and ads for evening performances "Tickets to be had at the usual places."[143] Despite the legal ban
on theater, performances proceeded smoothly throughout the fall of 1792.

However, Governor Hancock was growing increasingly frustrated with
the Tontiners' open defiance of the state's anti-theatrical legislation. In a
letter to the newspapers he complained:

Whether the apprehension of the evils which might flow from Theatrical
Exhibitions...are well founded or not...the Act is now a law of the
Commonwealth...and surely it ought to claim the respect and obedience
of all who happen to live within the Commonwealth.
No measures have been taken to punish a most open breach of the Law,
and a most contemptuous insult upon the powers of the Government.[144]

Hancock's letter provoked one effort to squelch the theater – an utter failure.
On December 5, 1792, the Boston sheriff attended the evening performance
and tried to close the theater and arrest the manager, Joseph Harper. The
outraged audience rioted, and in their fury tore down Governor Hancock's
portrait and coat of arms and trampled them.[145] The founders of the theater

could hardly have asked for more direct proof that the old order had lost its hold on public opinion. The "trial" of Joseph Harper was a farce, with Tontine member "Judge" William Tudor, who was as embroiled in supporting the offending entertainments as anyone, defending Harper and securing his release. Based on advertisements which ran in local papers, performances resumed just a few days after the incident, and proceeded for the rest of the season without opposition.[146]

The Tontiners made one last official effort to secure a repeal of the anti-theater law in early 1793. Their petition made it through the Assembly by a vote of fifty-seven to fifty-four, but was never signed into law.[147] On the surface, this denial seems to subvert the Tontiners' triumph. In fact, it reveals the extent to which their interests had polarized tensions in the Commonwealth, tensions between old and new, urban and rural, and central and peripheral factions. Like the Philadelphia elite, whose triumphs in the debates over the Bank, the Constitution, and the theater had positioned them to assume control of the Revolutionary Center, the Tontiners' tacit victory in the December theater riot shifted them to a new position of power. The rioting audience members demonstrated to the Tontiners and the Boston community their desire to maintain a Boston theater. When the rioters trampled Hancock's coat of arms – the quintessential emblem of the old order – they elevated the theater space into a realm of action and claimed it as their own. After Hancock's death in 1793, no other official attempts were made to close the theater.

To demonstrate their new status as cultural arbiters, both the Tontiners and the Philadelphia elite planned theater buildings to serve as showpieces of their respective cities. Philadelphians opened subscriptions in 1791 for their new theater, and Bostonians in April, 1793 for a theater to replace the one in Board Alley.[148] In citing their reasons for building a permanent playhouse, Philadelphia's Robert Morris and Boston's John Gardiner mentioned the positive impression that a beautiful playhouse would make on foreign visitors.[149] Plans for both theaters were grandiose, and modeled after their European counterparts.[150] While the Philadelphians constructed their theater opposite to their capitol, the Tontiners placed their theater literally at their doorsteps.[151] The Federal Street Theatre was built directly opposite a new row of townhouses on Franklin, Milk, and Federal Streets, known as the Tontine Crescent (designed by Charles Bulfinch), and modeled after the urban architecture of Bath, England. Together the Tontine Crescent and the Theatre formed a new urban neighborhood, which offered a monument to the Tontiners' vision for Boston's cultural and aesthetic growth.[152]

Subscribers wanted to make certain that they had the most elegant appointments possible, thus they sent to Europe for items such as "crimson tabray, fringe and tassells, chandeliers, girandoles," as well as scenery and furniture for the card and assembly rooms that the theaters also housed.[153] In addition to their luxurious trappings, the theaters were constructed to maintain distinctions between different social classes among the audience. The Chestnut Street Theatre proudly advertised: "The entrances are so well-contrived and the lobbies so spacious, that there can be no possibility of confusion among the audience going into different parts of the house."[154] It is also interesting to note that both the Philadelphians and the Bostonians insisted on having their own companies, under their supervision. Though splinter companies from the Old American troupe tried to establish themselves in Philadelphia in the late 1780s and early 1790s, they received no support from the Dramatic Association. Moreover, when Wignell contacted Bostonian Perez Morton about the prospect of bringing the Chestnut Street company to Boston for a season, Morton declined on behalf of the Tontiners, noting that it was Boston's ambition to establish its own private company.[155]

In their impatience to enjoy their new playhouses, the subscribers harried the builders, who appear to have put up both theaters in a record amount of time. As Philadelphian Abby Hamilton observed to her friend Sarah Bache, "The New Theatre is a superb building and only wants Wignell's return to open. The old ones groan as they pass, and say had it been for a church, it would have been years finishing."[156] But the price of this grandeur quickly mounted. Architect Charles Bulfinch's projected costs for the Federal Street Theatre had been between $15,000 and $20,000, but by January, 1794 the subscribers had already spent $35,000, and anticipated spending an additional $5,000 before the theater's completion.[157] Initial estimates for the Chestnut Street Theatre had ranged around $20,000, but Brooks McNamara estimates the final cost at approximately $135,000.[158] Subscribers for both theaters were repeatedly asked to contribute additional funds so that the buildings could be finished. Small wonder that their impatience to see their new playhouses occasionally got the better of them. For example, when Thomas Wignell and the new company were delayed in London, Reinagle was forced to open the theater for concerts to pacify investors who wanted to see the interior of the building.

It was after Reinagle opened the Chestnut Street playhouse briefly in February of 1793 that the Pennsylvania State Constitutionalists launched their last major offensive against the theater. Spurred by the luxurious appearance of the building, the State Constitutionalists proposed a bill that would permit a practice known as "partial taxation," or taxation directed at specific institutions and corporations, rather than a universal tax. The target was the New Theatre, which the legislature proposed taxing a fee of fifty dollars per performance. The revenues of this tax were earmarked for the construction of a presidential residence for George Washington. It is important to note that this new tax targeted the Chestnut Street Theatre only; no mention was made of imposing a tax on the Southwark Theatre, which was still in operation during this period. Moreover, the government had borrowed over $40,000 from the Bank of North America and other sources to fund the cost of the President's house. The Bank was also under renewed attack in 1793. Letters to *Dunlap's Daily Advertiser* accused the Bank's directors of using their monopoly to "aid their friends and ruin their enemies," and of deliberately excluding new subscribers.[159] A tax on the Chestnut Street Theatre would, in essence, allow the government to "rob Peter to pay Paul," simply taking revenues from one hated institution to repay a debt to another, without inconveniencing the government itself. It was a clever way for those men who objected to the financial and cultural plans of the elite to punish them. They attacked the elite's cherished new theater *and* their bank, and did it in the name of the Revolution's most revered figure, George Washington.

The Chestnut Street Theatre's supporters were outraged, seeing the proposed law as an attempt to destroy the new theater, and as a dangerous precedent that would open the way for future attacks on the Bank, their new turnpike corporation, and their growing land development companies.[160] They argued against the invocation of Washington's name, claiming that Washington as a known advocate of the theater would not wish his new home to profit by the theater's demise: "It would not be surprising...if he never entered a dwelling completed in so degrading a manner."[161] The theater's backers questioned the motives of the men who had introduced the tax, suggesting, "They indulge a hope that this act will amount to a prohibition of the amusements of the stage."[162] Reinagle submitted a petition, pleading against the tax and observing that such a tax would ruin two essentially "innocent" men, himself and his partner, Thomas Wignell. Reinagle's supporters asserted that since the fifty-dollar-per-night tax was not a condition under which the theater had originally been planned, such a condition should not be imposed retroactively.

The State Constitutionalists ultimately lost the battle over the tax, and the theater opened successfully, while the President's house remained unfinished for the next five years. More than any other individual struggle involving theater in post-war Philadelphia, the contest over which structure would assume greater importance, the President's house or the theater, suggests the extent to which the Philadelphia elite had succeeded in imposing their cultural priorities on the rest of the state. In that, it resembled strongly the Tontiners' victory in the 1792 Boston theater riot.

Yet just when it seemed that the Philadelphia theater might open without further controversy, the worst yellow fever epidemic since 1762 swept into the city. Death tolls reached into the thousands, and those men who had the financial wherewithal abandoned the city. The disaster prompted a storm of questions as to its cause. Was it evidence of divine judgment against the nation's leaders for being led astray by party and private interest? The clergy were quick to leap on a more local and tangible cause – the theater. Unfortunately for the theater's supporters, the outbreak of fever coincided with Wignell's return from Europe and with the plans for a gala opening of the new theater season.[163] As Martin Pernick notes, "The fever had miraculously appeared just as Philadelphia completed construction for what one Republican termed its Synagogue for Satan – the city's new Theatre."[164] The fever crisis rekindled the hopes of the anti-theater Quakers and clergy, who submitted new petitions against the imminent opening of the playhouse.

Nevertheless, despite the fever and the renewed efforts of the Philadelphia clergy, the Chestnut Street playhouse opened on February 17, 1794. Only two weeks earlier, Boston's Federal Street playhouse had opened to audiences so eager to view the new entertainments that they willingly paid up to twelve times the normal ticket prices.[165] It seemed, at long last, that citizens of Boston and Philadelphia would enjoy the "rational amusements" that they had craved for more than a decade. Unfortunately for them, the elites' heyday in the theater was fleeting, and a new swarm of troubles descended on the playhouses almost the instant they opened their doors. While these conflicts jeopardized the success of the Boston and Philadelphia playhouses, they also provided valuable object lessons for those elites in New York who were in the process of gauging the right moment to launch their own theatrical entertainments. Chapters 3 and 4 detail the political and cultural traps that the Boston and Philadelphia theaters encountered, and chapters 5 and 6 suggest the ways in which New York alternately emulated or avoided them.

3

"*A democracy of glee*"

T HE FIRST OFFICIAL YEAR OF OPERATION FOR THE FEDERAL Street and Chestnut Street houses might easily have been the last. In out-fitting their new theaters, the proprietors of both playhouses had imagined theatrical entertainments that would "advance the interest of private and political virtue"[1] in the new nation. But their vision clashed violently with the reality of party squabbles that prevailed between 1794 and 1795, and their ambitions for their theaters as sites of civic and cultural authority were chal-lenged by the invasion of factions that threatened to destroy the imagined community of the playhouse once and for all.

Yet the theaters' proprietors had no reason to anticipate disaster when the theaters opened their doors in early 1794. In both Boston and Philadelphia, audiences eagerly awaited the long-promised entertainments, and looked with evident pride at the handsome new playhouses that graced their cities. On January 29, 1794, six days before the opening of the Federal Street Theatre, Benjamin Russell's *Columbian Centinel* offered an enthusiastic description of the playhouse:

> The inside begins to display its brilliance. In convenience, elegance, and taste, the best judges have given preference to any in Europe – And the execution in style is equaled only by the excellence of the Architecture... For the honour of the town and the taste of our country, we shall endeavor to obtain such a description of it as will convey some idea of its beauty and elegance to those who cannot have the pleasure of seeing it.[2]

Russell's praise seemed to justify the labor and pains that the theater's founders had taken to bring the playhouse to Boston, and indeed Russell lauded the founders' diligence, commenting, "The Trustees have

"A democracy of glee": from a prologue written for the third season of the Federal Street Theatre, cited in Clapp, Jr., *Boston Stage*, p. 26.

71

spared no necessary expense."[3] He hailed the theater as an important monument to Boston's cultural enlightenment – a major shift from the scorn
heaped on the architectural "hovel"[4] that had been the first Board Alley
Theatre, and the inadequate entertainments housed therein. When audiences entered the theater for its first performance on February 4, 1794, they
found an interior that matched the outside appearance in luxury and modern style. The theater boasted a thirty-one-foot stage, "ornamented on each
side with two columns, and between them a stage door and a projecting
iron balcony." The ornate proscenium displayed "a flow of crimson drapery
and the arms of the Union and of the State of Massachusetts blended with
emblems tragic and comic."[5]

The deliberate intertwining of the American and State coats of arms with
the theatrical masks suggests an effort to claim the theater as an American
institution – to stamp a symbolic seal of approval on what was still, after
all, an illegal activity in Massachusetts. Not only did the building house
an impressive acting space, it also offered "a noble and elegant dancing
room ... richly ornamented with Corinthian columns and pilasters ... [with]
spacious card and tea rooms, and kitchens with proper conveniences."[6] The
creation of a ballroom, card rooms, and tea rooms *within* the theater structure also suggests that the Tontiners envisioned their playhouse as a gathering site for a certain wealthy class of patron, and that they hoped that their
theater would become the accepted cultural/social center for Boston's urban
elite.

While the Chestnut Street Theatre lacked the impressive outward appearance of its Boston counterpart, the Philadelphia playhouse was no less
impressive in its interior trappings. French traveler Moreau de Saint-Méry
recorded the following description of the house:

> The interior is handsome. The arrangement of the boxes is an agreeable
> semi-ellipse. The boxes are in three tiers, one above the other, fifteen
> boxes each ... The pit is raked from the first tier of boxes to the orchestra
> pit ... The auditorium is painted gray with a gold design. The third row
> of boxes even has slender gilt railings of some elegance. The boxes ...
> are papered in a tasteless red paper. The auditorium is lighted by small
> four-branched chandeliers.[7]

Though Saint-Méry's praise is not as unqualified as Russell's for the Federal
Street house, it is perhaps more useful, in that it offers the opinion of
a disinterested outsider – one of the "strangers and foreigners" that the
Boston and Philadelphia founders hoped their theaters would impress.[8]
Brooks McNamara notes one design feature that Saint-Méry overlooks: a

Inside View of the New Theatre. Philadelphia.

Figure 1. Interior of the Chestnut Street Theatre, Philadelphia

coat of arms above the stage, with the motto "The eagle suffers the little bird to sing."⁹ The Chestnut Street inscription was like the Federal Street coat of arms, a bid for legitimacy and for identification with the symbols of the new nation.

The new companies at both theaters held equal promise. The Federal Street Trustees had been intent on forming their own company to rival those of Wignell and Reinagle and Hallam's Old American Company. Perez Morton, member of the Union Bank and theater trustee, refused an offer from Wignell and Reinagle to play in the Boston house, commenting that the founders "have always been desirous of having a company of *their own* [*sic*], that they might command the Season of playing most agreeable to the inhabitants of Boston."¹⁰ The Boston trustees selected as manager Charles Stuart Powell, giving him a one-year, provisional lease on the theater, to be renewed if he proved a satisfactory manager. Powell was a veteran of the Theatre Royal in Covent Garden who had begun performing solo acts at the Board Alley Theatre in Boston in 1792. In 1793, Powell had traveled to England to secure a good company for the playhouse, which included his brother Snelling Powell and his brother's wife, Elizabeth Harrison.¹¹ Wignell and Reinagle had also made a strong bid to secure a good company for Philadelphia (and had perhaps been more successful than the Boston company, in the long run). Dunlap notes that Wignell's 1792 trip to England recruited a group of actors "more complete and replete with every species of talent for the establishment of a theatre than could have been contemplated by the most sanguine of his friends."[12] With their beautiful playhouses and promising acting companies, both Boston and Philadelphia looked forward to an active season of theatrical entertainments.

For its first performance on February 4, 1794, the Federal Street playhouse offered one of George Washington's favorite plays, Henry Brooke's *Gustavus Vasa, or The deliverer of his country.* Though Brooke's play deals with the liberation of Sweden from a tyrant usurper, it seemed to American audiences an excellent analogy to their own recent struggle with Britain. At the height of battle, Gustavus cries to his troops, who are outnumbered and outmatched:

> What are fifty, what a thousand slaves match'd to the sinew of a single arm that strikes for liberty? That strikes to save his fields from fire, his infants from the sword, his couch from lust, his daughters from pollution, and his large honours from eternal infamy? What doubt we then?[13]

To American audiences the hero, Gustavus, displayed manly virtues of republicanism not unlike their own presidential leader, and indeed, the last lines of the play echo Washington's self-sacrificing attitude: "O, I will of private passion all my soul divest, and take my dearer country to my breast."[14] Judith Sargent Murray,[15] a Boston author, whose satirical plays resembled those of Mercy Otis Warren, described the opening night audience's response to the play in *The Gleaner:* "I observed the marked attention, the solemn stillness, the tender tear upon the cheek of beauty, and the humid eye of manhood."[16]

New York, then enduring a season of "lamentably poor" scenic decorations, "of the lowest grade," and "black with age,"[17] looked on with some envy, since the scenes played in front of these uninspiring backdrops were not ones to excite patriotic fervor. The New York repertoire during the winter of the Chestnut Street and Federal Street openings featured: *Wild Oats, The Padlock, The Mourning Bride, The Irishman in London, The Fair Penitent,* and *The Chapter of Accidents.*[18] It was becoming increasingly apparent to New York audiences that their theater was both aesthetically and ideologically behind those of their sister cities.

Benjamin Franklin Bache's radical Philadelphia paper, the *General Advertiser* (later the *Aurora*), used the Boston theater opening to not only applaud Boston's patriotic choice of play, but to encourage the Philadelphia theater to emulate their patriotic display:

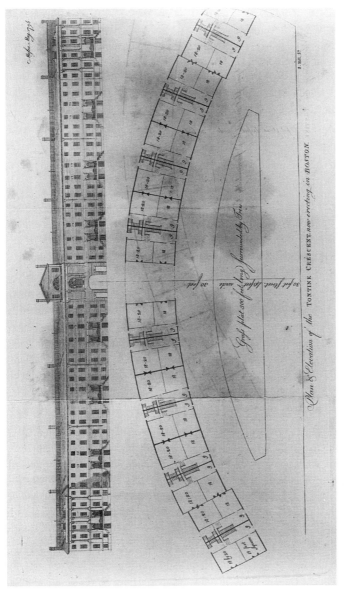

Figure 2. Elevation of the Tontine Crescent, Boston
Massachusetts Magazine, February, 1794

Figure 3. Federal Street Theatre and the Tontine Crescent, Boston

It is much to be wished that Messieurs Wignell and Reinagle may shortly favor the public with a representation of that admirable piece (*Gustavus Vasa*), and convince the friends of Freedom and Virtue that there are dramatic works which not only abound with pure and genuine sentiments in favor of liberty, but also powerfully advocate the cause of virtue and morality.[19]

Bache complained that the general choice of plays by Philadelphia's Chestnut Street managers did not reflect American sensibilities. The Philadelphia playhouse had opened on February 17, 1794, with O'Keeffe's popular comic opera *The Castle of Andalusia*, which lacked the serious republican tone of *Gustavus Vasa*.[20] During the first season the managers offered such British staples as *Venice Preserved*, *The Lying Valet*, *The School for Scandal*, and *The School for Wives*.[21] Of *The School for Wives*, Bache observed that "the play is not a mirror for an American audience. This to be sure is a fault common to most transatlantic productions." Bache noted that the play was useful in one respect: "by magnifying the deformities of vice abroad [it] may induce us to shun it at home."[22]

Bache's vision of the theater as a "school of Republican Freedom and Virtuous morality" differed from that of the theaters' founders.[23] From the beginning, the theaters' supporters had wildly optimistic hopes for the ways in which the theater could shape public sentiment in accordance with their views. Advocates such as Bostonian John Gardiner and Philadelphian Robert Morris, who touted the theater as a means of improving the manners and habits of society, expected the audience to receive material passively. They assumed that they would be able to use the playhouse to disseminate *their* version of nationalism: that government should be administered by a rational and detached elite which acted for the public good. Direct involvement by "the people" – whether in the government or the playhouse – was to be avoided at all costs, since the people were too often ruled by their passions, rather than reason. Yet articles and letters printed in Bache's paper, as well as various Boston newspapers, suggest that the theater came under sharp scrutiny from a public that believed it had every right to shape the form of its entertainments. This trend coincided with a rising tide of opposition to the Federalist political and economic agenda in 1794, and with the first stirrings of national party and class politics.

From 1794 to 1795, the tension between Federalist and anti-Federalist concepts of nationalism and political and cultural participation escalated rapidly. International crises over trade and foreign revolutions, coupled with domestic controversies over financial speculation and class divisions, demonstrated to Americans that the nation was not as united as they had believed, and that the process of securing the Revolution was not yet behind them. This tension quickly found its way into the playhouse, as every aspect of playgoing, from seating arrangements, to musical interludes, to script choice, to performance became a potentially problematic declaration of allegiance to a particular political, economic, or social agenda. Parties in the audience disputed the propriety of various plays and the inclusion of political songs in the program. Audiences already divided over the merits of the French Revolution attacked orchestra members for playing pro- or anti-French songs. Audience members who worried that an elitist "junto" was scheming for national power objected to plays which seemed to favor an aristocratic social hierarchy. Sometimes the objections to material were not simply political, but reflected divisions between "highbrow" and "lowbrow" tastes. For example, patrons at the Chestnut Street playhouse rejected the "complicated" operatic and orchestral music provided by Reinagle, in favor of "simple tunes."[24] Boston audiences expressed (sometimes violently) their preference for certain songs, performers, or productions that appealed to popular tastes.

The Federalists, who feared any form of factionalism and dissent (even within the playhouse), were alarmed by this trend, but were unable fully to prevent it.[25] When the members of the Philadelphia Dramatic

Association had asserted that they were the "approved guardians of their country," they had summarized the quintessential Federalist viewpoint, that as the guardians of virtue and rationality, they should steer America's cultural development. For the Federalists, a democracy which presumed that all men should occupy the same social and financial status was almost unnatural. They assumed that social and economic hierarchies helped to maintain order in a republican community.[26] Unfortunately for the Federalists and for their theaters, this outlook clashed with the system of direct participation which the Revolution had encouraged. The two most divisive issues of 1794–1795 which threatened to destroy the harmony of the Boston and Philadelphia playhouses were the fundamental disagreements over what kind of government control (centralized or de-centralized) should prevail in the states; and whether the fledgling nation should form alliances with either France or Great Britain.

Anxieties about a centralized *versus* de-centralized government system had reached one peak during the debates over the ratification of the Constitution. They re-surfaced with Alexander Hamilton's attempt to create a national bank in 1790. The creation of the Bank of the United States in 1791 underscored fears among agrarian districts that a central government which united both political and independent financial power would not act in the interest of the small farmer or merchant. It pitted these agrarian interests against the united urban factions who favored the national bank system. Though the bank issue did not create a formal party system, it pointed out the growing fissures among those who believed in a consolidated federal government and financial system (a group which, not surprisingly, included William Bingham and Robert Morris), and those who advocated a system of state and local banks (including Thomas Jefferson and James Madison).[27] The rift between these two nascent factions widened over the issue of American policy towards the French Revolution.

Americans had initially greeted the French Revolution with enthusiasm, seeing it as inspired by their own democratic experiment. But the French uprising quickly became too bloody and anarchic for many American Federalists, who also feared being drawn into a military conflict between France and Great Britain. Disputes over French *versus* British alliances polarized political factions in the states. Those who hoped to keep the United States relatively uninvolved in the European conflict supported the 1795 Jay Treaty with Great Britain (an agreement designed to protect American shipping interests against the depredations of British warships), and affiliated themselves with the Federalists. Those who feared renewed ties with Great Britain began creating what were known as Democratic-Republican Societies[28] or Constitutional Societies,[29] protesting America's seemingly conciliatory policy towards Britain. And those who believed that Americans owed too much to France to desert her in her time of crisis allied themselves with the Jacobin party.[30] When these three new parties met under the playhouse roof, they made a volatile combination.

Songs, scripts, and performers quickly became embattled by warring factions within the playhouse. In fact, the controversy over whether the popular French Revolutionary song "Ça Ira" would be played in the Federal Street Theatre began even before the house opened its doors. On January 23, 1794, the *Independent Chronicle and Universal Daily Advertiser* ran the following letter:

> CA IRA! However "jarring" the sound of *God Save the King* may be to the Republicans, it is presumed that the tune of *Ca Ira* will be agreeable to every Citizen who wishes well to the cause of France, and to the Rights of Man – it is therefore requested that the Theatre may be opened with the animating tune of *Ca Ira* accompanied with a FULL BAND; and it will be re-echoed by the loudest acclamations from every friend, to the tune of YANKEE DOODLE.[31]

A subsequent letter which appeared in the *Independent Chronicle* on January 30, 1794 suggests that the pro-French sentiment evinced in the call for "Ça Ira" may have provoked a mixed response from the Boston public:

> Some persons object to the playing of this Republican tune at the New Theatre because it is *imported*. Pray, let us ask, are not the players and the pieces to be performed imported also? Are not in fact the musicians imported? And shall we object to this tune merely because it is of foreign growth? Certainly no. Scarcely a tune that is played is manufactured in America – we must therefore have some imported tunes, and no one will so well please a republican ear as the French *Yankee Doodle* – alias CA IRA![32]

Once the theater opened, the controversy grew increasingly bitter. Bostonian Sarah Flucker recounted a struggle between the pro-Jacobin faction and the Federal Street orchestra that took place just eleven days after the theater's opening. In a letter to her friend Lucy Knox, she wrote of what was apparently a planned protest at the theater against England's Prince Edward (who was visiting Boston at the time and who had been scheduled to appear at the theater that evening).

On Monday I went to the Play, but alas, no Prince. He was doubtless prevented by the assurance that a large Party was forming in the Galleries to Govern the Music... There was an alarming opposition between the ragamuffins, the Loyalists, & Orchestra, and Peace was only obtained by the mortifying submission of the good to the bad. All *Gentlemen* [*sic*] were *silent* – the Jarvis clan gave the words of command. Fortunate for this Country that its innate virtue – and good government – has so far insured the comforts of Peace, that the discordant voice of a few rash men can do little in opposition.[33]

Flucker's letter mentions several interesting points. By noting that the protest against Prince Edward was planned, she affirms the theater as a site of political and social protest. Her observation that the "Jarvis clan"[34] was able to quiet the "ragamuffins" in the gallery implies that the Jarvises' republican sympathies were well known, and that they commanded the respect of the "lower class" Jacobins in the audience. Thus she confirms a system of social deference still operating in American society. Lastly, her observation that the "gentlemen" were silent suggests a reluctance on the part of Federalist members of the audience to engage in public debate, or perhaps to expose themselves as targets to the occupants of the gallery.

In another letter concerning the "Ça Ira" theater controversy, Increase Sumner described the same incident that had disturbed Sarah Flucker:

The design was first to avoid party matters, but the people in the galleries the other night prevailed, and after much noise and some confusion to the no small terror of the Ladies & obliged the music to play up "Ça Ira."[35]

William Cushing, a resident of Philadelphia, where similar demonstrations were occurring, responded that "the theater would be well enough if confined within the bounds of morality and decency, & not made an engine of party nonsense."[36]

Ultimately, the conflict between the Boston audience and theater proprietors assumed a violent character. Jacobins in the audience threw debris at the orchestra when they refused to play pro-French songs. The musicians responded with a somewhat piteous plea that they be allowed to play unmolested, assuring the audience "that it is not more their duty than their wish to oblige in playing such tunes as are called for, but at the same time they wish them to consider the peculiar poignancy of insult to men not accustomed to it."[37] The Federal Street proprietors listed the following advertisement in response to the violence against the orchestra: "50 Dollars reward – [for the] evil-minded person from the Gallery of the Theatre [who] threw into the Orchestra . . . a piece of Glass, and by that means destroyed one of the Kettle Drums."[38]

Philadelphia theater managers fared scarcely better, and were repeatedly forced to comply with gallery demands for "Ça Ira."[39] Bache's Republican paper, the *General Advertiser*, observed approvingly that the orchestra complied with audience requests for "Ça Ira," and that in doing so, they demonstrated "that they did not forget their audience was American."[40] On February 28, Bache reported: "Last Wednesday the House was again crowded. The orchestra opened with the President's March and then after repeated calls from the mountain, favored the audience with 'Ça Ira.' The Minister of the French Republic was present and was greeted by 3 huzzahs."[41] Bache's comments reveal the extent to which the Philadelphia managers had been forced to accommodate the noisy and politicized faction in the gallery. They also reveal the extent to which theater had become a site for debating and declaring political allegiances.

Yet theater managers in Boston and Philadelphia faced more worries than simply quieting the galleries. They had to strike a balance among all of the parties and factions represented in the playhouse. They could not afford to offend their wealthy Federalist patrons, nor could they afford to turn the tide of popular political sentiment against the theater. Some sort of compromise had to be reached that could appeal to all the different groups. Benjamin Carr's song "The Federal Overture" emerged as the solution. Liam Riordan has discussed the origins of Carr's tune – a medley of French Revolutionary and Federalist melodies that was popular between 1794 and 1798.[42] Lewis Hallam, manager of the Old American Company, had commissioned the work in response to a March, 1794 disturbance at the John Street playhouse in New York, in which Jacobin audience members rioted upon hearing the orchestra play English songs. "The Federal Overture" became popular with theater managers in Boston and Philadelphia, who were looking for ways to appease audiences from both the Federalist and Jacobin parties.[43] Managers also occasionally inserted pro-*American* songs into afterpieces and pantomimes, in an attempt to appeal to popular sentiment. For example, the song, "America, Commerce, Freedom" appeared in the 1794 pantomime *The Sailor's Landlady* by Susanna Rowson.[44] The words have little to do with commerce – the title is in fact the refrain to the drinking song that the sailors sing. Nevertheless, a story about American sailors having the freedom of the seas would certainly resonate with an American audience still smarting from British interference with American shipping.[45]

The managers of the Boston and Philadelphia theaters also tried to promote harmony in the playhouse through the use of celebratory prologues
and epilogues, designed to foster a sense of community among the audience.
The Federal Street proprietors created a contest, inviting submissions for
prologues and epilogues, and asked some of Boston's most respected citizens, including the Reverend Jeremy Belknap, to serve as judges (Belknap
declined). The prize for 1794 was awarded to Thomas Paine (Thomas Paine
of Boston later adopted the name Robert Treat Paine), and the prologue was
described as "highly creditable to the poet's genius."[46] In the prologue, Paine
draws a direct connection between Boston's new theater and the emergence
of theatrical/cultural genius in ancient Greece and Rome. He sees in the
Boston theater all the greatness of these ancient cultures reborn:

> And now, THOU DOME, by FREEDOM'S patrons rear'd
> With BEAUTY blazon'd and by TASTE rever'd
> APOLLO consecrates thy walls prophane
> Hence be THOU sacred to the MUSE'S reign
> In THEE *three ages* shall in *one* conspire...
> And ATHENS, ROME, AUGUSTA blush to see
> Their virtue, beauty, grace, all shine – combined in thee![47]

Paine wrote numerous other prologues for the theater, one of which appeared only ten days after the theater's opening, and is interesting because
it taxes the audience with the responsibility of monitoring the content of
the playhouse:

> If borne from far, the wit of ALBION'S race
> As dissolute as gay, these walls disgrace
> If foreign brogues and foreign manners strive
> Your speech to dictate and the *ton* to give
> If alien vices, here unknown before
> Come shameless to pollute COLUMBIA'S shore...
> Indignant rise!...
> And save while ye yet may, your spotless name
> Your own chaste Virtue, and your country's fame.[48]

The theatrical prologues and epilogues of the early national period
saluted the audience, addressed pressing concerns of the day, and affirmed
the audience's participation in a specific set of beliefs and values.[49] They
also provided the opportunity for commentary that could contextualize the
play for the audience. For example, in her prologue to the 1794 *Slaves in
Algiers*, Susanna Rowson juxtaposed the tyranny that the American

captives suffered with the freedom offered under America's democratic system, and within the walls of the playhouse:

> Shall the noble Eagle see her brood
> Beneath the pirate kite's subdued?
> View her dear sons of liberty enslaved
> Nor let them share the blessings which they saved? . . .
> Tonight our author boldly dares to choose,
> This glorious subject for her humble muse;
> Though tyrants check the genius which they fear,
> She dreads no check, no persecution *here*;
> Where safe asylums every virtue guard,
> And every talent meets its just reward.[50]

Rowson's prologue admitted only two points of view: that of the tyrant and that of the American patriot/audience member. The prologue united the American audience in an imagined community against the tyranny of foreign powers who would impinge upon its liberty. Her words affirmed the audience's participation in that community, while still reminding the audience that participation is an earned privilege.[51]

In addition to the political controversy affecting the playhouse, the theaters' founders also encountered audiences of differing social and economic classes who were beginning to clamor for the right to shape America's cultural identity. When the Boston and Philadelphia theaters had opened in the winter of 1794, they opened to communities already dividing along lines of social, economic, and political tension. The theater, which brought divergent groups face to face under the same roof, only amplified existing differences.[52]

Political differences grounded in international political crises were underscored by a growing financial schism among the nation's "have" and "have nots" – a discrepancy which the opulence of the Boston and Philadelphia theaters did little to conceal. Speculation had escalated rapidly in the first years of the 1790s, to the point that many citizens (not involved in speculation ventures) feared the advent of a new wealth-based aristocracy. A 1791 poem characterized speculation as a "baleful pest, [that] has pour'd his dire contagion in the breast/That monster that would everything devour," and as a phenomenon that would "pave the way for aristocracy and despotism."[53]

The Boston Tontine had initially been viewed with suspicion, since it represented a speculative, "get-rich-quick" scheme, which allowed its wealthy members to profit without manufacturing or owning any actual goods or property. Banks (like the Bank of North America and the Bank of the United States) often loaned money to their powerful shareholders to support additional speculative ventures. In February 1793, Philadelphia's *Dunlap's Daily Advertiser* accused the Bank of North America of functioning like a tontine, and of plotting to despoil poor farmers and acquire their property, by overextending credit, then foreclosing on property. The paper also complained that "the monopoly which the [Bank] enjoys enables the directors to aid their friends and ruin their enemies."[54] As Karen Weyler has suggested, "Speculation and its companion vices avarice and greed dismayed republicans throughout the United States as the self-sacrificing civic virtue of the war years gave way to more profit-oriented forms of individualism."[55]

In addition to the banking ventures of the 1780s and early 1790s, land speculation deals were gaining popularity among the Philadelphia and Boston elite. Among the most notable in Philadelphia were the four land companies formed between 1794 and 1797: the Asylum Company, the Pennsylvania Population Company, the Territorial Company, and the North American Land Company.[56] Almost one-third (twenty-nine out of ninety) of the original shareholders in the Chestnut Street Theatre owned stock in at least *one* of the land companies mentioned above.[57] Part of the popular objection to the land companies arose from the fear among the residents of the western territories that the men in charge of them would have too much sway in deciding how the western lands in the state should be run. Opponents feared that the financial monopoly the elite had created would be transformed into a territorial one as well. The controversy over land companies polarized not only the city and country factions, but also the urban rich and poor.

In Boston, Federalist candidates for state government were mocked for boasting that they were "the only real friends to their country," when, as the *Independent Chronicle* accused, they had "speculated in funds and spurned the common means of their citizens for the procurement of wealth." The paper noted with scorn that the Federalist candidates "presumed wealth, without any other pretensions, would qualify an individual for the duties of a Senator." The *Independent Chronicle* observed that out of the eleven candidates proposed by the Federalist *Centinel*, eight had ties to the Union, Massachusetts, and Branch banks. The *Chronicle* observed, "How far this particular interest is the 'real' representation of the people at large, let every candid citizen judge."[58]

How did the anxiety about wealth and speculation manifest itself in the theater? Class and economic divisions carried over into the playhouse most obviously in the dispute over theater boxes. Though Philadelphia's

Chestnut Street Theatre offered no privately maintained patrons' boxes, it was generally understood that box seats were reserved for members of the elite. The regulations of the theater noted that places in the side boxes could not be offered to fewer than groups of eight (or smaller groups who could afford the fee). On February 24, 1794, a concerned "middle class" patron wrote to the *General Advertiser*, complaining that the costs of the boxes and the eight-person rule precluded his bringing his family to the theater. "I have not the least ambition to hurt the feelings of the well-born by placing my family too near, but I think it hard that we should be excluded because [of] my retired situation." The writer suggested that if the managers feared "giving offense to their opulent friends by subjecting them to sit in the same boxes with the less wealthy," they should create separate but equally well-placed boxes for the middling sort, who also wanted to enjoy the theater.[59] His comments suggest that there was a perceived schism between the elite and the rest of the audience. The writer also acknowledged his own lack of social ambition – or perhaps his recognition that he could not aspire to the wealth shared by the occupants of the boxes. Nevertheless, he obviously resented the notion that distinctions of wealth should create an artificial division among patrons of a "democratic" theater. The playhouse, which had been planned to provide "rational and innocent amusement," suddenly faced the challenge of papering over the class, social, and financial differences among the audience. This was a task for which it was ill suited, though the managers did their best.

Perhaps the best clue to how the managers planned to cope with the multiple complications of the early national playhouse can be found in the texts that they chose for production. Some studies have examined the text of plays such as Royall Tyler's *The Contrast* (perhaps the best-known early American script) as a means of extrapolating information about both early American society and the early American playhouse.[60] While Tyler's work *does* offer insights into the theater of the 1780s – most notably the famous scene in which Jonathan the Yankee attends a play without realizing it – it is important to note that Tyler's play received only four recorded performances in Philadelphia between 1787 and 1796.[61] Assuming that the performance sites (the City Tavern, the Southwark Theatre, and the Chestnut Street Theatre) were filled to capacity on all three occasions, no more than 3,000 people in Philadelphia would have seen the play in production over a period of seven years. Few other early American dramatists (such as Susanna Rowson, Judith Sargent Murray, William Charles White, or John Murdock) fared better. Their plays were hailed for their novelty value, but they did not secure a permanent place in the repertoire. This may seem a strange choice on the part of the managers, not to actively cultivate the work of new American authors, yet they were to a large extent following the dictates of public taste. To a sizable part of the theater-going public (and certainly to the Federalists), part of maintaining a theater that rivaled its British counterparts meant producing the *same* plays that were available in European playhouses. An angry audience member complained to the Chestnut Street managers in 1794, "We have heard of new plays and farces which were performed many months ago in England, and which we had hoped before this time to have seen here ... unless you speedily alter your mode of conduct, your company will play to empty benches."[62]

Faced with such threats to their financial well-being, managers struggled to combine the most popular plays of the old British repertoire with current British works. They relied on a repertoire of pre-war favorites from Britain, including such works as *The School for Scandal*, Sheridan's comedy of scandalmongers, adulterers, and cheats among the British aristocracy; *The Busybody*, Susannah Centlivre's lewd satire on wooing and matrimony (which spawned her most popular character, Marplot); *Jane Shore*, Rowe's popular and tragic account of the life of Edward IV's mistress; and *The Gamester*, Moore's tragedy of a young, middle-class husband who ruins his family by his gambling addiction. The theater also offered a selection of new British works and new translations of French and German drama. Often the playbill would incorporate a familiar play as the main piece of the evening, enlivened by new dances, songs, or afterpieces. With these limited tools, the theater managers tried to accommodate their diverse audience.

Often they tried to re-style old favorites into forms more suitable to the contemporary taste of the audience. They also frequently cut or re-wrote certain passages in newer scripts to make the works conform to American tastes, while still allowing the audiences to feel that they were getting the best of "British" theater.[63] These changes were made to the theater's promptbooks – the master copy of the script, kept by the stage manager/prompter. Since the promptbooks were not generally intended for publication, the amended versions of the plays would only have been witnessed by the audience attending the performance.[64] For example, the popular English opera *Rosina* premiered at Covent Garden in 1782, and played in America twenty-one times between 1787 and 1799.[65] It had already been playing in America for seven years by 1794, but by that point, America's political and social climate had changed sufficiently that Thomas Wignell thought it prudent to cut 194 lines from the text. The opera tells the story of the virtuous and beautiful Rosina (who is, unbeknownst to her, a member of the gentry). She lives among simple harvesters (having lost her parents and her fortune), and is courted by two brothers – one a dishonorable captain who tries to kidnap her, and the other the virtuous Belville, who hopes to marry her. Wignell's major cuts to this script include references to the British class system, and derogatory remarks about farmers and the poor.[66]

Wignell also cut the following passage from Cumberland's *The Carmelite* for obvious reasons:

> DE COURCI: On England's throne
> No tyrant sits, deaf to the widow's cause
> But Heaven's viceregent, merciful and just.
> MATILDA: Thanks to thy royal sender! On my knee
> I offer prayers to Heaven for length of days
> And blessings shower'd on his anointed head![67]

From Richard Cumberland's *The Box Lobby Challenge*, Wignell eliminated the following undemocratic sentiments:

> SIR TOBY: In old times, everybody sat silent in company with their superiors, nobody spoke until they were spoken to; no tongue was heard at the table but the master's of it; now they are all talkers and no hearers, such as gabble and din; every priggish puppy gives puppily opinion.[68]

These texts play a crucial but complicated role in examining the marketing and production strategies of theater managers in the early Republic. The judicious cuts that they made to the texts allowed them to appeal simultaneously to American patriotic sentiment, since the plays were being purged of their English taint, while at the same time permitting them to take a cosmopolitan pride in the fact that their theaters were producing the latest European plays. Some claimed the pared scripts as entirely "American" – for example, in 1794, printer Mathew Carey advertised "A beautiful collection of plays," entitled *American Theatre*, which featured *Gustavus Vasa*, *The Belle's Stratagem*, *The Provok'd Husband*, *Natural Son*, *She Stoops to Conquer*, *The Busybody*, *Barbarossa*, *The Foundling*, *The West Indian*, and *Hamlet*. While some of these plays could be said to incorporate American themes (*Gustavus Vasa*), or in some cases, characters (if the title character of *The West Indian* can be admitted as American), none are actually written by Americans![69] Carey's claiming of popular and newly adapted scripts as "American" suggests the fluid nature of American identity during the early national period. It also suggests how difficult it was to define what did and did not constitute "American" theater during the 1790s.

For example, sometimes managers' efforts to propitiate their audiences with altered scripts backfired. John Hodgkinson visited the Federal Street Theatre in Boston in November of 1795 (before becoming manager of the theater). Like Wignell, Hodgkinson tried to alter standard British fare to suit what he thought were American tastes. But his alterations were so obvious and clumsy that they drew attacks, rather than praise. In particular, Robert Treat Paine noted: "When we see him scouring and patching a second-hand compliment to make it awkwardly fit us, we cannot but be disgusted at his fulsome adulation." Paine added, "Instead of compliments, they are insults to our nation." He cited with indignation a foreign visitor's account of travels in the United States which painted a dim picture of America's taste for altered dramas: "The Americans have so poor a sense of national dignity, that in their dramatic entertainments, their vanity is highly feasted with the offals from the complimentary repasts of other nations."[70] Paine's words are a caution to the American theater-going public not to accept blindly the superficial praise of the theater managers, or to allow that praise to lessen their vigilance in demanding a worthy theatrical product.

The founders of the Boston and Philadelphia theaters hoped to bring their audiences into what David Waldstreicher has termed a "magic circle of agreement,"[71] and to establish themselves at the center of that circle. But they failed to realize that what constituted central and peripheral positions of power in that circle were in flux, and that to try to establish a theater of "the people" is, in many ways, a self-defeating proposition, since the theater cannot appeal to every audience member, any more than a government can realistically represent every citizen. David Brigham has noted in his work on Peale's Museum in Philadelphia that the key to running a successful public entertainment in the early Republic was to attract a "democratic" range of spectators, while maintaining an implicit class structure. The secret was to promote a rhetoric of inclusiveness, but to make that inclusion dependent upon participation in the community (whether of the museum or the playhouse), under a certain set of established conditions or behaviors.[72]

Despite the efforts of the managers and founders, by the end of their first year of operation in 1795, both the Philadelphia and Boston theaters faced financial and managerial difficulties. The Chestnut Street managers had incurred heavy debts as a result of the yellow fever epidemic which had postponed the theater's opening. In 1795, Wignell and Reinagle were forced to appeal to the Trustees to re-finance the theater with a loan of $43,600.[73] In exchange for the loan, Wignell and Reinagle mortgaged the theater.

The Federal Street house faced similar challenges at the end of the 1795 season, but in this case the Trustees blamed Charles Stuart Powell's inadequate management for the theater's difficulties. In a letter to Powell, Trustee William Tudor declared that the proprietors of the theater were only willing to extend Powell's lease for one more year, and on the condition that he make several alterations to the running of the playhouse. Among the demands listed were:

2. That you make an addition to your company of at least six good actors. The Proprietors consenting for your own sake as well as the public, to the discharge of four in your present set.
4. That you present every week a pantomime or in its stead a musical drama. We suppose a Regard to your own profits would suggest the advantage of occasionally introducing an opera dance or some short entertainment between the Play and after piece.
5. That you dismiss one half of the present Band & engage an equal number of persons who shall understand their business and not disgrace the Orchestra by their incapacity or affront the audience by their ebriety.
6. That you bring out no new production without first submitting the same to the judgement of the Trustees, and no play or farce is to be considered a stock piece without their consent.[74]

The reason for these conditions, Tudor noted, was that "the Town and the Proprietors for two successive seasons have been greatly disappointed, and that we can no longer submit to the humiliating Idea of the Boston Theatre being considered as the most inferior in the United States."[75] Tudor's complaint neatly summarizes the dilemma facing Boston's and Philadelphia's theater founders at the end of their debut seasons. How could they reconcile their idealistic notions of what their theaters *could* be, with the reality of what they had become? It was a question that would continue to plague them until the end of the decade, but which grew increasingly troublesome with the coming of theatrical competition in 1795–1796. The opening of Ricketts's Circus in Philadelphia, and the creation of the Haymarket Theatre in Boston, transformed the way in which theater would be viewed and used in the new Republic.

Although they were displaced by the onset of party rivalries, financial reverses, and the growth of new social groups, the theaters' founders in Boston and Philadelphia had achieved three important goals in their first official year. They had constructed physical monuments to America's cultural advancement that would stand as models for future generations. They had established theatrical entertainments as a legitimate expression of American nationalism. And they had laid the groundwork for the development of American drama. The "powerful engine" of the early national theater transformed the cultural, political, and urban landscapes in which it flourished. Ironically, the theaters' founders were *so* successful at establishing their playhouses as sites for political and social transformation that they ultimately lost control of their cultural product, as it continued to be molded and altered by shifting concepts of "American" identity.

4

Butcher, baker, candlestick maker: the Mechanics take on the theater, 1795–1797

I HAVE SUGGESTED THAT THE POST-WAR THEATERS IN BOSTON, New York, and Philadelphia emerged as a cultural product of American nationalism, and noted that this statement begs the question, "Whose nationalism?" The theatrical wars which plagued Boston and Philadelphia from 1795 to 1797 were, in large part, an effort to answer this same query. To whom should the theater belong, and for whom should it speak? The proprietors of the Federal Street and Chestnut Street Theatres had assumed that "the people" would follow their lead in the playhouse, automatically approving whatever cultural product they chose to display. To their surprise, they encountered audiences and factions who demanded input into how the theater should be governed and what it should offer to the public. At the same time, New York's elite audiences were coping with the increasingly in-solent attacks of the mechanic population on their long-established cultural hierarchy. A similar phenomenon was taking place in the post-war society and economy as well. New social and economic organizations began com-peting with the established post-war elite, as allied artisans in Boston, New York, and Philadelphia demanded the same access to social and economic opportunity that the elite enjoyed.

Perhaps the sensible solution in both arenas would have been compro-mise – the Federal Street proprietors might have yielded to audience requests for less expensive tickets, or the Chestnut Street managers might have responded to demands for more popular music, instead of operas. The Federalist elite audiences in New York's John Street house might have made some concessions to their Tammany mechanic rivals. Or the Tontiners might have supported new initiatives by the Boston Mechanics to fund their own private corporations. As Edward Shils notes, the successful creation of nationalism is predicated on the ability of the elite (controlling) group to incorporate "the mass of the population" into the "central institutions and value systems" of the society.[1] He suggests that the participation need not be direct, but that the general public must be allowed to identify with the cultural system it is being asked to perpetuate. Thus, the public identifies itself with the central authority, rather than in opposition to it.

Unfortunately, the Tontiners, the New York junto, and the Philadelphia elite were largely unwilling to grant broader access to the cultural and financial institutions which had built their power. And thus, peripheral groups such as the Boston and Philadelphia Mechanics, and the New York Tammany Democrats,[2] who had, in the past, allied themselves with the reigning elite, began to support their own "central institutions," including their own theaters and their own playwrights. Not only did they assert control over these institutions, they claimed that *their* cultural products would be more genuinely "American" as well.

Yet the intricate social and economic structure of the post-war theater had complicated any attempts to cultivate American "native genius" in the playhouse. Though ostensibly a democracy, the new nation retained a class-based social and political hierarchy which dictated that the wealthy would lead, while the poor would follow. This same mentality manifested itself in the cultural experiments of the new nation.

John Murdock and the Chestnut Street Theatre: a mechanic speaks out[3]

> Occasionally visiting the theatre, I was, at times, much disgusted to see and hear pieces performed so foreign to the circumstances of a republican people; which prompted me, at my leisure moments, to throw my ideas into a proper train to produce a drama, which would be more consonant with the ears of Americans.[4]

Thus wrote John Murdock, Philadelphia hairdresser, in the prologue to his 1800 play, *The Beau Metamorphasized; or The Generous Maid*. Murdock's words offered far more than an *apologia* for thrusting himself into the public eye. They were a defense of American artisan "genius" and a challenge to America's elite theater-going public. Murdock's plays, though relatively unknown, are among the most interesting of the early national period in their attempt to introduce mechanic culture and politics to the early national stage. They provide a striking contrast to the works of authors such as Royall Tyler or Susanna Rowson, whose social status or affiliation with the theater gained them a cultural access that Murdock and his compatriots were denied. Unfortunately, Murdock's name has been largely forgotten by contemporary theater historians. Daniel Havens describes Murdock's first play, *The Triumphs of Love*, as an "awkwardly constructed" play, categorizing it as a "minor comedy."[5] Yet to dismiss Murdock's work without viewing it in the larger context of post-Revolutionary American culture and politics risks overlooking the nuances of class conflict that shaped both the early national theater and an understanding of American "native genius."

John Murdock wrote three plays, *The Triumphs of Love, or Happy Reconciliation* (1794), *The Politicians, or A State of Things* (1798), and *The Beau Metamorphasized* (1800). Each of these plays presented the Philadelphia Murdock knew, a hodgepodge of recent German and Irish immigrants, slaves and free blacks, Quakers, artisans, and wealthy elite. Each of his plays reflected the pressing political concerns of the day, from anti-Irish prejudice, to abolition, to party politics.

Murdock's plays reflect the growing rift between the elite and working classes in the early Republic. Beyond that, they challenge the criteria for cultural legitimacy in the new nation. By examining the issues that Murdock confronts in his plays, and by tracing the rise of class awareness in post-Revolutionary Philadelphia, theater historians may gain both a greater appreciation for Murdock's own "native genius" as well as a clearer sense of the disjunction between the rhetoric of republicanism and its practice.

As a hairdresser, Murdock belonged to that class known as "artisans" or "mechanics." Though the mechanics had played an important role during the Revolution, both as soldiers and as "Sons of Liberty," the end of the war saw a diminution in both their political and economic influence. Additionally, the economic depression of the post-war period hit the mechanics particularly hard. Thus, by the 1790s, many of Philadelphia's "laboring sort" found themselves at the mercy of a wealthy elite, and increasingly resentful of the "consummate display of boldness and presumption on the part of the aristocratic junto"[6] that dominated Philadelphia society.

They might not have resented the elite to such a degree had they been allowed to share in their post-war prosperity or partake in their entertainments. As I have suggested, the theater's repertoire, as well as its class-based seating system, served as a constant reminder of the inequalities still present in America's democratic society. One telling example reveals the extent to which Philadelphia mechanics found themselves marginalized by the city's "aristocratic junto." When William and Anne Bingham gave the city's first masquerade ball in the early 1790s, "the strictest measures were used to keep out the mechanics and their wives."[7] This incident suggests that the mechanics had *hoped* to participate in the same social events as the wealthier members of Philadelphia society, but that the perception of class difference on the part of the *elite* led to their exclusion.

With social, cultural, political, and economic spheres dominated by the upper classes, how could Philadelphia's mechanics hope to assert their own influence? Some did so through popular demonstration both on the street and in the playhouse. Audience members in the galleries (generally drawn from the mechanic and laboring classes) often proved a disruptive force in the playhouse, clamoring for particular songs, attacking – sometimes with words and sometimes with missiles – those actors or orchestra members who refused to comply with their requests. Yet these displays only reinforced the elite perception of the "lower sort" as an unruly mob, unfit to guide the politics or culture of the new nation. In the absence of any middle- or lower-class contenders, it seemed that "high" culture (literature, poetry, and music) would remain the province of the elite. America's "native genius" would reside with the "approved guardians" of the country's political and civic spheres. Enter John Murdock and *The Triumphs of Love.*

The Triumphs of Love reflects three contemporaneous events that were of particular concern to the Philadelphia mechanics: the yellow fever epidemic of 1793, the Convention of Delegates from Abolition Societies in Philadelphia in 1794,[8] and the rise of the Democratic-Republican party. Though these three events may seem unrelated, they were in fact significant factors in the creation of a politically aware artisan class in the theater.

As I noted earlier, in 1793 Philadelphia faced one of the worst yellow fever epidemics in the city's history. The wealthy citizens of the city (including the elite sponsors of the theater) fled, leaving the poorer people, including the mechanics and the city's large free black population, essentially to shift for themselves.[9] Only a handful of the city's leaders, including Dr. Benjamin Rush and politician Tench Coxe, remained behind. The blacks helped to nurse the sick and bury the dead, winning commendations from Rush, who had stayed to treat the sick (and who was, incidentally, an abolitionist). In *A Narrative of the Proceedings of the Black People During the Late Awful Calamity in Philadelphia*, the authors, two prominent black citizens, Richard Allen and Absalom Jones, described their role in the plague time:

> Many whose friends and relations had left them, died unseen and unassisted. We have found them in various situations, some laying on the floor, as bloody as if they had been dip't in it, without any appearance of having had even a drink of water for their relief…We feel a great satisfaction in believing that we have been useful to the sick, and thus publicly thank Dr. Rush for enabling us to be so.[10]

The conduct of Philadelphia's black population during the fever heightened awareness of their presence in the community and helped to fuel the nascent abolitionist movement in the state.

Other prominent Philadelphians like Tench Coxe tried to help mechanics stranded in the city to escape the fever. One of John Murdock's few surviving letters thanks Coxe for helping to get his family out of the city during the epidemic.[11] In the wake of the Yellow Fever Crisis, the Democratic-Republicans gained support from the Philadelphia mechanics – both out of gratitude for their help during the fever, and in protest against the Federalist elite's abdication of responsibility during the crisis.

Many members of the Democratic-Republican societies also supported the abolition of slavery.[12] Both Coxe and Rush participated in the convention of delegates from the Abolition Societies which met in Philadelphia in January of 1794 to protest the continuance of slavery in America. The delegates published a pamphlet in which they decried slavery as "degrading to our rank as men" and "repugnant to the principles of Christianity."[13] Both Coxe and Rush also sponsored Murdock's play, which contains the first emancipation scene presented on the early American stage.[14] Thus, as Martin S. Pernick has noted, the yellow fever of 1793 fundamentally transformed Philadelphia's political structure, bringing to prominence a party whose outlook was more in keeping with the sentiments of the American Revolution, and fueling the state's growing anti-slavery movement. The events of 1793 and 1794 also underscored a growing opposition to the "aristocratic junto" in Philadelphia society.[15]

The strong local flavor and unique class perspective of Murdock's work make it especially intriguing for scholars of the early national period. For example, while many playwrights of the early Republic situated their plays in recognizable locales (John Daly Burk's *Bunker-Hill* and Royall Tyler's *The Contrast* being two of the best-known examples), little aside from the scene painting or references to American cities marks them as grounded in a uniquely American environment.[16] Murdock, on the other hand, explores Philadelphia from stable to parlor to tavern. Like Royall Tyler, Murdock tackled the Whiskey Rebellion and the genesis of party politics. Like Tyler, he satirized Americans who aped British manners and customs. But *unlike* Tyler, he did so from the mechanic's perspective – from a segment of American society not traditionally given voice in the playhouse or credited with cultural "genius."[17]

Murdock submitted *The Triumphs of Love* for Chestnut Street managers Thomas Wignell and Alexander Reinagle's consideration during the theater's first season in 1794, but the play was rejected.[18] On the surface,

Figure 4. Title page from *The Triumphs of Love* by John Murdock

The Triumphs of Love is a simple tale that revolves around the trials and tribulations of three pairs of young lovers. The couples include Patrick and Jenny (a recent Irish immigrant and his American sweetheart), George Friendly, Jr., a young man of Quaker background, and his ladylove Clementia (a refugee from the political crisis in Saint-Domingue), and Major Manly, a former Revolutionary officer, and his fiancée, Rachel Friendly (a young Quakeress, who fears leaving her religious community to marry outside her faith). Yet underneath the trappings of its sentimental plot lurk critiques of almost every aspect of Philadelphia's cultural and political life. Among the most interesting are Murdock's presentation of the relationships between Jenny, her Irish suitor, Patrick, and their employer, Mr. Peevish, and George Friendly, Jr. and his slave, Sambo.[19]

The Jenny–Patrick relationship raises questions of class and "American" identity in the new nation, as Patrick struggles to assimilate into American culture. Irish immigrants played a crucial and often problematic role in Philadelphia's post-war economy. They provided a cheap source of labor, but also created problems in already overcrowded working-class neighborhoods.[20] Though Irish immigrants came to America expecting to reap the benefits of increased wages and a democratic system, they frequently fell victim to the same kinds of economic exploitation that they had experienced in Ireland, and found that the "equality" of a democratic government applied only to the very wealthy. Relegated to stable hand status, Patrick laments that he ever left his "dare [dear] Ireland."[21] His employer, Mr. Peevish, attacks Patrick as a "blundering Irish fool," threatening to "send to England for servants I can depend on." He complains that it is "mortifying that people of fortune and family should be treated this way."[22] Peevish's attack on Patrick emphasizes the growing socio-economic divisions in post-Revolutionary Philadelphia society, as well as the mechanics' resentment at the artificial distinctions made between the wealthy and laboring classes. As Patrick observes after Peevish storms away, "I heard the paple spaking [*sic*] in the kitchen, that he never had a fader [*sic*], and that his moder [*sic*] was a fish woman and sold tripes in the market."[23] To Patrick, Peevish's origins place them on the same social level; only Peevish's wealth enables him to "lord" it over Patrick, an attitude out of keeping with true republican spirit. Murdock's depiction of the negative treatment of Irish immigrants in the new nation reflects a pressing concern of the period. The discrimination practiced against Irish immigrants may also explain why so many Irish-Americans flocked to the Democratic-Republican party, which held as its motto the "Equality of Man."[24]

A comparison between the Patrick–Peevish relationship in *The Triumphs of Love* and that of Colonel Manly and Jonathan in Royall Tyler's *The Contrast* may offer some insights into the way different socio-economic groups perceived the interaction between classes in the early national period. Tyler, a Harvard-educated member of the upper-middle class, presents Jonathan as an entertaining rustic, but one who adamantly rejects the notion that disparity in wealth in any way indicates inferior social or political status. When Jessamy describes him as a "servant," Jonathan replies indignantly, "Servant! Sir, do you take me for a neger [*sic*] – I am Colonel Manly's waiter...No man shall master me: my father has as good a farm as the Colonel."[25] Manly seems to share Jonathan's understanding, and never tries to draw an overt distinction between them. However, Manly's "Federalist" outlook manifests itself in his patriarchal attitude towards both his "waiter" and his former comrades in arms. Moreover, Manly belongs to the Society of the Cincinnati, an organization of Revolutionary War officers that excluded common soldiers.[26]

Murdock, on the other hand, as a member of the mechanic class, understands the gap between the rhetoric of republicanism and its practice. Patrick's fiancée, Jenny, becomes the means through which Patrick is "reconciled" to the democratic system. As a wedding gift, Peevish offers his patronage to Patrick and Jenny, so that they can open a small shop. Though Patrick becomes independent of Peevish by the end of the play, he must still rely on the patronage system both to start and sustain his business. *Without the goodwill of his employer, he would not have had the opportunity.*

The George–Sambo relationship in *The Triumphs of Love* also raises the question of how different groups defined democracy and American identity in the post-war period – but it revolves around the thorny question of slavery. During one scene, George watches hidden as Sambo dances and cavorts in front of a mirror. Contemplating his reflection, Sambo asks, "Sambo wonder, he berry often wonder, why black folk sold like cow or horse." He adds that his fear of being sold to a cruel master "almost broke his heart."[27] Moved by Sambo's grief, George reveals himself and declares Sambo free. While the George–Sambo subplot reflects one of the pressing political issues of 1794, the question of why a *hairdresser* would choose to include a scene of emancipation in his play is an intriguing one, and may be traced back to the yellow fever epidemic and the crisis of authority during that period. Moreover, in championing the cause of abolition, Murdock allied himself with two groups anathema to the reigning Federalist elite who governed the Philadelphia theater: the Quakers and the Democratic-Republicans.

Murdock's venture into playwriting reflects another trend of the 1790s: the gradual separation of post-Revolutionary American society into separate spheres, based on social and economic status. Many mechanics had sought to establish their independence from the "aristocratic junto" through the creation of charitable organizations that fulfilled a host of both official and unofficial functions. These organizations provided structures for regulating prices, wages, and pensions, but more than that, they "formalized personal networks," and created a parallel system of interest-related ties to those that linked the members of the Philadelphia elite.[28] The mechanics also used their charitable and business connections to strengthen their own cultural rituals. Most focused on public celebrations, such as parades, which could be used to demonstrate solidarity among a select community, and as a vehicle of protest against their exclusion from the nation's "democracy of glee."[29] Murdock's *Triumphs of Love* emerges as an effort on the part of the mechanic class to give a more democratic representation of Philadelphia society. Unfortunately, the play and its author appealed to just that sort of American that the theater's founders did not want represented in their class-regulated theater.

After *The Triumphs of Love* was rejected for the first season, Murdock re-submitted it in 1795, recruiting a number of Philadelphians to plead his case. He complained that he perceived in the managers "a confirmed temper...to trample upon native productions."[30] Murdock was not the only one who sensed a reluctance on the part of the managers to accept "American" works. Benjamin Bache, editor of the pro-Jacobin *Aurora*, criticized the theater managers for their play selections, demanding, "Why do not Americans form for themselves a national taste in an age as enlightened as this?"[31]

At the urging of Murdock's supporters, *The Triumphs of Love* went forward in the spring of 1795.[32] Yet Murdock noted bitterly that though the play was finally presented, it was given at the "eleventh hour," and was "shoved into the world most unmercifully dissected by the managers."[33] Reviews of the play observed that while the comedy voiced "sentiments that do honor to the writer's heart as a man and a citizen," and addressed "several interesting topics such as negro slavery and our glorious revolution," the plot "wants interest and incident, and the sentiments are also rather trite." The writer added that the opening night production had been "received with wonted indulgence."[34] (While the critic's comments sound patronizing, in many ways the responses given to Murdock's work were not atypical of those given to other native authors.)

The Triumphs of Love received only one public performance on the Philadelphia stage. When Murdock petitioned the managers to revive it for the 1796 season, they refused. He penned a series of letters to local papers, exhorting the public to rally to his support and force the managers to re-stage his play. He asserted that "with all the imperfections which they [the managers] or those who influence them may charge it with...[the play] has the undoubted right of taking its place or chance in the early part of this season with other pieces."[35] While one citizen writing in support of Murdock's play commented, "The subject is so characteristic of our situation, that it makes us love our country," adding, "Genius in our own country ought to be patronized,"[36] another correspondent dismissed the play as unworthy of so much attention, observing that "the author certainly misplaces his abilities when they are employed in the production of dramatic production."[37] What is most interesting about this exchange is Murdock's implied attack on the proprietors of the Chestnut Street house, whom he describes as "those who influence" the managers, as the real party interested in the suppression of his play – and the retaliatory snubbing administered by the critic who urges Murdock to turn his attention back to his true talent: hairdressing.

Indeed, the presumption of a hairdresser to dictate to theater shareholders such as Robert Morris and William Bingham (two of the richest men in America) may have rankled among members of Philadelphia's wealthy class. Murdock, as a mere artisan, was not one of the "approved guardians" of his country's virtue, as the theater's founders had styled themselves in 1789.[38] Yet Murdock obviously believed that he was well within his rights to comment not only on the state of Philadelphia politics, but on its cultural future as well. Murdock's attitude reflected the growing dissatisfaction among the artisans of the young republic with the cultural assumptions dictated by their "betters." In Boston, the growing rift between the mechanics and the merchant elite produced a schism in the theater that led to the creation of a new playhouse. In Murdock's case, it led to his claim of a mechanic's share in American "native genius."

Murdock's "career" in the theater represents one example of the way in which the Philadelphia artisans were beginning to re-align their political and financial interest, but separating the personal from the political from the financial is a difficult process in unraveling the various strains of the debate that formed the controversy between the Philadelphia Mechanics and the Philadelphia elite between 1795 and 1797. The Mechanics seem to have formed political connections with the Democratic-Republicans partly out of genuine conviction, but partly out of political expediency, since they lacked the resources to effect widespread change on their own. The financial policies of the Democratic-Republicans were also compatible with the concerns of the mechanics, valuing the prosperity of the entire community, rather than one dominant class.[39] For their own part, the Democratic-Republicans made use of the mechanics' popular appeal, staging demonstrations with the mechanics to undermine the Federalist cause. One such occurred on July 4, 1795. Philadelphia mechanics, Jacobins, and Democratic-Republicans commemorated the day by burning a figure of John Jay in effigy. The statue of Jay represented him selling the United States to Britain. The Federalists sent in troops to quell the fire and demonstration, but their forces were beaten back, and had to yield to the crowd. But the event was hardly a celebration; as the *Independent Gazetteer* noted, "it appeared more like a day of mourning than that of rejoicing."[40]

Small wonder that with such a high level of tension operating between the mechanics and the merchant elite, Murdock's plays would be refused by the managers. Charming though they might be, and timely in their discussions, they nevertheless represented a segment of Philadelphia society that the elite were unwilling to include in their long-term plans for the state.

By the winter of 1795, the anti-Federalist and anti-elite sentiment espoused by the mechanics and the Democratic-Republicans had begun to crystallize into a dislike of what were perceived as elite activities and entertainments.[41] At the beginning of the theater's second season, Bache's *Aurora* had criticized the theater's managers for not offering more French dramas, and for producing plays which occasionally attacked the French.[42]

By November of that same year, Bache seems to have concluded that the Chestnut Street managers were no longer willing to work towards fostering an "American" national theater and that they were interested merely in aping British ceremony and styles. He accused Washington of perpetuating this pseudo-aristocratic system among the Federalists, claiming that the hallmark of Federalism was "an implicit and obsequious devotion to the President."[43] He accused the President of encouraging those "speculators and stock jobbers who have amassed ministerial wealth," through government posts or government-sanctioned ventures such as land speculation.[44] But most importantly, he drew a direct connection between the pageantry of Philadelphia's "Republican Court" (as Washington's coterie had come to be known), and the Federalist-dominated Chestnut Street Theatre. He complained: "The pageantry of life may answer the purpose of the scenery at the playhouse, and keep the vulgar of the world from beholding the grandees before they are dressed and made up for public exhibition . . . [It is] highly efficacious in deluding the vulgar."[45] To Bache, and his supporters, Federalist society and entertainments had become suspect – designed, as the earliest anti-theater protestors had feared, to make people "forget their political duties."

Where then could Philadelphians who, whether for political or economic reasons, resisted the Federalist regime turn for entertainment? Ricketts's Circus provided the answer. John Ricketts had brought his circus to Philadelphia before the Chestnut Street Theatre had been established, and had offered shows at a temporary site near what are now Twelfth and Market Streets.[46] In 1795, he returned to Philadelphia to build a new amphitheatre, known variously as the Art Pantheon, Ricketts's Circus, and Ricketts's Amphitheatre. The spot he chose for his circus was directly opposite the Chestnut Street Theatre, an open challenge to the exclusive Federalist entertainments. The *Aurora* predicted happily that the new amphitheatre "will add considerably to the beauty of this part of the city."[47]

When the circus opened in October of 1795, Ricketts received overwhelming praise for his efforts to please the audience (efforts which might be sharply contrasted with the perceived resistance of the Chestnut Street managers to conform to popular tastes). One telling letter to the *Aurora* suggests that the circus's supporters viewed it as a site in which the differing elements of Philadelphia society could be reconciled:

> This small tribute of applause is offered by a friend to the innocent amusements that give our citizens occasionally a fillip to life and bring together such numbers of persons who have never had any opportunity of seeing each other, that the consequence must be advantageous to society by producing a more general acquaintance amongst the people, and gradually wearing off the unsocial reserve of many in this city whose prejudices have formerly given to Philadelphia the unhandsome character of being too much tinctured with an illiberal and inhospitable kind of the *mauvaise honte*, which of late is disappearing.[48]

The letter, from a correspondent who signs himself "Z," paints, perhaps for the first time, an American theater as a truly *democratic* imagined community. The writer notes that the theater brings together disparate elements of society, and projects that the shared experience of performance in the theater will translate into more amicable social relationships outside the theater.

The managers of the Chestnut Street house (not surprisingly) took a somewhat dim view of Ricketts's efforts to recruit their audiences. In December of 1795, Wignell penned and staged a satirical piece entitled *T'Other Side of the Gutter* (a reference to the theater's location in relation to the circus). In it, he mocked the entertainments offered at the amphitheatre, but at the same time, tried to offer his own novelty equestrian acts in competition. Despite his efforts to reclaim the Ricketts audience, it was clear from the tone of his advertisements for *T'Other Side of the Gutter* that he regarded Ricketts's offerings as decidedly "lowbrow" in comparison to the repertoire at the Chestnut Street Theatre.

Yet the need for the benevolent atmosphere of Ricketts's became even more apparent in January of 1796, when open warfare broke out between the Chestnut Street managers and the gallery audience. As had happened in the past, the orchestra refused to comply with audience requests for specific tunes. Yet this time, they "threw down their instruments, with all the indignation that offended dignity can inspire," and left the stage. They were persuaded to return, but again refused to play the desired tunes. Upon this second refusal, "the audience now in earnest felt exasperated at the indifference, not to say the contempt with which they were treated," and so, "many gentlemen of the pit and boxes *united with the gallery against the band* [emphasis mine]." According to the newspaper account of the incident, this "formidable alliance" finally induced the orchestra to play the audience's requests.[49] This incident demonstrates a new alliance among members of the Chestnut Street audience against the policies of the managers. It suggests that despite their political or class differences, the Chestnut Street audience held the common opinion that the players and orchestra were the servants of the people, and that they, as audience members, were entitled to expect obedience and courtesy in exchange for their admission fee. The writer's observation that the gentlemen of the pit and boxes joined with those of the gallery suggests a forging of ties across traditionally separated sections of Philadelphia society against the "outsiders" in the theater company.[50]

In contrast to the disputes at the Chestnut Street house, Ricketts continued to please the public, who commended him for his "extraordinary exertions and attention."[51] Ricketts offered both equestrian demonstrations, as well as afterpieces like *Catherine and Petruchio* or *Robinson Crusoe*. Ricketts also offered patriotic displays of the American flag and a "Liberty Pole."[52] Ricketts was even able to appropriate the task of celebrating Washington's birthday (formerly the province of the Chestnut Street Theatre). On February 22, 1796, the Art Pantheon was the site of a grand ball, and of triumphant recitations and tableaux. An ode to Washington, recited at the circus, imagined the amphitheatre as a site safe from the stirrings of party debate: "Hence! Pale Envy's step profane/Hence! Foul faction's slanderous tongue/Within these joyous walls be found/No hand that gives the secret wound."[53]

Again, the success of Ricketts's Circus stood in sharp contrast to the increasingly disappointing efforts of the Chestnut Street managers. On February 27, 1796, a review in the *Philadelphia Gazette and Universal Daily Advertiser* complained that the theater's production of *Jane Shore* (once a popular pre-war drama) had featured "dull and heavy" musical accompaniment. The reviewer suggested that Reinagle "introduce those Scotch and Irish airs which light up pleasure in the countenances of 19/20th's [*sic*] of those who fill the house." He added that "the will of the majority ought to prevail in a place of amusement as well as a Senate."[54]

On April 7, 1796, the *Aurora* ran an advertisement for Philadelphia mechanics to meet at Myers Tavern to form a union for their protection. Their action may have come partly in response to the escalation of land speculation deals among the Philadelphia elite, who, as Ronald Schultz notes, were the "traditional animus" of the city's mechanics.[55] Again, the mechanics and their Democratic-Republican allies drew a connection between Federalist elite economic policy and Federalist entertainments. A letter printed in the *Philadelphia Gazette and Universal Daily Advertiser* satirized the recent spate of land speculation deals, under the guise of "Theatrical Intelligencer." Supposedly describing the "New Theatre over the Allegheny," which had opened "under the direction of the managers of the Population Company," the writer asserted that the "principal characters were ably supported by many of the leading and knowing ones of the state."[56] Yet, as the writer observed, few of these land deals had progressed unchallenged – bankruptcies and financial crises had resulted (Robert Morris and John Nicholson were among the most notable failures in the land speculation craze).[57] As a result, he commented, "the managers have . . . removed to the Old Theatre, Philadelphia." He added that the "New Stage has been occupied by several strolling companies in succession . . . who, it is said, have no managers." This last comment may be an allusion to the Democratic-Republicans or to the ongoing, but often incoherent, opposition to the settlement policies in the western part of the state.[58]

The conflict between the Federalists and their opponents escalated throughout 1796. In preparation for the presidential election, the Federalists had proposed a system to choose electors based on a general election. The

Republicans, who had fewer representatives, advocated a district system. The Federalist bill passed, and Republicans protested that the self-styled "Friends to Order and the Constitution," as the Federalists called themselves, were "forming a nationwide conspiracy" to affect the outcome of the presidential election.[59] By the time of the state election of October, 1796, the Federalists had secured all of the Assembly seats in the city of Philadelphia (although the Republicans had made important inroads in the outlying counties).[60] Yet the Federalists lost in the battle to choose electors for the presidential race. The national election of 1796, in which Adams triumphed over Jefferson, in many ways did not reflect the prevailing Republican mood of Pennsylvania.[61]

How did these political changes within the state and the nation affect the theater during the 1797 season? Oddly, political and class debates seem to have temporarily deserted the theater that year. Instead, controversy centered around Wignell and Reinagle's resentment of Ricketts's Circus. At the beginning of the season, Wignell and Reinagle decided to change their traditional performance dates to compete with the circus. Traditionally, the two houses had played on alternate nights. In response to Wignell and Reinagle's announcement, Ricketts, who had confined his performance nights to Tuesday, Thursday, and Saturday, advertised that he would offer entertainments on the Chestnut Street's traditional Monday, Wednesday, and Friday. Wignell and Reinagle's decision proved ill judged. Their ticket sales plummeted, and they were forced to declare defeat and return to their old performance schedule.[62] Once again, Ricketts's lively and democratic atmosphere had triumphed over the Federalist, class-regulated system at Chestnut Street. The other excitement of the 1797 season was the opening of Lailson's Circus. Inspired by the success of Ricketts, the new circus was designed on a massive scale that made the Chestnut Street house look "quite small" by comparison.[63] Lailson's opened in April, 1797 and offered pantomime and equine circus entertainments until the following April. Unfortunately for Lailson's company, the Philadelphia theater-going community could not sustain two circuses and a playhouse. The company went bankrupt, many of the circus performers (who were French) returned to France with Lailson, while other members of the acting company were absorbed by other troupes. The enormous building collapsed on July 8, 1798.

Despite the disputes between Wignell and Ricketts, and the brief competition provided by Lailson's, 1797 was a relatively "peaceful" year in the playhouse, as far as political debates were concerned. Party controversy reentered the theater in 1798, and by that point it was the Federalists who appeared to be struggling to maintain their cultural and social legitimacy in the playhouse.

"There you will find your Friends": the Boston Mechanics *versus* the Federal Street Theatre[64]

On October 6, 1796, a correspondent wrote to the Boston *Polar Star*, "The Theatrical Campaign has been opened in this town with considerable spirit. Two Generals dispute the empire of the Drama."[65] Those "two generals" were John B. Williamson, manager of the Federal Street Theatre, and Charles Stuart Powell, manager of the new Haymarket Theatre; the territory up for grabs was the Boston audience. The founding of the Haymarket Theatre in 1796 marked a division in Boston's theatrical realm, rather than a blossoming of healthy interest and competition. This division soon imperiled not only the financial stability of both theaters but the public taste and tolerance for any kind of theatrical entertainments whatsoever. By 1799, both theaters were on the verge of bankruptcy, and by 1803 the gigantic Haymarket Theatre had been torn down and sold for scrap lumber.

Unlike the Mechanics of Philadelphia, who patronized entertainments at Ricketts, the Boston Mechanics mobilized to establish their own alternative theatrical entertainments (the Haymarket Theatre) between 1796 and 1798. And more importantly for their new theatrical venture, unlike their brother artisans to the south, the Boston Mechanics did not subscribe to a broad Republican agenda. Rather, the artisan founders of the Haymarket Theatre represented the rising Federalism of a middling respectability: a group who would cast a shadow in the greater Boston public far into the nineteenth century.[66]

Both traditional histories and recent scholarship have attributed the rivalry between the two playhouses to political animosity, suggesting that the Haymarket flourished as a Jacobin response to the intolerably smug Federalist atmosphere that dominated the Federal Street Theatre.[67] William Warland Clapp wrote in 1853, "It was believed by many...that the Federal Street was managed by those opposed to the Jacobins, and that the Trustees, *who were all of the federal school of politics*...upheld and justified the manager in the introduction of pieces, tending to provoke...their political opponents."[68]

Though Clapp was correct in noting that party tensions plagued the theater during this period (indeed, they had invaded the Federal Street almost from the time of its opening), his explanation for the founding of the second theater ignored one important point; while the Federal Street Theater *did* number such arch-Federalists as Stephen Higginson among its supporters by 1795, it also laid claim to some of Boston's most prominent Republicans, including Perez Morton, William Tudor, and Charles Jarvis.[69] The Haymarket's proprietors, on the other hand, included such Federalist allies as future politician Daniel Messinger, and editor of the Federalist mouthpiece, the *Columbian Centinel*, Benjamin Russell.[70] Neither theater could submit a list of proprietors with exclusive allegiance to one political agenda.

What the proprietors of each theater did have in common, however, was their socio-economic status. The proprietors of the Federal Street, the Tontiners, were joined through a network of common financial ventures, such as the Tontine, the Union Bank, the Tontine Crescent Buildings, and the theater, as well as interlaced family connections. They had opened the doors of cultural and economic advantage in Boston in the early 1790s. Though their political interests diverged as the decade progressed, they maintained their connections, built on shared social and financial interests. The proprietors of the Haymarket Theatre, on the other hand, were composed primarily of artisans and small merchants and professionals. The Mechanics, along with their satellite merchant associates, occupied a different and more nebulous social space than the Tontiners, one that they were struggling to define in the mid-1790s. Lacking the cohesive web of family, school, and civic ties that linked the Tontiners,[71] they sought other methods of association. Through participation in such organizations as the Massachusetts Charitable Mechanics Association, the Ancient and Honorable Artillery Company,[72] and ultimately through their proprietorship in the Haymarket Theatre, they found a means of stamping their identity on the Boston public. Yet the question remains: why were these two groups unable to coexist peacefully in Boston society? If political disputes were not the prime motivating factor, what accounts for the often acrimonious nature of the rivalry between the two playhouses?

By the mid-1790s, possession of a theater had come to represent a certain status in Boston society, as did the power to oversee its repertoire and functioning. The proprietors of the Federal Street Theatre, the Tontiners, had made their bid for this status between 1791 and 1794, as they consolidated their power and resources to force a permanent playhouse on a somewhat skeptical public and a resistant government. Their efforts had been rewarded; as the editor of the *Columbian Centinel* noted, the Federal Street playhouse was an achievement to be proud of: "In convenience, elegance, and taste, the best judges have given preference to any in Europe." He added, "The Trustees' [demonstration of] liberality must receive the plaudits of their fellow citizens, strangers, and foreigners."[73] But despite its promise, the theater opened to an audience divided by political tensions between pro- and anti-Jacobin factions. As I noted earlier, party tensions were present in the playhouse from the time of its opening, and even occasionally resulted in violence in the theaters. However, these episodes, while attention-getting and troublesome, were not the primary cause of the division in Boston's theater culture in 1796.

The Haymarket Theatre and the Boston theater wars had two main points of origin: the rise in power of the Massachusetts Charitable Mechanics Association, and the thwarted ambition of Charles Stuart Powell.[74] Powell had come to Boston as the manager of the Federal Street Theatre. A reasonably talented actor, but a poor manager, he soon earned the enmity of the Federal Street Trustees, who dismissed him in the summer of 1795.[75] He was humiliated and took out advertisements in the *Massachusetts Mercury*, threatening to write a "tell-all" book about his treatment at the Federal Street.[76] He pieced together solo performances in and around Boston, and waited for a chance at revenge.

His opportunity came through an unlikely source: the Boston Mechanics. In Clapp's history of the Boston theater he offers an interesting, though unqualified, comment about the founding of the Haymarket Theatre. He observes, "The Boston Mechanics were not partial to the Federal Street [playhouse]."[77] As noted earlier, party controversy in the Federal Street Theatre was confined primarily to outbursts from the gallery – a group generally composed of apprentices, servants, sailors, and other less wealthy (and less respectable) citizens, or as Robert Treat Paine described them, a crowd "unlac'd by Fashion, unrestrain'd by art."[78] The mechanics and minor merchants who attended the theater would have been more likely to secure seats in the pit – removed from the rowdyism of the upper stories.

Yet, unlike the gallery occupants, who stayed and fought it out in the Federal Street Theatre – insisting on their right to participate – the Mechanics decamped. Their sense of alienation from the Federal Street house speaks to their growing realization that they would never be allowed to become full-fledged participants in Boston culture, as designed by the Tontiners and Federal Street proprietors. This lesson had begun one year earlier, in 1795, when the Mechanics first attempted to incorporate.

In 1795 the Boston mechanics had created a mechanics' "constitution," ostensibly designed to allow mechanics greater legal authority over their apprentices. In fact, the apprentice issue formed but a small part of the mechanics' larger purpose. The constitution of the Mechanics Association outlines a similar function to that of the Boston Tontine Association: the creation of a group which could oversee the management and distribution of funds on behalf of the organization, funds which might be used for public or private benefit.[79] The Tontiners had raised nearly two million dollars to fund their plans: the Mechanics raised a mere two hundred.[80] Nevertheless, the Mechanics' plan to incorporate alarmed Boston's wealthier merchants and professionals, many of whom were affiliated with the Tontine, the Union Bank, and the Theatre. To the wealthier citizens of Boston, it seemed as though the men of the "middling sort" were aspiring to positions of power that threatened their own. They were not merely aping their betters, they were potentially usurping their financial and cultural authority.

In 1795, before any proposals had been made for a rival theater, the Mechanics circulated copies of their constitution to the twenty wealthiest merchants in Boston, soliciting their patronage.[81] They were rejected, and their repeated efforts to carry the petition for incorporation to the legislature also met with refusal.[82] Thwarted in their wish for official recognition, as the Tontiners had been three years before, the Mechanics formed an "unofficial" association. They collected dues and sponsored lavish dinners and events to which they invited Boston's leading Federalist lights, from John Adams to Harrison Gray Otis.[83] And they eschewed party debates, believing that politics were irrelevant to their larger charitable and financial goals. Their constitution explicitly prohibited "any debate or conversation upon any political subject whatsoever."[84]

Who were these mechanics intent on finding their niche in proper Boston society? There were eighty-three members of the original Boston Mechanics Association, whose professions ranged from bricklayer to hairdresser, to blacksmith.[85] Among the most well known and powerful of the original Mechanics were Benjamin Russell and Daniel Messinger.[86] Daniel Messinger was the son of a Massachusetts farmer. As a boy, Messinger was apprenticed to a Boston hatmaker. He was eventually able to start his own business, and by 1797 had saved enough money to purchase his own estate on Newbury Street for £1,000, where he set up both shop and residence. In the early nineteenth century, he served as a member of the Massachusetts state legislature and as an advisor on numerous charitable committees. Joseph Tinker Buckingham describes him as "a firm, active and consistent Federalist."[87]

Benjamin Russell had been apprenticed under the well-known editor Isaiah Thomas during the American Revolution. After the war he founded the paper that became the pro-Federalist *Columbian Centinel*. Russell was an important figure in the Sons of Liberty (as the Boston mechanics had called themselves during the Revolution), and after the war he remained an advocate for the mechanics,[88] as well as a spokesman for the emerging faction known as the "Essex Junto" (arch-Federalist enemies of the Democratic-Republicans).[89]

Both Messinger and Russell enjoyed relatively comfortable lifestyles which allowed them the leisure for involvement in the political and cultural spheres of Boston society. However, the members of the original Boston Mechanics Association encompassed a diverse group of men, whose incomes generally restricted their ability to support a wide range of investments or enterprises. In her essay, "From Carpenter to Capitalist: The Business of Building in Post-Revolutionary Boston," Lisa Lubow suggests that while the balance of wealth in Boston resided in the hands of the top 10 percent of Boston's taxpayers, who, in turn, controlled 65 percent of the town's wealth, the majority of the town's population belonged to the "middling sort." An impressive estate for a man of the "middling sort" might range in value from $400 to $1,000, while those of the "better sort" soared anywhere from $9,000 to $17,000.[90] A review of the tax records for the proprietors of the Haymarket Theatre suggests that many of the founders fell into the "middling" category.[91] Yet to assume that the disparity in wealth between the "middling" and the "better" sort automatically translated into political allegiances is misleading. As Gary Kornblith writes, "the Federalist party was not merely for the rich," and "the main current of artisan republicanism . . . in the *1790s* was artisan *federalism*."[92] Artisan Federalists, Kornblith argues, "cared . . . deeply about promoting equitable economic development . . . They regarded balanced economic growth as virtually a panacea for current problems of social injustice and political conflict."[93] Though these men of the "middling sort" could not compete financially with the town's elite, they could learn to maximize their influence in other ways, such as the formation of associations and incorporations.

The specific impetus for the founding of the Haymarket Theatre remains something of a mystery. Powell may have seized on the Mechanics as the only united faction in Boston society likely to compete with the Tontiners. He may have observed that they were beginning to sponsor separate entertainments, such as the February 1796 Washington's Birthday fete at Concert Hall, which was staged in direct competition with the celebration offered at the Federal Street Theatre the same evening! Powell actively courted the Mechanics, referring to them as the "Sons of Liberty," pledging to name the playhouse the "Liberty Theatre" in their honor, and promising that the new theater would accommodate the mechanics and their families. In all his proposals for the new theater he emphasized that it could be built to rival the luxury of the Federal Street house (but for less money), and he noted the potentially lucrative nature of the investment.[94]

Several aspects of the building and management of the Haymarket suggest that its founders viewed the theater as both a promising business venture and as an opportunity to establish themselves as a viable and contributing force in Boston culture. In a letter to Benjamin Russell's paper, the *Columbian Centinel*, Powell took aim at the Federal Street house. He observed that though the founders had promised that the theater would "be a school of virtue and morality," it had not fulfilled its mission. He added, "Whether these assurances have been realized, or whether indeed any were so credulous as to expect it – are questions which do not perhaps require the acuteness and penetration of a philosopher to determine."[95] Powell and the Mechanics asserted that *their* theater would correct the "licentiousness" of the stage, substituting "chaste morality and sentimental humor" instead.[96] Thus the Mechanics boldly appropriated the cultural mission of the Tontine Gentry.

In addition to its moral improvements over the Federal Street, Powell and the Mechanics promised increased accessibility as well. The Haymarket's seating capacity doubled that of the Federal Street, approaching approximately two thousand seats.[97] This expansion suggests that the Haymarket's proprietors hoped to target a broader audience than the Federal Street, as do its oft-advertised promises that it would never raise its ticket prices and the assurance that ladies could come in any style of dress. In fact, the *Massachusetts Mercury* praised Powell's plan to build two galleries for the theater, rather than the traditional single gallery, since it would permit "many respectable citizens' wives . . . an opportunity of going to the theater at a very inconsiderable expense without being obliged to suffer the expense necessitated to dress for the boxes."[98]

The building itself, located at the corner of Tremont and Boylston Streets, has been described somewhat disparagingly as "an immense wooden pile," perhaps because in many cases the Mechanics offered their skilled labor and materials in lieu of cash investment.[99] Yet other contemporary accounts compared it to the Opera Houses of Paris and London, claiming that it promised to "exhibit a finish of elegance and design hitherto unknown in the new world."[100] Its only fault appeared to be that its ceiling was too high, and "the voices are lost before they reach the remote part of the audience."[101] Yet that flaw notwithstanding, the building met with general approval among its supporters. As one observer noted, "Last evening I attended the rehearsal at the Haymarket Theatre, and was highly delighted with the . . . grand appearance and the richness and brilliance of the scenery, it looked like a national edifice." The observer added, "I felt all the pride of an American dilate around my heart."[102] The evident pleasure that the Haymarket proprietors took in the luxury of their playhouse and in its ability to stand on a par with the Federal Street suggests that they viewed it as an alternative but comparable site for establishing their social and cultural connections.

But what would they put on the stage of their glorious new theater? Though the Mechanics had decried the "contemptible tribe of mountebanks, ropedancers, mimes, buffoons, and Merry-Andrews"[103] populating the Federal Street stage, ironically, the Haymarket's repertoire remained strikingly similar to its competitor. Historians who have imputed a "Jacobin" agenda to the Haymarket might be hard-pressed to justify its opening night production of Hannah Cowley's *The Belle's Stratagem*.[104] The play, set amongst the nobility of England, chronicles the romance of the worldly Doricourt and the modest Letitia Hardy. The last line of the play, "Cursed be the Hour, should it ever arrive, when British ladies shall sacrifice to foreign graces the grace of Modesty," affirms the virtues of Englishwomen over all others. This play hardly seems an appropriate choice for a theater fostering a hotbed of Jacobin sentiment. However, it seems a perfectly natural one for a "middling sort" audience who wanted access to the popular plays that their betters were seeing, but wanted them on their own terms.

The Haymarket and the Federal Street houses occasionally presented the same plays within the same week. A play such as *The Mountaineers* or *The Merchant of Venice* which had been particularly successful at one theater would be snatched up by the other, three to five days later.[105] This box-office-based competition points to a class and social schism between the two houses, rather than a political one. A telling episode, recounted by Representative Thomas Dwight, points out the class differences perceived between the two theaters:

I happened in the Barber shop the other day to say that I intended to visit the Haymarket Theatre once before I left town – "Poh, said Joseph Coolidge, (who was present) go to the <u>Old House</u>, There you will find <u>your Friends</u> [emphasis original]." As soon as Mr. Coolidge left the shop – the boy said, "Mr. Dwight, you may believe Mr. C. if you have a mind, but the new players are a damned sight better than the old." Go where we will, we find the partisans of both theatres disputing their respective merits.[106]

Initially, the competition between the two theaters seemed to spur each company to greater efforts. As the *Polar Star* remarked, "The entertainment at the Old Theatre was said to be excellent on Monday evening. It seemed as if all the talents of the performers had been unfolded and developed by competition."[107] The *Columbian Centinel* reported that "both Theatres... are well attended. There is much ability in both. But the style of dancing and the pantomimic exhibitions at the large theater [are] the most elegant ever seen by an American audience."[108] Responding to the popularity and success of the new house, the Federal Street lowered its ticket prices to try to attract the Haymarket crowd. On December 31, 1796, three weeks after the opening of the Haymarket, the Federal Street proprietors announced that "from an earnest desire to submit to...whatever is for the public accommodation," they would lower ticket prices by approximately half their original cost. They promised that "should any further reductions be deemed needful for the general satisfaction, they will be made with the same cheerful observance and attention."[109]

The two theaters also tried to outdo each other in their patriotic displays – each claiming a greater fervor than the other. For example, on Washington's birthday in 1797, the Federal Street Theatre announced that it would present "an evening in the style of masonic and dramatic spectacle, worthy of the glorious nativity of that illustrious man."[110] Dwight commented that the playhouse had been as "full as it could be stowed without packing the bulk like dried goods." He described the spectacle as follows:

> The curtain was drawn, and exhibited a statue of General Washington on horseback, on each side of him some beautiful transparent paintings of all the goddesses of liberty, etc. The Tree of Liberty was planted, covered with garlands and the most beautiful wreaths of flowers – around it was performed a rural dance with such art and agility...I never saw before. In fact, I was much more delighted with the play and its accomplishments than I have ever been with any theatrical exhibition.[111]

For that same evening, the Haymarket announced that it would revive the popular *Bunker-Hill* production. Of that performance, Dwight observed that there were reportedly "not less than two thousand people" in attendance on that evening. He expressed his amazement at the amount of money being spent by the residents of Boston on theatrical entertainments, "The extravagance of the people of this town in their amusements has got beyond all rational bounds." He reckoned that the costs of celebrations planned for Washington's birthday could not "be estimated at less than seventeen thousand dollars."[112] It seemed – for a while – that Boston audiences would spend and spend, as long as the houses were willing to offer ever more extraordinary entertainments.

Yet what might have been a profitable rivalry between the two houses soon proved disastrous. Not only were the Federal Street and Haymarket Theatres competing with each other, after 1795 a profusion of entertainments, ranging from equestrian shows to fireworks displays, vied for their share of the popular market. A string of managers at both houses bankrupted themselves in trying to attract audiences. The luckless Charles Stuart Powell lasted only one season as manager of the Haymarket.

Moreover, by 1797, both the Tontiners and the Mechanics had shifted their focus to other ventures and concerns. Though the Tontiners still maintained an interest in the Federal Street Theatre, they had suffered a series of financial setbacks in 1796 which made them unwilling (or unable) to bolster the depleted accounts of the Federal Street house. Samuel Hewes of the Massachusetts Democratic-Republican Society complained: "This town is in a distrest [sic] situation, Money is unusually scarce, produce has fallen 50 per cent – The whole tontin [sic] Company have shut themselves up & many tendermen are nearly ruined by it."[113] Thomas Dwight reported that "several persons in this town who have been very respectable . . . have within a few days past failed . . . All this is the effect of speculation in Eastern lands and Georgia Lands, Tontine Buildings, &c., to carry on which they have borrowed money at a monstrous percent and are now unable to fulfill their contracts." Dwight's letters to his wife report the bankruptcy of a number of Tontine affiliates, including Charles Bulfinch, the architect of the Federal Street Theatre and the Tontine Crescent, and merchant Joseph Barrel.[114]

Both theaters struggled through the 1796–1797 seasons, the highlights of which were the Haymarket's celebration of the launching of the frigate *Constitution*, and the Federal Street's fund-raising efforts to aid families of Americans being held captive in Algiers, the premiere of John Daly Burk's *Bunker-Hill, or, The death of General Warren*, and the debut of actor and playwright William Charles White, Boston's first real star.[115] Though they enjoyed only a short heyday on the Boston stage, both Burk's and White's careers merit some discussion for what they reveal about Boston's conflicted theater world at the end of the eighteenth century.

A recent Irish immigrant, John Daly Burk infused both his newspaper, the *Polar Star*, and his plays with patriotic zeal and an active reformist spirit.[116] Burk's work appealed to popular (and generic) republican sympathies. He wrote for a nation that he described as a "moral, intrepid, and enlightened community, ranged under the banner of equality and justice."[117] *Bunker-Hill* debuted at the Haymarket Theatre on February 17, 1797. As the title suggests, it chronicles the brave campaign waged by a handful of poorly armed American soldiers against a powerful British army. The play also offers a romantic subplot between a British soldier (Abercrombie) and an American girl (Elvira), whose conflicting allegiances underscore the pathos of the struggle. Despite a largely negative response from critics (including William Dunlap), who labeled it "vile" and "execrable," *Bunker-Hill* enjoyed tremendous popularity among its mechanic audience at the Haymarket, who rejoiced in seeing themselves and their compatriots – the foot soldiers and Sons of Liberty – portrayed as heroes on the American stage.[118]

If Daly's work appealed to the uncomplicated tastes of a mechanic audience, William Charles White's debut at the Federal Street seemed to promise more sophistication. Unlike John Murdock and John Daly Burk, White boasted the requisite breeding, education, and social status that could make his sponsors in the theater proud to claim him as a "native genius," as a cultural product comparable to the best that Britain had to offer: in other words, as "the Garrick of America."[119]

The son of a prosperous merchant and established citizen of Boston, White combined claims to a respectable social status and refinement with the advantage of having been "born" an American in 1777. For the frustrated audiences in the galleries, weary of watching British plays and British actors, White's debut offered the chance to pit American talent against stale British tradition, to re-invigorate the Boston stage with a dose of homegrown inspiration. For the audiences in the pit and boxes, White's standing as a young gentleman of Boston seemed to prove the theater's claim to "polish the manners and habits of society . . . and to improve and refine the literary taste of our rising republic."

Such high expectations naturally placed a great deal of pressure upon their object. All the more so, since White's debut on the Boston stage in the winter of 1796 was not the calculated move of a patriot, devoted solely to the cultural enrichment of his country, but rather the impulse of a stagestruck youth taking advantage of his father's prolonged absence from the city.

While on a trip out of Boston in December of 1796, William White, Sr. received a spate of letters from concerned friends, informing him of his son's decision to take the stage. One observed, "Since your departure, he appeared to me a little deranged...It was yesterday noon that he made known to us his determination of acting the part of Douglas in the tragedy of that name."[120] Young William told one well-meaning advisor who bade him think of his father's sorrow at his decision: "Oh, you kill me! Do not mention my father. I love him, but I must go on the stage or I shall be wretched all my life, nay I shall die, for I would rather stab myself than do business."[121]

Thus, apprehensively, young William's advisors watched him make his debut at the Federal Street Theatre on December 14, 1796. White played Norval in the tragedy of *Douglas*, and to the relief of his friends met with "unbounded applause." Samuel Parkman wrote to White's father to assure him his son's performance had rivaled that of England's most noted thespian and that "'twas the general observation that [young William] would be the Garrick of America."[122] John Daly Burk's *Polar Star* noted with approval: "He did not merely please, he astonished an elegant and discriminating audience." The *Star* added that "his declamation was correct, classical, and pathetical, his tones full of harmony," concluding: "The writer does not hesitate to affirm that there has scarcely ever been a better first night of *Douglas* in Europe."[123]

The *Polar Star's* review raises telling points about both the performance and the audience in the Federal Street playhouse. The description of the audience as "elegant and discriminating" implied that the audience knew *how* the part ought to have been performed, and that young William was not merely pleasing an unsophisticated local crowd, but a cosmopolitan one with refined tastes. The observation that William played the part "correctly" suggests that there were certain accepted conventions for playing tragedy, and that William demonstrated the same *craft* and *technique* that one would expect of a professional actor. But the last comment is perhaps the most significant. By comparing an American production, featuring an American actor, to the playhouses of Europe, the writer made an important claim to his readers: that Americans did indeed have the ability to compete with European culture, and even perhaps to outdo it. Yet at the same time, he subtly reinforced the notion that the European cultural pattern remained the accepted standard: William's merit as a performer appeared only as he fit the European models.

The *Polar Star* review and audience reaction to White's performance epitomize what Richard Bushman has described as the post-Revolutionary tension between European notions of gentility and refinement and

American images of "republican simplicity."[124] White, in many ways, seemed to straddle this awkward division, but what an "American" theater might be (aside from a temple of virtue), what aesthetic standards it might profess, had, even in 1796, to be determined. In justifying his work in the theater to his father, William had claimed that his goal was to "reform" and "improve" the morality of the stage, and diffuse its corrupting European influences. The Haymarket's founders had observed with asperity that, despite the claims of the Federal Street proprietors, their theater had never become the temple of republican virtue they had promised: perhaps White would be the answer? As Bushman observes, "the contradiction between republican simplicity and genteel elegance was the central problem for many American men of letters trying to conceive a consistent American character."[125] Just how William might improve and reform the stage to reflect American sensibilities remained to be seen.

By January of 1797, William's fame had spread from Boston to New York. Notices appeared in the New York *Argus*, again labeling him the "Garrick of America." More importantly, however, the paper noted, William had aspirations to write for the stage. The *Argus* reported that William had already written a tragedy, and boasted that this youth, "of the most reputable connection in town . . . will do honor to America."[126]

William's tragedy, *Orlando; or, Parental persecution*, debuted at Boston's Federal Street Theatre on March 10, 1797, as William's benefit performance. Notices appearing in the *Columbian Centinel* observed that "expectation is on tiptoe for this juvenile production of theatrical genius."[127] The play tells the story of young Orlando, whose secret marriage is opposed by a tyrannical father and wicked brother, who plot to betray him, his wife, and his closest friend. Although White and his Federal Street sponsors touted the play as "void of foreign arts,"[128] the script is in fact highly derivative of earlier English tragedies such as *Venice Preserv'd* and *The Gamester*. Most of the characters are murdered, executed, or drink poison by the end of the play.

A telling silence greeted *Orlando* after its first performance. The Federal Street audience, which had held such high hopes for the play and for White's genius, was unsure how to receive a script which so clearly fell below its expectations for a rising American author. No reviews appeared in the papers which had been so eager to proclaim White's work as the "first American play" written in Boston.[129] But clear evidence of White's failure appeared when the Haymarket Theatre advertised a new "afterpiece" which satirized *Orlando*. Entitled *Chrononhotonthologos: King of Queerumania*, the play was described as "the most tragical tragedy that ever was tragedized after a

Figure 5. Illustration from the manuscript of *Orlando*, by William Charles White

tragical manner by any tragical company of comical tragedians." The playbill also promised that "a young gentleman of Boston" would play the role of the "King of the Antipodes, or the gentleman who carries his head where his heels should be."[130] The death knell for *Orlando* sounded when White sent the play to the American Academy of Belles Lettres and was informed that "the grand fault of *Orlando* is... the plot is not sufficiently interesting."[131]

Thus ended William Charles White's brief career on the Boston stage. By 1797, William's father had begun to suffer a reversal of fortune. He had bought a considerable amount of property in Boston between 1785 and 1795, but by 1796 had begun to default on debts, and his land was being seized as payment. Perhaps out of consideration for his family's reduced circumstances, or perhaps discouraged by the negative response to his first dramatic efforts, William retired from the Boston stage after only one season, and turned to the study of law. Any further ventures into theatrical activities seemed unlikely.[132]

White's failure with his first play raises intriguing questions about the role of the native author in late 1790s America. If Murdock's plays had been blocked by his class allegiances and perhaps by his too-familiar local allusions, what could explain White's failure, as a young gentleman of the city undertaking a classical theme? White's failure with *Orlando* emphasizes a crucial distinction between aesthetic and commercial genius in the early Republic. As Michael Warner notes, while Americans "*wanted* a distinctively indigenous culture," in the years following the Revolution the nature of the "Americanness" that they expected to see was still undefined. Although William Charles White was hailed as an "American genius," in the 1790s such a label often had more connection to a product's commercial viability than the presentation of a new, "national" aesthetic sensibility. Thus, for a Boston theater manager to proclaim White in 1796 or 1797 as an "American author" or an "American actor" was more probably an advertising tactic than, as Warner observes, an invitation to partake in a "specially indigenous cultural good."[133] Though its progress in the eighteenth century was problematic, Warner suggests that an American literary and cultural aesthetic evolved during the first half of the nineteenth century, as the "national imaginary" grew under Jefferson and Jackson.[134] This evolution was mirrored in the national drama as well, and appears in White's later plays.[135]

But in the meantime, not even the "cultural product" of a native Boston author could rejuvenate the jaded Boston theater audiences in the late 1790s. By 1797, neither the Federal Street nor the Haymarket was in stable financial condition. The Federal Street house distributed chandelier lamps from the theater lobby to the trustees, in lieu of financial dividends that year; and in March, 1797, the proprietors of the Haymarket were forced to call a meeting of the subscribers "to determine some mode of raising funds, competent to the discharge of any debts which have already accrued..."[136] Nevertheless, according to John B. Williamson, the manager of the Federal Street house, the Tontiners still had the advantage over the Haymarket proprietors, since the Federal Street Theatre was "paid for to the uttermost shilling." He urged the Federal Street Trustees to continue to invest in productions at the playhouse, with the goal of edging out the Haymarket competition: "How far the proprietors of the other house can cope with you in that advantage, you who are intimately acquainted with the laboring part of this community can best judge."[137] In Williamson's assessment, the "laboring part" of Boston, the mechanic proprietors of the Haymarket, would not be able to sustain any prolonged contest with the Federal Street. This sentiment was echoed by Williamson's successor, John Hodgkinson, who observed that there were "very few monied or influential men" involved in the Haymarket.[138] Yet both theaters clung on through that difficult year.

In addition to the financial crises facing the owners of both houses, Boston's theatrical culture suffered another setback in February of 1798, when the Federal Street house caught fire and burned to the ground. Some ministers in the town regarded the fire as a judgment on the Tontiners: "We desire to thank thee O Almighty God [for] suffering to be destroyed by fire the monuments of human pride and dissipation," as Thomas Dwight wrote to his wife Hannah.[139] The total value of the land and the building was estimated at some $70,000 – only one share of which had been insured.[140] Nevertheless, the Tontiners paid for the theater's reconstruction, which further diminished their resources.[141] Interestingly, they rejected suggestions from manager John Hodgkinson that they simply purchase the Haymarket Theatre (which itself was teetering on the brink of bankruptcy). In a letter from Charles Bulfinch to the Trustees of the Federal Street house, Bulfinch states that Hodgkinson "begs me to suggest to you whether it would not be...a very practicable thing to purchase shares in the Haymarket Theatre by means of a secret agent." Hodgkinson claimed that this plan would give the Federal Street Trustees "command of a majority of votes." His plan was for the Federal Street owners to transfer all of the moveable props and scenery from the Haymarket, and sell the building for some other purpose.[142] Hodgkinson had noted, with some desperation, "Boston cannot maintain Two Theatres [*sic*]."[143] Yet despite Hodgkinson's plea that the public was "exhausted" by the rivalry between the two houses, the Tontiners persisted in their plans to re-build the theater, and on an even grander scale than the original structure. Moreover, the Trustees denied Hodgkinson's petition to lower the theater's rent, in response to the financial losses he had suffered as manager. Hodgkinson ultimately threatened to resign, commenting that he would not "run that risk as an <u>individual</u> [*sic*] which a numerous body of <u>rich men</u> [*sic*] think it dangerous to share."[144] The Trustees finally acceded to Hodgkinson's pleas, but, unfortunately for them, Hodgkinson's predictions were correct: the Boston public *was* tired of the wrangling between the two houses and of mediocre and unoriginal entertainments.

While the proprietors of the Federal Street Theatre were foundering, the Mechanics too saw a gradual shift in their focus away from the activities at the Haymarket. Part of their original constitution had called for annual festivals, and unlike the Tontiners, they had experienced a growth in economic prosperity.[145] They turned to the planning of their winter festivals (which coincided with the opening of the traditional theatrical season), and left the running of the theater to a series of managers who were unable to fill the theater's enormous capacity, or to negotiate a successful working relationship with the Federal Street proprietors.

Additionally, party tensions had escalated in Massachusetts during 1798, with the imposition of the Alien and Sedition Acts. Though, as noted earlier, neither theater boasted a completely "Republican" or "Federalist" list of trustees, nevertheless, as Hodgkinson observed, "the doubtful state of public affairs" had produced an "apathy" among Boston's theater-going population, who had more pressing concerns.[146]

What began as a decade of promise for Boston's cultural growth ended in chaos. Though the supporters of the Federal Street and Haymarket Theatres had envisioned their playhouses as significant symbols of cultural and social achievement, they lacked both the understanding of the form and the momentum to sustain them. Nevertheless, the competition among the early Boston theaters points to a broader struggle within Boston society – a struggle to determine who would control its social and cultural development in the years to come.

The Federalist swansong

By the beginning of 1798, the elite theaters in both Boston and Philadelphia were again in serious difficulties. However, in this case, the problems were no longer simply those of finance. Instead, the elites were fighting to maintain their hegemony in a society which had profited by their example and was rapidly evolving cultural systems that surpassed their own. The years from 1798 to 1800 witnessed the Boston and Philadelphia elites' last efforts to secure their cultural and social legacy, and saw the constant influx of new and diverse elements into the theaters' "democracy of glee."

5

A commercial community: the New York difference

THUS FAR, I HAVE TRACED THE HISTORIES OF THE BOSTON AND
Philadelphia theaters from their inception to the brink of financial failure.
I have suggested that the post-war antipathy to theater in both cities could
not withstand the efforts of "new men" who viewed the theater as a means
of promoting republican rhetoric and the "native genius" of the new nation.
New York, on the other hand, offers a different model of both wartime
occupation and post-war recuperation. Like Boston and Philadelphia, New
York felt the humiliating sting of wartime occupation. Like their fellow
citizens in Boston and Philadelphia, patriots in New York had chafed under
the British army's flouting of its anti-theater prohibitions. But unlike Boston
and Philadelphia, New York emerged from the war with a fragmented social
and political structure that owed less to differences in ideology, and more
to nascent capitalist and class divisions that would produce a strikingly
different theatrical and civic culture in the city's early national period.

In many ways, the post-Revolutionary New York resembled the pre-
Revolutionary one. Boston and Philadelphia had experienced major shifts
in political and cultural power during the Revolution. The Tory faction in
Boston had been dethroned, making way for a new generation of monied
men, determined to wield their power for both private and public good.
The Quaker faction, while still vocal in Philadelphia, had largely lost its
political sway, and the radical republican experiment of the Revolution had
fundamentally transformed Pennsylvania's post-war political parties and
rhetoric. New York, on the other hand, emerged from the war physically
decimated by the fires that had swept the city under the British occupation:
"Late in 1783, New York had lain scarred with fire, some of its weed-choked
streets the pastures of roaming cows, its fences and orchards long since
destroyed for fuel, its wharves decaying and its treasury exhausted."[1]

As I suggested in chapters 1 and 2, New York's wartime political scene showed a pattern of shifting allegiances, as traditional ties among family networks (like the DeLanceys and the Crugers) ruptured and re-framed themselves along lines of loyalist and patriot. I also suggested that the uncertainty that had dominated the colony during the war years continued to impact its post-Revolutionary structure. Numerous books have chronicled New York's post-war ambivalence, labeling the state "The Reluctant Pillar," for its hesitancy during the process of ratifying the Constitution. Historians from Charles Beard to Jackson Turner Main have identified New York as the "exception" in studies of the process of ratification.[2] In part, New York's "exceptional" status seems to hinge on the tensions between merchant Federalists who saw the advantages of union, and mechanic and yeoman classes who feared the implications of the Constitution.[3] The tensions in the city also seemed to replicate its pre-war pattern of family and business alliances. However, it is important to note that the crucible of war had brought new men to power, and had sifted and sorted pre-Revolutionary alliances. Post-war New York saw descendants of powerful families who had been bitter enemies before the war forming pro- or anti-Federalist alliances based on common social and financial interests. Those who found their economic interests furthered by ratification were primarily New York's merchant, banker, and lawyer class, and included old family names like Cruger, Livingston, and Low. Other members of the nascent Federalist party included Comfort Sands, Josiah Ogden Hoffman, John Jay, Richard Morris, Peter Vandervoort, Richard Varick, William Duer, Isaac Roosevelt, and Alexander Hamilton.[4] On the other side, the "anti's" were another group of old families and "new men" headed by Governor George Clinton, and including Samuel Jones, John Lansing, and Brockholst Livingston (not all of the Livingston family were Federalists).

The contending parties of the immediate post-war period represented a combination of "old" and "new" men, who formed interest-based alliances that superseded traditional ties and overlooked long-standing feuds. Of the "new" men brought to power in New York, Alexander Hamilton and George Clinton, who eventually came to stand at the heads of their parties in the state, are among the most interesting. Of Alexander Hamilton, the future Secretary of the Treasury, much has been written, ranging from stories of his supposed illegitimacy to his virulent hatred of his rival Aaron Burr. Some histories debate his scruples in the handling of the nation's post-war economy and his own financial speculations in the state of New York. Yet few challenge his genius either in structuring the nation's new financial system or in helping to form the Bank of New York. Of Clinton, less has been written. He was not as "new" as Hamilton, in that he was a native New Yorker, and had married into one of upstate New York's most influential families, the Tappens.[5] Clinton had served on New York's Assembly in the 1760s as a radical Whig, and was known as "a sturdy republican and unqualified democrat."[6] While Clinton's politics had garnered the loyalty of the Sons of Liberty and the mechanic and agricultural interests during the war, his post-Revolutionary policies left him vulnerable to attacks from the "aristocratic" section of the population that had been elbowed aside during the Revolution.

"It soon became evident that the Federalist group had but little in common with Governor Clinton."[7] The financial crisis that spanned the four years after the Revolution divided the state of New York among Federalist and anti-Federalist loyalties. In some ways, the post-Revolutionary sectionalism of New York resembled that of Pennsylvania, in that its largest Federalist contingency resided in the eastern part of the state, while its largest anti-Federalist factions dominated the west. The highest concentration of pro-Federalist supporters resided in New York County, Kings County, Suffolk County, Richmond County, Albany, Columbia, and Montgomery. Most of these counties were either border areas (bounded by Connecticut, Massachusetts, or Vermont), or seaport areas. On the anti-Federalist side were many of those counties along the Hudson River with a strong agricultural contingency, including Ulster County, Orange County, Dutchess, Westchester, and Washington.[8]

In addition to the Federalist/anti-Federalist schism, the eastern and western counties divided on a number of other issues – among the most important, the question of what to do with the loyalist population that had remained in the state after the war (and after the mass exodus of refugees to Canada). As Julius Goebel notes, "By 1783, New York patriots had committed themselves to a policy of retaliation against those who had opposed them during the war for independence."[9] The western counties in particular had a difficult time reconciling their post-war outlook with their radical Revolutionary philosophy. On January 27, 1787 the state Assembly voted on whether or not ex-loyalists could serve in the legislature and the majority of votes for disqualification appeared in the western counties. Eastern New York Federalists like Hamilton, on the other hand, sought ways to reconcile former Tories with the new political regime.[10] Hamilton actively campaigned for the rights of former loyalists, defending them both in the courtroom and in print. In an open letter to the citizens of New York, Hamilton observed:

> The idea of suffering the Tories to live among us under disqualifications is...mischievous and absurd...Viewing the subject in every possible light, there is not a single interest of the community but dictates moderation rather than violence...Were the people of America with one voice to ask "What shall we do to perpetuate our liberties and secure our happiness?" The answer would be GOVERN WELL, and you have nothing to fear from either internal disaffection or external hostility.[11]

One of Hamilton's most famous and controversial early cases involved a loyalist named Joshua Waddington, sued in 1783 under the Trespass Act. Hamilton carried the day, and Waddington subsequently enjoyed a successful career as a merchant, a member of the New York Tontine, a subscriber to the Bank of New York, and a shareholder in the Park Theatre.

While a discussion of New York's post-Revolutionary political turmoil may seem tangential to the development of its post-war theater, I suggest that the very ambiguity and controversy that surrounded the question of how (or whether) to re-integrate former loyalists into the government mirrors the controversy over how to re-introduce a traditionally "British" pastime into a newly republican nation.

As I noted in chapters 2 and 3, theatrical entertainments had returned to the old John Street playhouse immediately after the end of the war. Perhaps anticipating the least resistance there, Lewis Hallam, Jr. attempted to re-establish theatrical entertainments in New York in 1785. Yet he had reckoned without the damage – physical and psychological – done by the occupying British troops. On October 14, 1785, Hallam received a formal rebuke for offering theatrical entertainments "without a license or the permission of the civil authority." His action was deemed "unprecedented and offensive... while so great a part of the city still lies in ruins."[12] Hallam tried to climb into the good graces of the Assembly by offering a "donation" to aid the destitute, but the city returned the gift. Though theatrical entertainments in post-war New York never attracted the same level of opposition as they did in Boston and Philadelphia, two cities with an entrenched history of anti-theatrical sentiment, the war and the shift in power towards the Whiggish Clintonites had temporarily turned the public taste away from "aristocratic" entertainments.[13]

Despite the initial resistance, Hallam re-opened the John Street Theatre on November 21, 1785, with, according to *McLean's Independent Journal*, "unremitted plaudits from every part of the house." The writer also noted that the company had gone to "vast expense" to ensure that the John Street house had been "repainted, beautified, and illuminated in a style to vie with European splendour."[14] For the next nine years, Hallam continued to operate the John Street house as part of his larger circuit of theaters up and down the east coast. Though, as I have suggested earlier, numerous changes occurred within the company during that time (the departure of Thomas Wignell for Philadelphia, the advent of John Hodgkinson, etc.), the company seems to have paid little attention either to creating a more "American" repertoire (with the notable exception of Royall Tyler's *The Contrast*, which premiered at the John Street Theatre in 1787), or to renovating or re-locating the house to adjust to New York's shifting landscape. Thus, by 1794, Hallam found himself the proprietor of a theater that no longer represented the city New York had become, and that could no longer contain its schisms, rivalries, and multiple agendas.

Three major changes transformed New York society between 1783 and 1794: the creation of the Bank of New York, the establishment of the New York Tontine, and the ratification of the Federal Constitution. These events shifted the balance of power in New York, sharpened the growing distinctions between the "haves" and the "have nots," and ultimately drove one faction from the John Street Theatre in search of their own, uncontested space.

"New York has always been a commercial community," observes Mrs. Archer to her son Newland in Edith Wharton's *The Age of Innocence*.[15] Mrs. Archer derides those who describe New York as an "aristocratic" society, asserting that *financial* interests, not familial ones, had formed the bonds between "the respectable English or Dutch merchants who came to the colonies and stayed . . . because they did so well."[16] Indeed, Wharton's description of nineteenth-century New York society provides a clue to the formation of the city's post-Revolutionary society and to the origins of the Park Theatre.

Like its counterparts to the north and south, the pre- and post-Revolutionary New York theater formed part of an intricate web of social, political, and economic considerations. The origins of New York's post-war theater, like those of the Boston and Philadelphia playhouses, can be linked to ventures as diverse as the creation of banks, tontines, and political

parties. However, *unlike* its sister cities, New York produced a theatrical environment surprisingly devoid of republican ideology. The founders of New
York's Park Theatre espoused no overt political or ideological motives for
the creation of their theater. Instead, their choice to build the Park Theatre
was a natural outgrowth of their economic plans for their own select portion
of New York society. While I do not dismiss their accomplishments in the
creation of the Bank of New York or the Tontine Coffee House, ventures
which eventually benefited more than a narrow circle of investors, I suggest
that their vision, and thus ultimately their theater, was a more personal and
private one. Their outlook was shaped by their understanding of commerce
as the driving force in the new nation, and they saw economic power as
the way to access opportunity in the political and social spheres. Ironically,
their surprising absence of idealism clashed directly with that of the most
idealistic figure to emerge from the early national theater, Park playhouse
manager William Dunlap, a passionate believer in the power of the theater
to transform its audience.

But who were these men whose idealism encompassed profit but not
patriotism? In his diaries and in his *History of the American Theatre*, William
Dunlap mentions only a few of the names of the over 100 shareholders
associated with the Park Theatre. Nor do subsequent histories record many
additional names. The archival record also seems curiously blank, compared
to the fairly extensive records available in Boston and Philadelphia. Thus
mapping the involvement of the post-war elite in the founding of the Park
Theatre has proved a challenging process. Interestingly, the largest record
of names that has appeared to date comes from the papers of Alexander
Hamilton, who, though he does not seem to have been a shareholder himself,
represented a group of the theater's proprietors in a lawsuit. His biography,
The Intimate Life of Alexander Hamilton, described his involvement in the
suit, and adds:

> Subscribers to the [Theatre] building fund included nearly every per-
> son of note in New York at the time. Some of them were: Stephen Van
> Rensselaer, James Watson, William Constable, Nicholas Cruger, William
> Bayard, Isaac Gouverneur, Elias Hicks, Gerret Kettletas, Robert S.
> Kemble, Nicholas Low, Dominick Lynch, Julian Ludlow, Stephen
> Tillinghast, Pascal N. Smith, George Scriba, Gulian Verplanck, Joshua
> Waddington, Nathaniel Prime, Rufus King, Charles Wilkes, DeWitt
> Clinton, Brockholst Livingston, Josiah Ogden Hoffman, John Watts,
> Nathaniel Fish, Thomas Lispensard, and about seventy others.[17]

Some of the other names not listed in Hamilton's biography, but found in Dunlap's diaries and other sources, include: Comfort Sands, William Henderson, Carlisle Pollock, Phillip Ten Eyck, Edward Livingston, Jacob Morton, William Dunlap, and John Hodgkinson.[18]

The list of names above is suggestive for what it reveals about the *type* of subscriber that the Park Theatre attracted. Of the thirty-four men listed above, nineteen were members of the New York Tontine and fifteen held stock in or served as officers of the Bank of New York. Many had overlapping connections via business concerns or membership in various social and civic organizations, and many served in local office. And while some had shown initial allegiance to the anti-Federalists, most espoused the Federalists' cause, especially their economic policies.

Between 1783 and 1794, these men consolidated their influence in the state, until they became, as one paper called them, an aristocratic "Junto."[19] Like their compatriots in Boston and Philadelphia, their ventures often blurred the boundaries between public and private good. But, also like their colleagues, they had to wait for the ratification of the Constitution to launch them into true power. The showdown over the Constitution in 1787 mobilized the Federalist merchant faction and transformed the face of New York's political and economic landscape. Examining the history of their rise to power may help to reveal the forces that shaped their theater.

In the years immediately following the war, New York fell into the hands of the anti-Federalists, who dominated the western region of the state. Yet even though the "anti's" occupied the largest geographical region of New York, they could not squelch the increasingly powerful merchant party rising to challenge the power of the Clintonians, and to campaign for ratification of the Constitution. New York's Federalists had two ostensible reasons for advocating ratification and union. The first was the state of the post-war economy. Prolonged occupation by the British and skirmishes across the state had interrupted every aspect of New York's trading networks, from lumber to fur to livestock. Moreover, once the war ended, Spain and France, which had created shipping alliances with the colonies for the duration of the struggle, revoked their agreements, leaving merchants with neither the goods to trade, nor the market to trade in.

Their second reason was also connected to their anxieties about the economic welfare of the state, but encompassed a broader concern about its post-war political development as well. In the political vacuum left by the withdrawal of British troops, corruption and vice seemed to consume the city. Black market trading and bribery ran rampant. Citizens lamented that "public faith and honor and public credit were replaced by local interest and avarice."[20]

E. Wilder Spaulding has suggested: "Politics in the state of New York immediately before and after 1783 is the story of the struggle of a propertied, intelligent minority to maintain itself against a less well-to-do, less sophisticated majority."[21] Yet to some extent, this argument overlooks the intelligent leadership of the anti-Federalist party, which also hoped to maintain its outlines against the pressure of post-war society. It might be more accurate to suggest that the political war waged in New York between 1783 and the time of its ratification of the Constitution in 1787 represented a battle between the commercial hub of the state and its agricultural interests. It also represented a movement away from the radical Whig politics that had dominated the state since 1777, towards one more focused on advancing the economic interests of a relatively small group of New Yorkers. This transition of power, and the state government's subsequent shift in focus, had a profound impact on the development of the state's political and economic spheres, which in turn manifested themselves in the city's post-war cultural endeavors.

Like their counterparts in Boston and Philadelphia, New York's postwar elite interested themselves in financial ventures that promised them both autonomy and influence. In the wake of the war and during New York's painful period of reconstruction, a group of wealthy men pooled their resources to form two corporations that ultimately secured their position as both the civic and cultural leaders of the city's post-Revolutionary society. Those two ventures were the Bank of New York and the Tontine Coffee House.

Initially founded in 1784, the Bank of New York met the same kind of popular resistance that the Bank of North America encountered in Philadelphia. Agrarian interests maintained that only a land bank could quell dangerous tendencies towards speculation, and up through the ratification of 1787, Clinton's faction supported the agrarian position. In fact, the Livingstons (Chancellor Robert Livingston in particular) had lent their support to an earlier land bank project capitalized at $750,000.[22] Thus, when the announcement for the founding of the Bank of New York appeared in the *New York Packet* on February 23, 1784, it met a skeptical response. As Robert Livingston observed, such a venture would turn "merchants from Commerce to Stockjobbing."[23] Livingston's fears seem to have been justified, as Cathy Matson has suggested: "It was conceived not as a commercial corporation, but to facilitate speculation by discounting merchants' notes and bills of exchange, and by paying specie for government certificates. It was run, then, for the profits of the stockholders."[24]

The original framework of the Bank of New York allowed its funds and stock to be consolidated in the hands of a relatively small number of wealthy men who could in turn use the funds for their own ends. Among the bank's first subscribers and directors were an intriguing combination of "old" and "new" men – a combination of former loyalists, like Joshua Waddington and William Seton, and former Sons of Liberty like Alexander McDougall, who became the first president of the organization.[25] The other directors were: Samuel Franklin, Robert Bowne, Comfort Sands, Alexander Hamilton, Thomas Randall, William Maxwell, Nicholas Low, Daniel McCormick, Isaac Roosevelt, John Vanderbilt, and Thomas B. Stoughton.[26]

But for all their wealth, in 1784 the founders of the Bank of New York lacked sufficient influence to secure a charter for their venture. The Clintonians, who continued to dominate the state government, supported two successive paper currency projects (secured by land, including the estates confiscated from former Tories).[27] Repeated efforts on the part of the bank's directors to secure a charter met with refusal. Part of the state's reluctance to grant a charter may have been the fault of the bank's directors and stockholders, who did little to dispel public perception of banks as sites for stockjobbers and speculators. In particular, shareholder William Duer caused a public scandal through his crafty manipulation of stocks and specie. Duer accumulated hundreds of thousands of dollars in debts (some estimates ranged as high as three million), buying and selling notes, plotting to undermine land bank systems, and even scheming to take over the Bank of the United States. He drew at least two of the bank's other shareholders into his plan: William Constable and Comfort Sands. Nor were they the only ones who felt the effect of his manipulation. Duer played fast and loose with the fate of New York's banking system for a period of almost eight years. When his affairs finally collapsed in 1791–1792, much of the New York market crashed with him: "Real estate prices fell, credit became tight, housing starts were ruined, and rancorous accusations and lamentations continued for months."[28] It is worth noting that New York entered its financial crisis just as Boston and Philadelphia were experiencing surges in their post-war economy (as the rapid rise of the Tontine, the Union Bank, and the Bank of North America suggests).

New Yorker Henrietta Maria Colden wrote to her friend John Laurance, describing both her own economic difficulties and the chaos in the city:

The most opulent men in this city are wholly ruined. Mr Macombe declared his bankruptcy today at the coffee house...Mr. Brockholst Livingston declares he is not worth 1,000 dollars on earth if his debts are paid...How many bankruptcies must follow in this city, Philadelphia, and Boston, it is impossible to say; the whole fabric of speculation has been so connected that a general failure is supposed to be inevitable issue among the dealers in stocks.

The speculators are daily boxing in the streets, cursing and abusing each other like pickpockets and trying every fraud to prey on each other's distress. Your imagination cannot picture a scene of such mingled distress and turpitude in this unhappy city.[29]

Yet Duer and his cohorts were not the only source of controversy that plagued the city's merchant elite. New York had become the *de facto* capital of the new nation, but in the process had also sunk into a "vortex of folly and dissipation," as the *Boston Gazette* noted disapprovingly.[30] The city had rapidly resumed its role as a center of commerce and offered a staggering array of British luxury goods. Its elite maintained their homes in a style that smacked of aristocratic luxury.[31] Could such a city provide a permanent home for the capital of the young republic? Ultimately, the answer was no. As part of a complex series of financial negotiations related to the repayment of the nation's war debt, the New York Federalists (chiefly Hamilton) agreed to relocate the nation's capital to Philadelphia. Angry broadsides portrayed Philadelphia moneyman Robert Morris running away with the capital on his back.[32] Thus the city was left without the gaiety of the fetes and ceremonies that had abounded during its years in the spotlight, and fell instead into the hands of an increasingly daring group of "moneyed men," ready to take advantage of the financial gains that the swap of capital city for debt relief had brought.[33]

These men, who included the founders of the Bank of New York, succumbed to a fit of what became known as "scriptomania" – buying and trading subscription shares (also known as "scrip") from the Bank of New York and the Bank of the United States. Plans for new banks and new stock companies arose seemingly overnight, and though Duer was the chief instigator behind many of the most outrageous ideas, he drew a considerable following of men who hoped to get rich quickly by exploiting the city's need for ready money. As the *New-York Journal* noted: "It may be said with propriety that a Tontine and Bank mania now rages in this city."[34]

When the speculation bubble collapsed in late 1791/early 1792, the city fell into an economic depression. Paradoxically, however, the very fears and apprehensions that had led the state government to reject the Bank of New York's pleas for a charter so often in the past now prompted them to pass one that would outline solid legal guidelines for the Bank's operation, and that would assign a portion of the Bank's stock to the state authorities. The dangers of unsupervised speculation were all too clear, and a scenario in which the government could maintain at least a small measure of control over the Bank's operations now seemed desirable. The Tontine Coffee House also emerged from the wreckage of the 1791 crash. Created in 1792 at the corner of Wall and Water Streets, the Tontine Coffee House venture drew together 153 merchants and lawyers, at least eighteen of whom would later become proprietors of the Park Theatre.[35]

Unlike the Boston Tontine Association, which functioned in cooperation with the Union Bank as much more of a private lending institution, the Tontine Coffee House venture became the site of both public stock trading and public conviviality. It drew representatives from all classes and political parties, and in the early 1790s became a site of political demonstration, and sometimes political violence.

In the wake of their success with both the Bank of New York charter and the Tontine Coffee House, it might seem logical that New York's merchant elite would take the same next step as their Boston and Philadelphia counterparts and establish a theater. But although they had secured a measure of financial stability, the political climate of the state remained unpropitious. Despite, or perhaps because of, the success of the Tontine and the Bank of New York in the early 1790s, the political situation in New York remained unsettled. Though the merchant elite had triumphed in the ratification debates of 1787, and though they had successfully navigated the Panic of 1791 and established their financial organizations, their artisan counterparts had not been so fortunate, and the growing gulf between the wealthy merchant capitalists and the mechanic population led to the rise of Democratic-Republican organizations, bent on re-shaping New York's unequal social system.[36] The political discontent of the mechanics and Democratic-Republicans manifested itself on the streets, in the papers, in the Assembly, and in the playhouse, and it is in this last site that the Democratic-Republicans were perhaps most effective at routing their wealthy Federalist enemies.[37]

Though the New York Federalists had enjoyed a brief period of ascendancy after the ratification of the Constitution, they had failed to uproot the Clintonian faction completely. After the Panic of 1791–1792, Clinton joined forces with the mechanics and the Livingston family (the majority of whom

Figure 6. Tontine Coffee House, New York City, 1797
Painting by Francis Guy

remained enemies of the merchant elite), as well as Madison and Jefferson, to re-assert the anti-Federalist (now Democratic-Republican) agenda in the state. The Clinton faction's contempt for the merchant elite manifested itself in a variety of ways, ranging from acts of government to public harassment. As Josiah Ogden Hoffman (future Park Theatre patron) complained in a letter to Stephen Van Rensselaer (future lieutenant-governor and Park Theatre patron): "The Clintonians . . . have resorted to falsehood and personal abuse" to discredit "the mercantile part of the city."[38]

The mechanics, who also opposed the "mercantile part of the city," campaigned for their own charter of incorporation in 1791, much as Boston's mechanics attempted in the later 1790s. They were rejected and their pique led them to support the Tammany Society, perhaps the most powerful (and certainly the most visible) of the city's new republican organizations. Though best known today for its associations with the corrupt "Tammany Hall" politics of the late nineteenth century, New York's Tammany Society originated as an apolitical group, created to "cherish the great principles of civil liberty . . . and give exercise to the divine emotions of charity."[39] Named for the Indian chief known as "Saint Tammany," the society claimed a truly "American" origin, since its name and ceremonies owed nothing to European saints and symbols. Members wore bucktails on their hats, the leaders of the organization were known as "sachems," and members frequently dressed in Indian costume when attending ceremonies for the Fourth of July or Washington's birthday.[40] It also incorporated former soldiers and Sons of Liberty who had fought during the Revolution and, unlike the Society of the Cincinnati, was open to enlisted men, rather than wealthy officers.[41]

Although it *began* as an apolitical organization, the Tammany Society quickly became a thorn in the side of New York's wealthy merchants. Denied access to institutions like the Bank of New York and the Tontine Coffee House, its members proposed creating their own separate financial organizations. As the *New-York Journal* noted on January 18, 1792: "A tontine was opened by the Tammany Society a few days ago for the purpose of erecting a great wig-wam, or Tammany Hall." The Society also proposed creating a new bank.[42] Unfortunately for the members, they lacked sufficient capital to realize their plans – a fact which exacerbated their sense of the inequality of New York's social and economic environment (as did the fact that the cornerstone was laid for the wealthy Tontine Coffee House only a few months after the Tammany tontine venture collapsed).[43] Denied access to potentially lucrative financial opportunities, confined to a meeting hall disparagingly described as the "Pig Pen,"[44] the members of the Tammany

Society vented their frustrations on those most visibly to blame for their misfortunes: the merchants of the Tontine Coffee House and the wealthy patrons of the John Street Theatre.

On June 11, 1793 Alexander Anderson recorded in his diary, "[L]ast night there was an affray at the Tontine Coffee House between Whig and Tory, or to modernize it, aristocrat and democrat."[45] Supporters of Tammany and the French Revolution climbed to the top of the Coffee House and hung a French Liberty Cap from its roof – a symbol which pro-Jacobin and pro-Democratic-Republican newspapers applauded and which they begged the Tontine proprietors to leave in place. On December 21, 1793, the *Columbian Gazetteer* complained that the Tontine Coffee House had been divided by party schisms, and that "only persons of the same party" would now associate cordially in the building.[46] On March 7, 1794, John Anderson (brother of Alexander) recorded in his diary that while passing the Tontine Coffee House on his way home, he had heard a noise, and upon going in, had found "a number of people dancing...the carmagnole" (to celebrate the re-taking of Toulon).[47] Anderson's entry suggests that the Coffee House had ceased to be merely a site of economic transaction, and had become one of political and social interchange as well. Only four days before John Anderson found dancers in the Tontine Coffee House celebrating a French victory, the Tammany crowd had launched its most effective and devastating attack against the merchant Federalists.

On March 3, 1794, the John Street Theatre premiered *Tammany; or The Indian Chief*. No surviving text of the play exists, but theater historians have commonly categorized the opera as an early example of the use of "native" subjects in American drama.[48] Yet the contemporary response to the play suggests that *Tammany* had strong political overtones and may have been instrumental in driving the merchant elite from the playhouse. The day of the play's debut, a letter signed from "A Republican" appeared in the New York *Daily Advertiser*, lauding the "first dramatic presentation that America can boast from the pen of a woman," and warning those who planned to "hiss" the production that to do so would "reveal aristocratical principles, which at this crisis I would conceive to be rather dangerous."[49] The author's words contain a clear warning that those unsympathetic to the French or Democratic-Republican cause would face violence in the theater if they displayed sentiments that showed them at odds with the rest of the audience. On March 6, the *Daily Advertiser* described the play as a "Symbol of republicanism."[50] On the following day, the *Daily Advertiser* made a point of noting that the audience had, in fact, been made up entirely of members of the same political party and social class: "The audience was of one complexion in point of sentiment. In the pit and in several of the boxes I saw a considerable proportion of respectable mechanics and other industrious members of society." The paper goes on to note that there were some of the "poorer classes of mechanics and clerks" who had been too vociferous in their approval of the material, and "would be much better employed on any other occasion than disturbing a theatre." But, most importantly of all, the writer added, "The Junto were kept aloof."[51]

If the turning point in the history of the Boston theater had come when its angry audience tore down Governor Hancock's coat of arms and trampled them, then the symbolic shift in New York's theater world appeared when its mechanic population took control of the theater boxes, the site traditionally reserved for the wealthiest, most "well-born" patrons, and when the Tammany Society crowd successfully drove the "junto" from the playhouse.

The Tammany Society continued to vaunt their success, touting the play's author, Ann Julia Hatton, as the "poetess of the Tammany Society," inviting her to give recitations on the victory at Toulon, and to celebrate the achievements of the Society in poetic presentations. Tammany's highly visible appropriation of a cultural form traditionally reserved for the elite, and their patronage of their "own" playwright, did much to boost the morale of the Society, and heighten their sense of their power in the city.[52]

By the summer of 1794, the Tammany crowd had made the theater inhospitable for its wealthier patrons. On July 8, 1794, a small advertisement appeared in the *Daily Advertiser* announcing subscriptions for a "New Theatre," and calling for interested parties to meet at the Tontine Coffee House. Rumors of a new theater appear to have circulated at least two months earlier, as Henry Wansey's diary suggests. On May 19, he recalls attending the theater with Mrs. Comfort Sands (wife of the future Park Theatre proprietor) and her daughter. He described it as "a very bad theatre," adding that "a new one is going to be built by subscription."[53]

Unfortunately, though a group of subscribers expressed interest in creating a new playhouse, no adequate location presented itself to the investors. An announcement ran in the *Daily Advertiser* on August 19, 1794: "No place that is to be purchased can be found as eligible as where the present theatre now stands."[54]

In 1794 New York remained in a state of transition in terms of its civic development. Areas traditionally occupied by the elite prior to the Revolution (below the Wall Street block) had fallen into greater and greater disrepair, and were increasingly the province of the mechanic and free black populations of the city.[55] The Tontine Coffee House had marked the starting point of more "upscale" development of estates, new and wealthy churches, and the future City Hall. As Elizabeth Blackmar describes it, "The Tontine Coffee House became the landmark by which all other commercial activity sited itself for the next twenty-five years."[56] Though in 1794, when the theater subscription opened, the site of the future Park playhouse was in an undeveloped area, surrounded by "the poorhouse and the Bridewell, and a scattering of squatters in their canvas tents,"[57] the city was in the midst of a class-based structural transformation that would soon make that neighborhood one of the wealthiest in the city. "Manhattan's merchant proprietors asserted a distinctive class interest in the organization of the city's geography which bore down on the town's 'productive' classes."[58] The wealth and power of the city's merchants manifested themselves in their design of new neighborhoods, parks, and houses of worship. Henry Wansey observed in his journal that after the ratification of the Constitution, New York's elite had thrown themselves into urban development, and that "all their public works and undertakings have commenced in a more important style."[59] Englishman William Strickland, on a tour of the United States, noted with surprise the luxurious appointments of the homes of New York's elite classes: "The houses are in the stile [sic] we are accustomed to – within doors the furniture is all English or made after English fashions."[60] He also commented on the differences between New York's older Presbyterian Church and the new Episcopalian one that had opened on Ann Street in 1794 (part of the newly developed area of the city).[61] He noted that the Presbyterian congregation was of the "middling class ... not aristocrats, but good plain republicans," while the Episcopalian congregation comprised a wealthier group, as evidenced by the large number of black servants they brought with them to hear the service.[62] As Young notes, by the middle of the 1790s, the city was growing at an impressive rate: "Some two hundred and fifty mansions assessed at over £2000, a handsome Broadway, fashionable restaurants and gardens, the new Tontine Coffee House – all betokened a wealth that prompted one visiting Englishman to think of New York as 'London in miniature'."[63]

Despite the improvements to the area immediately above Wall Street, however, few thought to situate a theater there. Thus, according to the *Daily Advertiser*, since the subscribers failed to locate a satisfactory site for their new playhouse (presumably one sufficiently removed from the Tammany crowd, yet sufficiently close to their own homes), they agreed to "re-finance" the John Street.[64] On August 29, 1794, the *American Minerva* printed plans for a re-modeling of the John Street playhouse, under the direction of managers Hallam and Hodgkinson.[65] They would invite eighty subscribers to contribute a total of £12,000 to renovate the theater by the following spring. In exchange, the subscribers would receive a season's worth of free tickets, and a committee would be appointed by the new subscribers to oversee the operations of the theater. Subscriptions and plans were available for review at the Tontine Coffee House. Hallam and Hodgkinson's scheme was a clever one to lure disgruntled elite patrons back into the playhouse. Only the wealthiest men in town could afford the £150 shares on offer, and those men would then become the *de facto* owners of the playhouse, thus routing the Tammany Hall crowd. *They* would oversee the running of the theater, including perhaps the selection of plays for the season. On the whole, and in the absence of any more promising location, it seemed like the best option. Yet only three months later the *New York Magazine* offered the following tidbit: "The present time may be considered as an era in the history of the New York stage . . . A new house is to be built by the present [new] managers, with the assistance and under the patronage of men of the first fortune and taste in the city."[66]

Where had these men of "fortune and taste" found the land to build their theater? While they themselves owned sizable lots in the area surrounding Wall Street, their property was devoted to their expensive new homes and to their business ventures.[67] Land in lower Manhattan was at a premium by the end of the eighteenth century.[68] High rents and property values meant that no one could afford to waste an inch. Within the heart of the city's growing elite neighborhood, who had land to spare?

The sponsors of the new Theatre had found a block of land owned by a loyalist widow named Ann White, a woman not mentioned in either Dunlap's or Odell's histories of the New York theater, but one whose personal wealth and influence provided the necessary "raw material" for the construction of a new, elite theater in post-Revolutionary New York. White, whose property adjoined that of some of the wealthiest men in the city, members of the Tontine and the Bank of New York, owned what appears in a map of the site drawn in 1798 as the entire city block at the corner of Chatham and Ann Streets, conveniently near the new homes and businesses of theater shareholders such as Isaac Gouverneur, Nicholas Low, Gulian Verplanck, and William Henderson.[69] White's property, listed in one New York Registry of Deeds as "Blocks 89 and 90," was near Trinity Church (listed as "Block 87") and diagonally across from the site of the future City Hall.[70] Thus the land that she could offer for the construction of a new theater would place the playhouse in a strategically important site for New York's wealthy elite, intent on establishing a haven away from the threats and humiliations of the John Street house.

White is an interesting, if obscure, figure in the creation of the Park Theatre, and tracing her connection to the theater has proved challenging. There were three Ann Whites listed in the city directories during the period between 1794 and 1798, and while the Deeds and Conveyance Records list her husband's name as Thomas, the two Mrs. Whites of greatest social prominence in the New York histories seem to have been married to men with other first names. However, the New York City census lists an Ann White as the head of a household of three women (plus servants) in the 1790s, and the *Journal of the Senate of the State of New York* records a "memorial of Ann White, widow and relict of Thomas White, late deceased... read and committed" in 1784.[71] Thomas White, a Philadelphia loyalist who first bought property in New York in 1762, left Philadelphia for New York permanently when his loyalist politics threatened to get him into trouble in the Quaker City.[72] Before the Revolution, his family had been members of Philadelphia's elite inner circle, as their membership in the exclusive City Dancing Assembly suggests.[73] Thomas White's death in 1784 left his wife heir to considerable property, and she retained control over the majority of her holdings for forty-four years, as the *Minutes of the Common Council*, which make constant reference to various parts of her property, attest. Her personal estate was known as "The Vineyards," and was apparently one of the most splendid private homes in the city.[74] In addition to her considerable property holdings, she was also invested in the Bank of New York, owning at one time as many as ten shares (considerably more than even some of the theater's future proprietors).[75]

Perhaps an investigation of White's history and identity seems strange, given that she appears to have played no major role in the theater's history beyond providing the land for the playhouse. But the nature of her transaction with the theater's founders contributes to the air of mystery and secrecy that surround the theater's origins. According to the Deeds and Conveyance Records in the New York City Register's Office, there were *no* transactions recorded on the theater site between 1793 and 1798, nor do the records show a *sale* of the property at any time immediately after the theater's opening. Yet by 1798, when a new map of Ann White's property was drawn, the theater appears on the map. Thus the nature of White's financial and business dealings with the theater's founders remains unclear. She appears to have leased and/or sold various pieces of her property throughout her residence in New York, and those transactions are recorded, yet the names of the theater's founders do not appear in any legal document securing the land for the playhouse, suggesting perhaps an informal arrangement between the two parties: one not intended to publicize the founders' names or agendas.

Her family's political leanings may also explain some of the lack of formal information surrounding the source of the land for the Park Theatre. As the wealthy widow of a prominent loyalist and one of the few female stockholders in the Bank of New York, Ann White had connections among the very men behind the Tontine Coffee House, the Bank of New York, and the new theater (men like Joshua Waddington, for example). These connections may have encouraged her to rent or loan the property to help establish a new elite playhouse for her circle of acquaintances. Though her motives in giving or renting the land to the theater's shareholders may never come to light, her contribution enabled the subscribers to the new theater to proceed with their plans for a playhouse that would reflect their interests and would shield them from the hostile attacks of their political opponents and social inferiors.

Unraveling the mystery of Ann White's property and identity illuminates one part of the story of the Park Theatre. But it leaves a larger question unresolved. Why, with the financial backing of the city's elite, with the land primed for development, did the Park Theatre, conceived in 1794, not open its doors for four more years? Why did its founders, alienated from the John Street house, allow such a lapse between the impulse to establish a new site and the fulfillment of their wishes? Why, when it *did* open, was it still unfinished? The proprietors of the Boston and Philadelphia theaters erected their playhouses in record time, building and opening them in less than a year, and furnishing them with the best supplies and decorations they could buy. But the Park Theatre languished and eventually opened in a still rudimentary state, and its long delays have yet to be fully explained.

On May 5, 1795, three of the Park Theatre's commissioners, William Henderson, Carlisle Pollock, and Jacob Morton, and two of the theater's managers, John Hodgkinson and Lewis Hallam, Jr., presided over the laying of the cornerstone of the Park Street playhouse.[76] By 1796, etchings of the theater were in circulation and drawings of the Manhattan "cityscape" showed the partly finished roof of the playhouse.[77] Letters from 1796 mention that the roof of the theater had been completed.[78] Such progress might suggest that the theater would soon be ready for its new audience. But in the intervening period between the completion of the roof and the theater's opening, several events put the entire project's existence into jeopardy. The combination of these incidents may suggest why the proprietors delayed so long in the opening of their playhouse, and why, when they did throw open its doors on January 29, 1798, they encountered almost immediate disaster.

Part of the reason for the delay in finishing the theater lay outside the founders' control. Yellow fever returned to the city in late 1795 and again in 1796, killing hundreds of citizens, and driving others from their homes into the countryside.[79] Much as the yellow fever epidemic of 1793 had postponed construction and opening of the Chestnut Street Theatre in Philadelphia, the yellow fever scares in New York necessarily slowed progress on all projects in the city.

Yet the yellow fever episodes fail to provide a complete explanation for both the ongoing delays in the building of the theater, and the proprietors' seeming lack of concern at the lengthy process. One explanation for their seeming inattention to the progress of their new playhouse may be that by 1796 they had become embroiled in a new series of financial speculations that completely overshadowed any venture as "minor" as a playhouse.

If scrip speculation had been the trend of early 1790s New York, land speculation became the craze by the middle of the decade. Merchants rushed to gobble up enormous tracts of undeveloped land, planning to recoup their investments by leasing or selling the property to the immigrants flooding into the country, or to those lower- to middle-class citizens seeking increased opportunities in undeveloped areas. While, in theory, these land speculations promised their investors huge rewards, they required an immense outlay of cash investment, an investment that might not reap results for years, thus leaving speculators at the mercy of their creditors and their speculation ventures in danger of collapse.[80]

Over one-third of the Park Theatre proprietors became embroiled in land speculation schemes between 1796 and 1798. Among the men who participated were: Comfort Sands, James Watson, William Constable, William Bayard, Nicholas Low, George Scriba, Josiah Ogden Hoffman, Nathaniel Prime, and John Watts. The ventures ranged from the Black River Tract development project, a 300,000-acre site in western New York state, to the Yazoo Land Company. The Black River Tract project involved Nicholas Low, William Henderson, and Josiah Ogden Hoffman. They borrowed over $100,000 from the Bank of New York to finance the deal. By June of 1798, they owed more than $137,000 which they could not afford to repay. Hoffman defaulted on the loan, which left Low and Henderson responsible for their shares. The fact that both men were shareholders in the Bank of New York had facilitated their borrowing money for speculation.[81]

However, their inability to repay it caused them personal embarrassment and the bank financial difficulties.

The Yazoo Land venture proved an even greater debacle financially and politically. Comfort Sands, Nathaniel Prime, and William Constable were three of the theater's proprietors who got drawn into one of the most notorious financial scandals of the early national period. Speculators in Georgia had arranged, by dint of bribery and graft, to secure large, undeveloped tracts of land in Georgia. With the promise of sizable financial returns they lured speculators from states like Massachusetts, Pennsylvania, and New York. Some investors thought that they owned the rights to as much as 4,000,000 acres of land. Nathaniel Prime invested $100,000 of his own money in the scheme. Prime, Sands, and Constable signed a bond for over $300,000. When the venture collapsed in 1798, New York felt the repercussions. Sands, Prime, and Constable had been among the city's wealthiest merchants, and they were now in debt for close to half-a-million dollars.[82] The theater's chief representatives, Comfort Sands and William Henderson, were among the hardest hit, and in light of their experiences with the all-consuming land deals and subsequent lawsuits of those two years, it is perhaps not surprising that the theater's construction should have languished or that its proprietors should have been reluctant to sink additional funds into what was rapidly becoming an incredibly expensive project that showed little hope of returning their investment.

Reviewing the records of the Bank of New York during the period from 1795 to 1798 suggests the enormous amounts of money changing hands during this period. Between March and November of 1795, William Henderson and Carlisle Pollock deposited $87,000 on behalf of the Park Theatre building project.[83] Yet by the following year (by the time the roof had been put on the building in 1796), the fund had declined to a *deficit* of $43.93.[84] In June of 1797, Henderson and Pollock borrowed an additional $20,028 to cover the expenses of finishing the theater (or at least getting it ready to open its doors). During that same period (June, 1797), Comfort Sands borrowed $50,000 on his own behalf and William Henderson borrowed $100,000. Many of the other Bank shareholders and New York Tontiners were also borrowing heavily during this period; for example, Edward Livingston borrowed $39,655.56 and James Watson borrowed $9,000. The Bank was also facing serious financial difficulties in the form of defaulted or worthless stock, owing $1,054,662.27 in 1797.[85]

On top of the land scandals and bank troubles, many of the city's merchant elite also faced increasing difficulties in their businesses due to the interference of the Barbary pirates, who had brought trade in the southern Atlantic and Mediterranean to a virtual standstill. The shipping records of the period suggest that many of the city's wealthiest men were stretched to breaking point financially, and that they could not afford any additional expenses.

Moreover, in the intervening period between the groundbreaking for the Park Street house and its opening, the New York theater world had not remained idle. Conditions in the John Street house degenerated to the point that in 1795 Hallam was forced to put locks on the *inside* of the theater's boxes in order to protect wealthier patrons.[86] As the *Daily Advertiser* noted, "They [the managers] wish the theatre to be esteemed a moral, rational, and instructive amusement, free from the least riot or disorder." Hallam promised that the locks would ensure that "no persons of notorious fame will be suffered to occupy any seat in a box where places are already taken."[87] The addition of locks on the inside of the box doors suggests at least two possibilities: that either Hallam still had elite patrons who occupied the box seats, but who were complaining because other, lower-class members of the audience (including prostitutes) were intruding on them; or that Hallam's elite audience had fled due to the rowdiness in the theater, and he hoped that a promise of protection and privacy would lure them back in. Hallam's measures appear to have been only marginally successful. Elihu Hubbard Smith's diary complains of a riot "in one of the boxes" on April 18, 1796.[88] Alcohol in the theater may have been partly to blame for the increasing unruliness of the John Street audience. Newspapers in 1796 began to feature notices from the management, warning patrons that: "Much confusion having arisen from the introduction of LIQUOR [*sic*] into the house during the performance, the managers respectfully hope gentlemen will not call for any until the conclusion of the first piece." Hallam added: "The Doorkeepers are in the strictest manner ordered to prevent its admission."[89]

Ricketts's Circus gave the John Street Theatre additional competition between 1795 and 1797, and on June 13, 1796 the *American Minerva* announced the opening of a new playhouse at Freemasons' Hall.[90] While chaos reigned at the John Street house, other theatrical venues opened around the city, ranging from the circus (also known as the Greenwich Street Theatre),[91] to concert halls, to learned pig shows. The city opened a pleasure garden called the "New Vauxhall," which offered firework displays for its patrons. The Tammany Society continued to stage its own entertainments, including readings and playlets by their poetess, Mrs. Hatton.[92] The city soon boasted more theatrical entertainments than its population could hope to attend, yet these were composed primarily of visiting companies who occupied the flexible space at the Greenwich Street Theatre, including Ricketts's Circus, Wignell and Reinagle's company, and John Sollee's troupe.[93] John Anderson's diary records the wide variety of performances that he attended between 1795 and 1798, including the circus, the John Street Theatre, the Tammany Society events held on the Fourth of July, the "vocal and instrumental" concerts conducted by John Hodgkinson for the Freemasons at the Brick Meeting House, a display of automatons, performances at Greenwich Theatre, etc.[94]

Odell's *Annals of the New York Stage* and Ireland's *Records of the New York Stage* chronicle both the wealth of offerings during this period, as well as the continual bickering among the theater managers and visiting companies that threatened to squash public interest in the theater altogether. Wignell and Sollee engaged in a bitter public dispute in 1797 about which company had the right to perform which play. On September 12, 1797, Wignell accused Hodgkinson and Sollee of deliberately undermining his company, by "circulating handbills on the day of representation, charging us with opposing them, when in fact they were opposing us."[95] The New York *Argus* publicly rebuked the theater managers for allowing their "personal animosities" to disrupt the theaters' business, and the editors of the paper adamantly refused to become tools in the managers' war against each other (noting that they had been flooded with letters from "both sides").[96] Hodgkinson and Hallam's disagreements over the management of John Street ended in a lawsuit, and resulted in Hallam's removal as co-manager of the projected Park Street house.

How could the new theater at Park Street hope to profit in such an environment? What emerges from the various controversies and quarrels of the mid-1790s is the impression that both audience and managers alike had lost their sense of theater as a medium to "polish the manners and habits of society," and to teach audiences how to become good republican citizens. Theatrical entertainments had become synonymous first with party, then with profit, and by the time the Park Theatre opened on January 29, 1798, the playhouse seemed as little likely to resolve the problem of the one, as to realize the potential of the other.

In the weeks immediately preceding the Park Theatre's opening, fresh disaster struck. William Dunlap had joined John Hodgkinson as manager of the theater in 1797 (theirs was a partnership doomed to end in failure, as Dunlap's diary suggests). Shortly before the opening of the playhouse,

William Henderson and Carlisle Pollock approached Dunlap to demand free tickets for the theater's proprietors, "about 130" in all.[97] Henderson suggested that the free tickets might help to mollify the proprietors, noting that he wanted to have them "in a good humor" for "when they [the theater committee] should call the proprietors together to state accounts and require a settlement." Henderson and Pollock's request suggests that they knew the building of the theater had not gone as planned and that the expenses would exceed the proprietors' expectations. Moreover, Henderson implied that the proprietors had been led to expect the free tickets, and that if Dunlap refused to give them, they might in turn refuse to contribute any additional funds to the theater. Dunlap protested vociferously: "I told Mr. H. that I could not conceive that the gentlemen who had subscribed to the building could be so selfish as to withdraw their patronage ... from the theater because not complimented with a free ticket." According to Dunlap, Henderson showed little sympathy: "He said that when people employed their money, they expected something in return for it."[98] Dunlap was finally forced to give in and grant the free tickets, a concession that cost him a substantial amount in ticket revenue.

Why the proprietors were so willing to bully Dunlap remains an interesting question, and suggests a degree of detachment on the part of the investors from the activities of the theater, as well as a lack of understanding concerning the theater's finances. Henderson's threat that "when people employed their money, they expected something in return for it" suggests that the theater's shareholders viewed it as just another investment that should yield a return, either in free tickets or cash. Elihu Hubbard Smith, a close friend of Dunlap's and an amateur author in his own right, noted in his diary that the theater had been built by "a group of businessmen," and his description seems particularly apt, given their treatment of Dunlap and their expectations for the playhouse.[99] Henderson and Pollock were in the unenviable position of having essentially bungled the theater's construction in allowing it to drag on for so long, and in allowing so much of the investors' money to go to waste in the process. They were more than willing to sacrifice Dunlap to the proprietors, shoving the responsibility for the theater's financial success onto his shoulders, and delivering free tickets to their financially taxed colleagues until such time as Dunlap would transform the theater into a money-making enterprise. Unfortunately for both the Henderson and Pollock team, as well as for Dunlap, their theater would be plunged into financial difficulties immediately after opening night.

As I suggested earlier, it is ironic that the most business-driven of the three major post-war playhouses, the Park Theatre, should have been given into the care of the most ardently idealistic dramatist of the early national period.[100] Dunlap's mission, to create a theater that would become a "school of wisdom," where "the lessons taught must be those of patriotism, virtue, morality, religion," seemed a virtually impossible one in light of the proprietors' expectations. Indeed, Dunlap eventually came to see a "democratic" theater as incompatible with private patronage:

> But the question arises – "How are the evils flowing from theatrical representations to be banished from them, and the good preserved and secured?" The answer is, to make the theatre an object of governmental patronage; take the mighty engine into the hands of the people as represented by their delegates and magistrates ... If a state or city government were to direct a theatre, nothing could be represented that was not conformable to patriotism, morality, and religion.[101]

He spoke feelingly, having been subjected to the whims of the proprietors in their demands for free tickets, and the edicts of the pro-Federalist audiences who condemned his politically controversial plays (like *André*), demanding instead simple and familiar comedies, or European translations.

Often called the "father of American drama," William Dunlap produced a staggering volume of plays during his career in the early national theater, writing, translating, and adapting over fifty during his lifetime. Dunlap wrote the first *History of the American Theatre* (1832), as well as a biography of a well-known British actor, George Frederick Cooke. Yet Dunlap was interested in more than the theater, and his career and diverse range of interests merit a brief discussion, since they suggest why he campaigned so actively to cultivate the arts in America. Initially trained as a painter, he created a number of his own works (based on religious or national themes), and was one of the directors of the American Academy of Fine Arts (1817), and a founder of the National Academy of Design (1826). In his *History of the Arts of Design* (1834), he claimed "industry, virtue, and talent" as the only true patrons of the arts, drawing a sharp contrast with the traditional European system of patronage, through which artists became the servants of wealthy aristocrats. Indeed, this nationalistic strain runs through much of Dunlap's writings on both art and the theater. Through his writings, he did much to legitimize theatrical entertainments in the new nation.[102]

Yet for all Dunlap's enthusiasm and talent, he stood little chance of making the beleaguered Park Theatre a financial success. At first the playhouse

attracted patrons, intrigued perhaps more by the prospect of seeing the
new building than by the artistic product inside. William Laight noted in
his diary that the theater opened to "an immense crowd of people."[103] The
Daily Advertiser observed: "The New Theatre was opened to the most overflowing house that was ever witnessed in this city." The author added that,
though unfinished, the house "exhibited a neatness and simplicity which
were highly agreeable."[104] The opening night performance of *All in a Bustle*
(an original play written by Mr. Milns) begged the indulgence of the audience members for the unfinished state of the playhouse. Set on the night of
the first performance, the playlet shows the theater in an uproar; the props
room is full of lumber scraps and is too cluttered to hold any props; a stray
dog has stolen the lead actress's wig; the coalman is demanding his money
or he will take back his coal; and the stagehands have crashed all of the
scenery together. As one character cries to the manager:

> All is in confusion above Sir, the Sky and Sea have run foul of each other –
> the garden scene has got entangled over the clouds! And trying to get
> them loose, the glass in the green-house has . . . scratched the clouds so
> they look like flying dumplings.[105]

Though the play may strike the reader or audience member as comical,
it expresses the very real financial and managerial difficulties that plagued
the house. Within the first week of the theater's opening, its receipts had
dropped by roughly three-fourths of the first night's income.[106] Nor did
business improve in the coming weeks. Panicked, the theater's proprietors
called a meeting on February 21, 1798 to review the debt of the theater.[107]
There was little that could be done to force the New York audiences to
patronize the house (especially the mechanic and lower-class audiences
who had received the emphatic message that they were unwelcome in the
elite theater), nor could the proprietors complain about lack of ticket sales,
given that they had appropriated the best and most expensive seats in the
house for their own use, *gratis*.

After its troubled opening in 1798, the Park Theatre continued to experience a series of financial reversals and personnel changes through the first
two decades of the nineteenth century. Yet during that time, it was able to
consolidate its coterie of supporters in a way that perhaps no other early
national theater managed to, and to define itself as *the* site for the city's new
elite to exert their financial and cultural control over American society. By
the 1820s, the most successful of the monied men of the post-Revolutionary
period had managed to establish new business and family dynasties that

helped to maintain their influence in the New York theater. While the Boston and Philadelphia elites lost their financial or political influence in the new century, the New York junto continued to expand its network of connections, and continued to identify the theater as an important site or symbol of their centrality.

Thus while it may seem strange to end a history of the Park Theatre on the eve of its opening, the explanation for much of what happened in the New York theater well into the nineteenth century lies in the *origins* of the venture. Dunlap's histories and diaries and Odell's and Ireland's chronicles map the fate of the theater after 1798.[108] My goal in this chapter has been to trace the complex social, political, and economic conditions surrounding its beginnings. I suggest that ultimately, the Park Theatre came into being as a retaliatory gesture against a certain section of New York society that had challenged the territory of its merchant elite. Unlike their compatriots in Boston and Philadelphia, the elite did not *need* a theater to cement their social status or to reinforce their cultural superiority. As members of a "commercial community," they valued the theater as an investment first, and as an extension of their own identities second. They never felt the need to link their theater with the rhetoric of republicanism, nor do they seem to have envisioned it as a site to "polish the manners and habits of society." They moved, as Wharton described it, in a kind of "super-terrestrial twilight" that made them largely impervious to the struggles taking place below. While the rantings of the mob might annoy or inconvenience them, they could not deter them from their pursuit of wealth and power.

If the post-war theaters of Boston and Philadelphia became a means for the self-appointed guardians of their country's virtue to imagine a democratic community in the playhouse, the post-war theater of New York became a means for the city's merchant elite to define who could and could not participate in their community. By the nineteenth century, their theaters would become means of defining those in the center and those on the periphery of political and economic power.

6

Into the hands of the people

In 1795, COLONEL J. S. TYLER OF BOSTON'S FEDERAL STREET
Theatre had implored playhouse audiences to "let austere politics one hour
flee, and join in free *Democracy of glee!*"[1] However, by the end of 1798, with
growing party divisions between Federalists and the rising Jeffersonians,
such an innocent union seemed almost impossible. Between 1798 and 1800,
as the Park Theatre was struggling to find its feet, both the Federal Street
and the Chestnut Street playhouses suffered as a result of the renewed
national political debate, as audience members waged open war against opposing political parties – wars which had evolved from the boisterous and
impetuous party conflicts of 1794 into the bitter and acrimonious wrangling
generated by the French XYZ Affair and the Alien and Sedition Acts.

Moreover, by 1800, many of the theaters' original supporters had lost
their financial clout, as private banks, land ventures, and speculation deals
collapsed. Philadelphian Robert Morris, once one of the richest men in
America, landed in debtors' prison, while Tontine stalwarts like William
Tudor were forced to sell their securities and call in old loans as land deals
soured. William Henderson, Carlisle Pollock, and Comfort Sands faced
lawsuits over unpaid debts, and the Park Theatre's $20,000 outstanding
construction loan from the Bank of New York remained unpaid.

As the political and financial might of the post-war elite waned, new
groups moved into power in the government and the playhouse. Thomas
Jefferson's election in 1800, sometimes called the Revolution of 1800, marked
a turning point in the development of America's early national drama. It
closed an era in which an elite minority had assumed responsibility for the
cultural progress of the nation, and it ushered in an age in which, as William
Dunlap prophesied, the time had come to "take the mighty engine into the

"Into the hands of the people": William Dunlap, cited in Witham, *Theatre in the Colonies*, p. 68.

hands of the people."² Dunlap stressed the importance of public rather than private patronage for the theater, noting that a privately sponsored theater was often susceptible to the whims – political or otherwise – of its owners, whereas a state-sponsored playhouse could preserve its moral, artistic, and political independence.³ His call for a state-sponsored theater seems a tacit indictment of the "approved guardians" of the nation's virtue who had failed to establish the "schools of Republican virtue" and "democracies of glee" that they had promised a decade before. Dunlap's accusation raises the question: how had these sites of "rational amusement" become political and social minefields that threatened to destroy the very unity that their founders were struggling to create?

Philadelphia's Federalist patriotism and the fight over "Hail Columbia"

In April of 1798, a new song debuted at the Chestnut Street Theatre – one which incited as much political controversy as the pro-French "Ca Ira" had four years earlier. "Hail Columbia," composed by Philadelphian Joseph Hopkinson for Chestnut Street player Gilbert Fox, created an overnight sensation among Federalists and an instant furor among Republicans. The song's refrain exhorted the audience:

> Firm – United – Let us be
> Rallying 'round our Liberty
> As a band of brothers join'd
> Peace and Safety shall we find.⁴

Its tone was stridently pro-Adams, at a time when he had never been more popular with his Federalist allies, or more unpopular with his Jeffersonian opponents. The recent scandal over the XYZ Affair, in which three French agents had demanded bribes from the United States (in an attempt to coerce the States into complying with French policies against Great Britain), had catapulted John Adams into a position of power unparalleled at any other point in his presidency.⁵ Jefferson's supporters had long resented Adams's suspicion of the French government and his inclination to forge an alliance with England. However, when the XYZ scandal proved Adams's fears justified, "the world in which John Adams had functioned since the start of his presidency was stupendously transformed."⁶

The surge in his popularity, and the discrediting of the French/Jacobin agenda, quickly manifested themselves in the playhouse. The House had commissioned the XYZ papers to be disclosed on April 2, 1798; by April 24, "Hail Columbia" had transformed the playhouse into a rallying site for pro-Adams, anti-French supporters. Whereas once the newspapers had decried any anti-French sentiment in the playhouse, they now joined with the theater audiences in mocking French politics, manners, and customs, and in affirming their loyalty to Adams's agenda.

William Cobbett, editor of the arch-Federalist paper *Porcupine's Gazette*, heralded "Hail Columbia" as a godsend for "the lovers of the drama," who "for much too long, have . . . been shocked and insulted with the sacrilegious hymns of atheism and murder."[7] In a letter to her sister, First Lady Abigail Adams described the scene at the Chestnut Street Theatre, during the playing of "Hail Columbia": "After the Principle Peice [*sic*] was performed, Mr. Fox came upon the stage to sing the song . . . The House was very full, and at every Chorus, the most unbounded applause ensued." Mrs. Adams noted that the song was repeated four times during the performance, "and the last time the whole [Gallery *canceled*] Audience broke forth in the Chorus, whilst the thunder from their Hands was incessant." She added that "at the close, they rose [and] gave 3 Huzzas, that you might have heard a mile."[8]

Bache's pro-Republican *Aurora* denounced the song as "Anglo-monarchical," accusing the theater audience of "Tory" sympathies and of acting "as mad as the priestesses of the Delphic god" in their enthusiasm for Adams and the tune.[9] Yet Bache, for all his vehemence, could not stem the wave of pro-Federalist sentiment engulfing the playhouse. In both Mrs. Adams's and Cobbett's accounts of the song's debut, it is worth noting that *each* mentions the fact that every section of the audience, pit, box, and gallery, applauded the pro-Federalist spirit of the song, and that little or no dissent seems to have been displayed within the walls of the theater. This event may suggest the extent to which the theater had succeeded in alienating and excluding those audience members not sympathetic to the political sympathies of its proprietors, or it may reflect the strongly pro-Adams mood of the city during this period. Abigail Adams wrote with satisfaction that the success of "Hail Columbia" in the playhouse signaled "death" to Bache's allies there.[10]

However, the suppression of controversy within the theater did not indicate an absence of dissent outside the playhouse, as Bache's anti-Adams diatribes and various popular demonstrations indicated. While the Federalists may have taken temporary control of the playhouse, both pro- and anti-French sentiments still ran hot in the popular press and in staged public celebrations.

For example, in May of 1798, a group of young Philadelphia Federalists marched to Adams's house to express their support for his agenda, then proceeded to attack Bache's print shop.[11] David Waldstreicher observes that this type of Federalist-backed demonstration was not uncommon during 1798, when "fistfights took place in the State House garden between wearers of different revolutionary emblems."[12]

The Federalists tried to parlay the anti-French sentiment created by the XYZ Affair into a renewed commitment to the Federalist agenda and to the Federalist interpretation of the Revolution. Fearing French threats to mobilize French immigrants (as well as Irish immigrants and American Jacobin sympathizers), the Federalists enacted a series of laws known as the Alien and Sedition Acts, which they hoped would allow them to squelch any potential opposition. The Alien Acts extended the period required for immigrants to achieve American citizenship, while the Sedition Acts permitted the prosecution and imprisonment of anyone found guilty of conspiracy to "write, print, utter, or publish" any material "designed to defame the government or make it the object of the people's hatred."[13] But although the Alien and Sedition Acts allowed the Federalists to silence political opposition for a brief time, they could not stave off the Republicans for long.

Throughout the spring and summer of 1798, the Federalists enjoyed a period of high popularity, and truly seemed the defenders of the Republic and the Revolution. American sentiments had been alienated from France by the French ambassadors' high-handed conduct. Yet by the autumn of 1798, the Federalists had begun to lose their political momentum. The French had rescinded some of their more flagrant demands for tribute, and seemed to be re-establishing themselves in public favor in America. The Alien and Sedition Acts, which had initially been justifiable (to some degree) as an anti-war measure, now appeared as blatant attempts at censorship of the popular press. Even staunch Federalist Alexander Hamilton feared the "tyrannical" turn that the Federalist party seemed to be taking.[14]

But what role did the Chestnut Street Theatre play in this conflict? How did a company that had begun the year with such a conspicuous affirmation of Federalist policies in the playing of "Hail Columbia" cope with the crisis in Federalist leadership? Unfortunately for the theater, the yellow fever returned to the city in the autumn of 1798, and the theater remained closed until February of 1799, when Wignell, Reinagle, and their diminished company[15] returned to Philadelphia to an utterly bankrupt playhouse.

The year 1799 did not begin well for Philadelphia's theater-going public. Lailson's Circus had collapsed in December of 1798, and at the start of the 1799 season, Wignell made the mistake of attacking the *Philadelphia Gazette*, which had criticized his company. According to Pollock, Wignell announced that he would offer a play entitled *Retaliation, or A peg at the Printers*. The *Philadelphia Gazette* ran the following caution to him:

> Good Tommy Wignell, don't attack the printers!
> As well might *drunkards* be revil'd by *vinters*!
> Believe me friend, in spite of all your witticisms,
> They'll bear too hard upon you by your criticisms.
> 'Tis they can raise a player and a poet –
> You're wrong, believe me, and they'll let you know it.[16]

Wignell was forced to back down, and the company mounted a season that seemed lackluster compared to the ever more elaborate pantomimes offered at Ricketts's Circus.[17] By the spring of 1799, the theater's debts had grown too large for Wignell and Reinagle to manage. On May 2, 1799, the Chestnut Street Theatre was sold by the sheriff of Philadelphia to a new group of forty shareholders, which included only seventeen of the original ninety-one members of the 1788 Dramatic Association and 1792 stockholders. The other twenty-three were new investors, who included both Republican and Federalist supporters. For the most part, however, these new investors lacked the traditional family and business connections that had bound Philadelphia's pre- and post-war elite.[18]

What had happened to the theater's original allies? A number of them had suffered financial setbacks, and could no longer afford to invest in the theater. By 1798, the popular land companies created during the early 1790s had collapsed and land claimed by the North American Land Company, the Pennsylvania Population Company, and the Asylum Company was confiscated in sheriffs' sales. As I noted earlier, among the original members of the Dramatic Association and 1792 theater stockholders, twenty-nine (almost one-third) had also held shares in the land companies. Unfortunately for them, the principal managers of the companies, John Nicholson and Robert Morris, were unable to pay their debts to the stockholders (debts which ran into the hundreds of thousands of dollars).

Robert Morris's humiliation, both financial and personal, was acute: "The Bank of Pennsylvania, the Bank of North America, and the Bank of the United States, all institutions which he had helped to found, brought suit against him."[19] His beautiful new marble house, begun in 1795, remained unfinished as his financial straits worsened, and it came to be known as "Morris's Folly."[20] Eventually, Morris retired to his country house on the outskirts of Philadelphia to hide from his creditors.[21] But on February 15, 1798, Robert Morris, once one of the wealthiest men in America, was taken to debtors' prison. There he met and befriended a young man named William B. Wood, who was destined to become one of the most prominent managers of the Chestnut Street Theatre. In his *Personal Recollections of the Stage*, Wood described watching Morris walk in the prison yard, noting that he would circle the square, "dropping from his hand, at a given spot, a pebble on each round, until a certain number which he had in his hand was exhausted." Wood noted that Morris often greeted and spoke to him with "great kindness" and "friendly notice."[22] His courtesy to Wood aside, it was a sad ending for the man once called the "Financier of the Revolution."

E. Digby Baltzell has referred to Morris and some of his contemporaries somewhat disparagingly as "cut flowers," meaning that while they may have achieved a certain distinction in their lifetimes, they failed to found significant family dynasties, or to perpetuate their connections or traditions beyond their own generation.[23] While Baltzell's observation has the advantage of hindsight, in many ways it summarizes the phenomenon that seems to have overtaken a section of the Philadelphia and Boston elite at the end of the eighteenth century. Although the Tontiners and the Philadelphia elite had built their post-war economic and social power on a network of interlacing family and business connections, *maintaining* those ties in the face of political and financial strife proved challenging.[24]

Disaster in Boston

The Tontiners fared little better than their neighbors to the south in the political and economic upheaval of the last years of the eighteenth century. Between 1798 and 1800, they saw their theater transformed from the "trophied monument of a well-informed people"[25] to a virtually abandoned shell, whose glory seemed past.

By 1798, political schisms threatened the placid surface of Federalist Boston. Perez Morton, Charles Jarvis, and William Tudor – all original Tontiners and theater supporters – had become involved with the Republican party. Their associates, including Stephen Higginson, had become identified with the "Essex Junto," a group of extreme Federalists.[26] And even the Boston Federalists disagreed among themselves about how to handle American relations with France in the wake of the XYZ Affair. As Paul

Goodman observes, "Urban interests had never been monolithic; fissures had always existed . . . The prospect of war with France, however, heightened differences and polarized groups."[27] The Tontiners still struggled to maintain the financial alliances which had launched them, but "the old coalition . . . who had . . . erected the Union Bank . . . was foundering because local aristocrats combined with Tory factors to overpower the middling interests of young businessmen . . . and honest mechanics."[28] As of January 1798, bills submitted to the Union Bank were being protested for non-payment.[29] The rising post-war elite that the Tontiners had created was fracturing under pressure from outside, wealthier trade interests, some of whom opposed the political leanings of its founders.

The Tontiners were undergoing a similar challenge to their cultural authority in Boston. The competition from the Haymarket Theatre had undermined their monopoly on Boston's aesthetic development, replacing the theater's original mission to refine the manners and habits of the people with a shallow financial rivalry. The *Massachusetts Mercury* criticized the Boston theater, claiming that it was designed solely as a money-making venture, and had become too corrupted to be exposed to the public.[30] But a worse blow was yet to come. As I noted in chapter 4, the 1798 season began with the disastrous fire that gutted the Federal Street house, destroying the scenery, properties, costumes, and interior decorations, as well as large portions of the roof. The fire started when a porter left a damp basket of wood under a stove to dry.[31] According to Clapp, the burning theater was a memorable sight for many Bostonians: "citizens from Charlestown, Roxbury, Dorchester, and Cambridge were attracted to the spot by the great light."[32] Thomas Dwight wrote to his wife:

> This moment I returned from one of the most August sights that I have ever seen – the burning of the old Theatre. It took fire, or at least fire broke out about 4 o'clock this afternoon – the Senate and House of Reps adjourned immediately – We all ran – the column of smoke was a monstrous black cloud which from the State House view of it covered almost all of the town on the Northerly side of it . . . The players had been rehearsing for the evening's performance – the Wardrobe, which was a valuable one, is entirely consumed – the beautiful chandeliers and other ornaments of the Assembly room are all lost.[33]

He added that Mr. Gilman (one of the proprietors) had told him that replacing the wardrobe, theater machinery, furnishings, and building would cost at least $72,000. Dwight predicted: "The plays at Boston are considered as over for this season, if not forever."[34] Yet the Federal Street Trustees opted to rebuild the theater, planning it on an even grander scale than the first design.[35]

John Hodgkinson, who was struggling at the Haymarket Theatre, urged the Federal Street proprietors to buy the Haymarket space, promising that if they did so, "party will be destroy'd and...public amusements will no longer interfere with the private peace of [Boston's] inhabitants."[36] As I noted in chapter 4, the proprietors rejected suggestions to purchase the struggling Haymarket Theatre, preferring to maintain their own space, rather than ally themselves with the Haymarket's founders.[37] Even though individual members of the Tontine were experiencing financial difficulties, the proprietors proceeded with their plans to resurrect the theater, as the *Federal Gazette and Daily Advertiser* reported, "with all expedition, in an elegant and more commodious manner than it was before."[38]

The pause in the Federal Street Theatre's activities gave a temporary boost to the Haymarket house.[39] Like the Philadelphia audiences, Boston theater-goers had experienced a surge in pro-Federalist patriotism after the XYZ Affair. The song "The Launch," written to commemorate the launching of the Merrimack, hailed the "Sons of Columbia," urging them to "Let true Federal mirth be seen in each face/No *Jacobin* or *Traitor* [*sic*] your company disgrace."[40] On July 23, 1798, the *Boston Gazette* displayed the following announcement for the Haymarket Theatre: "At the end of the play, Mr. Hodgkinson will sing 'Adams and Liberty,' after which all Federal Americans are invited to a patriotic effusion in two parts, called 'The Federal Oath; Death or Liberty!'."[41] However, even these novelties could not attract sufficient audiences to support the Haymarket's 2,000-seat house, three nights per week. A summertime attack of yellow fever also kept audiences out of the playhouse. Faced with the prospect of dwindling box office receipts, Hodgkinson was finally forced to dismiss his company.[42]

The Federal Street Theatre re-opened in October of 1798, with Hodgkinson as manager, and with improved accommodations for the audience. But by that point party animosity had escalated in the crisis over the Alien and Sedition Acts, and was making itself felt in the theater. Audience members and reviewers were reading political messages into the most seemingly innocuous works, including Shakespeare. For example, the pro-Federalist *Massachusetts Mercury* recommended the Federal Street's production of Shakespeare's *King John* because "[m]any of its political sentiments with respect to the French Nation are not inapplicable to the Gallic character at the present day; some references have a peculiar point, and will undoubtedly be noted by the popular praise."[43] A letter to the *Constitutional Telegraph* on November 20, 1799 attacked the theater for its presentation of the farce *The Constellation, or America Triumphant*. The author wrote angrily that "the father of that farce must be some kind of rank Jacobin who has taken that method to ridicule the gallant and unparalleled deed of our American heroes." He further abused the theater for having "turned into a farce the most brilliant exploit that has ever graced the naval records of any nation."[44]

On December 11, 1798, a despairing Hodgkinson wrote to the Federal Street proprietors, "I think I have tried every effort possible to promote success in the Federal Street Theatre, but the opposition by a party to its politics" had conspired with various financial crises to turn the audience from the theater. It is important to note that during this period, the theater's proprietors still comprised a mixture of Federalists and Republicans, who seemed able to coexist fairly peacefully (at least as proprietors of the theater). The *audiences* were the ones who had become adept at reading political motivation into the playhouse offerings, and were taking issue with them, as in the case of *King John*. Discouraged by his inability to attract or to please the Boston audiences, Hodgkinson left Boston in April of 1799, at the close of the season, and never returned.[45]

New York's faltering steps

In addition to its financial woes, the Park Theatre could hardly have chosen a less propitious political moment to open its doors than the winter of 1798. Just as they had in Boston and Philadelphia, the Alien and Sedition Acts made it dangerous for playwrights and newspaper editors to express any political opinion for fear of how it might be interpreted.[46] From 1795 to 1798, political tensions between the Federalists and Democratic-Republicans had escalated to such a point that any dramatic material or public event or incident seemed open to interpretation and debate from both pro- and anti-Jacobin groups. New York's always uneasy class relations had erupted into outright warfare during this three-year period, as housing shortages and financial difficulties widened the gulf between those who aped the "aristocratical" principles of the Federalists and those who adhered to the "republican simplicity" of the Democratic-Republicans. One of the most bitter episodes of the period, the "Affair of the Ferrymen" (November, 1795), had nothing to do with the city's theatrical entertainments, but had far-reaching implications for its cultural and social development, and created a seemingly unbridgeable gap between the Federalist alliance and their Republican opponents. The "Affair of the Ferrymen" began with an altercation between Federalist alderman and Tontiner Gabriel Furman and the Manhattan–Brooklyn ferrymen, who refused to let the ferry leave early on a particular day when Furman was in a hurry to return to the city. Their disagreement escalated into a brawl, and Furman brought the ferrymen before the court for their "impudence" in refusing to accommodate him. They were sent to jail without a formal trial. Their plight drew the attention of the city's Republican faction, who viewed the incident as a clear demonstration of the Federalists' willingness to trample on the rights of the "lower classes." As Young notes, the Republicans seized on the ferrymen issue, linking it with other examples of Federalist "oppression." One letter to the *New York Journal* described the Federalist faction as "[p]eople in office ... guided by a British influence and aping the customs and manners of petty tyrants who exist under monarchy ... punishing citizens for daring to speak to them."[47] Another letter offered the sarcastic suggestion that the city's Federalist elite "hang gold chains around their necks inscribed 'I am born to govern, therefore approach me with reverence'."[48] The case created local Republican martyrs and stigmatized Federalist elite culture. It also prompted many of the "undecided" smaller merchants and yeomen to desert the Federalist cause.[49]

Additionally, by the late 1790s, the Democratic-Republican Society of New York had been largely absorbed into the Tammany Society. Tammany members had extended their civic activities throughout the mid-1790s, and by 1798 were in active competition with the Federalists who had tried to bar them from both economic and cultural opportunity.[50] The Tammany Society had also begun to practice political coercion to "persuade" mechanics to adopt the Democratic-Republican point of view.[51]

Given the volatile political climate of the period, it seems hardly surprising that a theater would have had to tread carefully to please its patrons, citizens already alert for the least whiff of political smoke in the playhouse. Yet despite the political ferment, Dunlap waded into the fray with one of the most politically controversial plays the young nation had seen: *André*. Many historians of the American theater are already familiar with the uproar occasioned by Dunlap's re-telling of the execution of the dashing British officer, Major John André, who was found guilty of espionage after a trial that Jeffrey H. Richards describes as "a blot on Washington's record."[52] Dunlap presented André in a sympathetic, even heroic, light and, more importantly, showed the American character, Bland, wavering in his loyalty to the American cause. The most controversial moment of the play came when Bland tore off his American cockade and threw it to the ground, renouncing his allegiance to "The General" (George Washington). In a time when the wearing of cockades or other Revolutionary symbols could generate public brawls, Dunlap's choice was a puzzling one.[53] Odell suggests that a string of box office failures (sinking as low as $99 per night in receipts) may have prompted Dunlap to gamble on material likely to draw larger audiences and greater attention to the theater. Unfortunately for him, he got his wish.[54]

Though its March 30, 1798 performance brought $817 in ticket sales, the play generated so much debate on its opening night (with members of the audience hissing at Bland) that Dunlap re-wrote the play to have the cockade restored to Bland.[55] Despite his efforts to make the play more palatable to the audience, "*André* played three nights in New York, with attendance falling off the last two."[56] Lucy Rinehart has suggested that Dunlap's own political ambivalence (he was the son of a loyalist, though himself an ardent supporter of the Revolution) may have colored his dramatic works.[57] It might also be argued, however, that Dunlap's *André* offers a similar plea to the prologue of the Federal Street Theatre in Boston that implored audiences to "let austere politics one hour flee, and join in free *Democracy of glee*." Bland learns in the play that the good of the many must outweigh the good of the one. Party divisions in the theater or in American society must be put aside so that the community as a whole can triumph, as McDonald reminds Bland: "How self intrudes, delusive on man's thoughts! He sav'd thy life, yet strove to damn thy country." McDonald tells Bland that his loyalty to his nation must outweigh his own personal desires.[58] However, as Rinehart notes, Dunlap does not suggest that loyalty to one's country should not be unquestioning or uncritical. Indeed, as she points out, Dunlap abhorred the blind worship of the " 'monuments of our ancestors' " that produced a " 'deadly stagnation' " in politics and society.[59] Unfortunately for Dunlap, he was operating a theater at a time when to be critical of the government was a dangerous undertaking, and certainly an unprofitable one in a theater dominated by the Federalist elite.

Dunlap's friend Elihu Hubbard Smith was both a sympathetic witness to his struggles, and himself an amateur dramatist who contributed prologues and plays to the theater. Though Smith played a relatively minor role in the history of the New York theater,[60] nevertheless, his contributions merit some attention as the efforts of a "native genius" to claim dramatic territory for American artists. Smith's first play, *Edwin and Angelina; or The*

Banditti had debuted at the John Street Theatre on December 19, 1796, and was, as Fredrika J. Teute suggests, a "dismal failure."[61] Smith's efforts to create a "textual hybrid of an English poem and a German play," while they may have expressed a synthesis of Enlightenment thought and Romanticism, failed to strike a uniquely "American" chord with his audience. Dunlap noted that the characters of Edwin and Angelina were "all too familiar to all readers."[62] Smith's challenge in creating his one failed opera mirrored those of other authors of the early national period: how to create something recognizably American that would still live up to European standards. Smith's thoughts on the role of the native playwright in the early national theater echo the sentiments of other American authors like John Murdock, William Charles White, Judith Sargent Murray, and Susanna Rowson: "Even the feeblest efforts of the American muse ought not to be absolutely discouraged. This might repress the genius and exertions of some who otherwise would acquire deserved eminence . . . Everything is to be hoped from [public] competition."[63] For Smith, the key to inspiring the "American muse" lay in accepting and developing all of its manifestations, trusting to a democratic system of open competition to foster the best and brightest specimens.[64] Sadly, in theaters run by businessmen, where profit and not "high art" was the motive, the "American muse" had few opportunities to try its wings.

Though Dunlap did his best with the Park Theatre, circumstances worked against him at every turn. The return of the yellow fever in the fall of 1798 meant a truncated theater season that could not begin until December (three months after its planned opening). Still smarting from his essay into controversial material with *André*, Dunlap had turned to translating the popular German dramatist, Kotzebue. While productions of Kotzebue's work attracted audiences, nightly receipts still averaged around $450. Such meager takings would never permit the theater to repay its debt to the Bank of New York, or to realize any profits for its investors.

Sic transit – the end of an era for the early national theaters

I have suggested that the Boston, New York, and Philadelphia theaters ended the century on notes of disharmony and failure, and that the communities their proprietors had hoped to foster (whether benevolent or self-serving) were also in disarray.

In January of 1799, Thomas Dwight had complained to his wife that the actors at the Federal Street Theatre were playing to almost empty houses,

On the 15 April 1800 —

		dollars . cents
Balance of Profit & Loss		84084 . 38
Discount received		42048 . 98
Five discount days, previous to 1 May, will amount to		6000 . —
Interest due on Walter Livingston's debt, about		15000 . —
do	on loan to the Corporation	2700 . —
do	on notes taken for the Havanna bills	575 . —
do	on loan made for building Tontine Tavern	6500 . —
do	on loan made for the Theatre	2800 . —
do	on loans made to the State of New York	10559 . 42
do	on loan to the Library	50 . —
do	on C Sands's debt	1600 . —
do	on C McGregor's debt, by assignment from Mr. Bronson	1633 . 33
Profit made on the House & Lot, Hanover Square, amount with the interest to		12000 . —

Dollars — 185551 . 11

Contingent Expences for the last six months
will amount to, about — 11,000 . —

Loss by deficiency of clerks, by Barber & Griffin's
note discounted, & by overdrawings about — 4000 . —

15000 . —

Dollars — 170551 . 11

Deduct, Dividend suppose of Nine ₱ Cent — 85500 . —

Surplus, on 1 May, 1800 — D₅. 85251 . 11

Chas. Wilkes Cashier
15 April 1800.

Figure 7. Profit and Loss Statement, the Bank of New York, April 15, 1800

and that the Haymarket Theatre had been attached for debt.[65] In May, 1799, Wignell and Reinagle had been forced to sell the Chestnut Street house to new subscribers. The 1798–1799 season had nearly bankrupted New York's Park Street house. The theater "boom" of the early national period seemed to be drawing to a close. But the last and greatest theatrical event of the century was yet to come, and it drew together (however briefly) Americans of every party and class. The event was the death of George Washington.

When word reached Philadelphia of Washington's death, the city was plunged into mourning and into ceremonies of remembrance. This included a pageant at the Chestnut Street Theatre which was, as Clapp observed, "literally full to overflowing."[66] The Chestnut Street house featured *The Roman Father* and *A Monody on the Death of Washington*. The theater was draped in mourning, and the stage tableaux displayed a tomb, surrounded by Grecian pillars, a portrait of Washington, and an American Eagle, shedding tears of blood.[67] The Federal Street Theatre was similarly decked in symbols of mourning, and also offered *A Monody on the Death of General Washington*, which lamented, "A nation's tears o'er worth *divine* are shed/For god-like, matchless WASHINGTON is dead."[68] Boston's Republican paper, the *Constitutional Telegraph*, noted with approval that the manager of the theater had "testified his respect for the feelings of the community" at Washington's funeral procession "by placing the representation of a Monument on the top of that Edifice [the theater], in front with suitable inscriptions."[69]

After New York received news of Washington's death the theater closed for ten days, re-opening on December 30, with the theater hung in black. As a tribute to Washington, the theater presented *Gustavus Vasa* on January 8. For the event the chandeliers and boxes were hung with mourning.[70] The house remained shrouded in black until Washington's birthday on February 22.

Through their displays and performances, the theaters offered audiences the chance to re-unite and re-affirm their loyalty to what Washington had represented: the strength and ideals of the Revolution. But in many ways it was a fleeting unity, since even as these ceremonies were taking place, funeral marchers in Philadelphia chose to divide themselves by party loyalty. It seemed, at least for the time being, that the theater proprietors' dream of a "democracy of glee" had died with Washington. And with the election of Jefferson in 1800, and the triumph of the Republican agenda, the Boston, New York, and Philadelphia theaters entered a new and challenging era.

A sentimental democracy: the transformation of American theater under Jefferson

How would America's fledgling theater evolve under the leadership of the Jeffersonian Republicans and under the influence of Jeffersonian democracy? The theater of the post-war period, 1783 to 1800, had been directed towards the education of the audience. As the "approved guardians of their country,"[71] the theaters' founders felt keenly their mission to mold and elevate the minds and feelings of their audience members. Plays ranging from *Bunker-Hill* to *Gustavus Vasa* celebrated the glory of the rising Republic in a way that encouraged audience members to reflect on their civic duty and their role in the new nation. To a large extent, these post-war theaters were a product of the Enlightenment ideals that had sustained the Revolution; and they were created (ideally) as a forum for disseminating those ideals to a broader audience.

Part of what was at stake after Jefferson's election – both in the statehouse and the playhouse – was possession of what Ronald Formisano has termed the "Revolutionary Center."[72] The Tontiners and the Philadelphia elite had made their bid for this center in the years immediately following the Revolution. The New York elite had launched their cultural ventures somewhat later, and had thus, in many ways, failed to put their stamp of cultural authority on the city. Now, in the aftermath of the Republican victory, the Revolutionary Center was re-defined and its ownership re-negotiated. Unlike the elites' rigid republican hierarchies, the Jeffersonian theater would reflect a more sentimental view of what a democratic society should be. Jeffersonian democracy, according to Lance Banning, "taught that power was a monster and governing was wrong."[73] Thus any attempt to "dictate" to Americans on how to fulfill their duties as citizens worked against the fundamental principles of democracy. The overwhelming popularity of German playwright August von Kotzebue, as well as a proliferation of new American plays, mirrors this changing outlook.[74] Kotzebue's work blended republican simplicity (touching scenes of domestic harmony) with emotion and pathos. As David Grimsted has observed, the chief attraction of Kotzebue's work to a Republican audience was its message that "[l]earning, position, social sanctions of any kind were unnecessary, even obstructive to the man who would do right."[75] Even though critics eventually turned against the cloying sentimentality of Kotzebue's work, his plays epitomized the simple and untutored virtue that would be the hallmark of Jeffersonian democracy.[76]

The enthusiasm for Jeffersonian democracy also found expression in a spate of pro-America plays, which celebrated America's native genius, military victories, and local heroes. Though Americans were still importing the majority of their dramatic fare from Europe,[77] there was a sharp rise in the number of original American productions during the first decade of the nineteenth century. Between 1800 and 1810, ninety-four new "American" plays were printed in the United States (compared to the fifty-two published in the seventeen years after the war).[78] In discussing the playwrights of the Jeffersonian era, Gary Richardson suggests that they were "consumed with describing, exploring, analyzing, and ultimately defining what it meant to be 'American'."[79] Political satires, such as *Jefferson and liberty; or, a Celebration of the fourth of March*, and *The Essex junto, or, Quixotic guardian*, embrace the tenets of Jeffersonian democracy, and offer a sharp critique of the repressive Adams administration. For example, in *The Essex junto*, the evil Duke of Braintree (a not-too-subtle figure for John Adams, a resident of Braintree) tries to kill the character "Patriot," who has left his daughter, Virginia, in the Duke's care. The Duke numbers among his allies the Federalist character Cockade (an allusion to the emblems worn by the Federalist party) and Junto. Virginia, meanwhile, is in love with a worthy young man named Monticello, but is kept from him by the Duke's treachery. Monticello, and his companions Rusticus and Agricola, contrive to rescue Virginia and her father, Patriot, from the Duke's clutches, and all ends happily as the evil Federalists are banished and the loyal Republicans rejoice.[80] *Jefferson and liberty* also features the evil Duke of Braintree. In this drama, the Duke plots against the American people, whom he refers to as "the swinish multitude." He is abetted by Alexander Hamilton and Peter Porcupine (arch-Federalist editor William Cobbett). However, once again the nefarious Duke is defeated; this time it is by the will of the people who elect Jefferson as president. The play ends with Jefferson's inauguration and features his complete inaugural address in the text.[81]

Other popular authors (including William Dunlap) eschewed political satire, and emphasized "the popularly accepted linkages between orderly families and stable political states," re-inventing the Revolution as a "family drama in which the founding fathers had rescued the general citizenry from potential aristocratic oppression."[82] Even Boston's William Charles White re-invented himself as a playwright during the early national period.

In 1810, White (now an ardent Republican and respectable lawyer) wrote *The Clergyman's Daughter*, a touching and melodramatic story of a simple "republican" family, betrayed by a ruthless aristocrat, bent on corrupting both the son and daughter of the house for the mere sport of it. Unlike the ponderous and self-conscious verse of his earlier play, *Orlando*, the characters in *The Clergyman's Daughter* speak with genuine feeling. Lamenting the ruin of his sister by the evil Lord Sidnal, the young Theodore proclaims, "Once sir . . . I was happy. Our little frugal home was the abode of unenvied felicity. Contentment crowned our table, gladness brightened our fireside, and peace shed its balm on our pillow." Theodore contrasts this image of republican contentment with Sidnal's behavior: "His very crimes were seductive, for they were concealed by the graces which embellished them."[83] The play, which enjoyed enormous success in Boston, may be read as a caution against corrupting European and party influences. Indeed, the sentiments in the play, and the image it presents of republicans' artless simplicity, struck the right note with nineteenth-century American audiences, attuned to what Jay Fliegelman has termed a "natural language" of sentiment and emotion.[84]

These sentiments also echoed the tone of White's own political writings, including his 1813 essay, *Avowals of a Republican*, in which White defended his loyalty to the Republican cause, and cautioned his fellow party members against believing the "applause of ignorant men," who would lead the Republican party into the excesses of Jacobinism, or leave the country prey to the machinations of the monarchists.[85] Though his writings draw upon the teachings and style of authors from Shakespeare to Rochefoucauld, White infused them with a sentiment and patriotism which appear entirely original and entirely *American*.

In many ways, White mirrors the transition in an American literary and cultural aesthetic during the early national period. White began his stage career as the "Garrick of America," an awkward, homespun substitute for the "real" thing, but as the national imagination evolved, White's true native genius emerged. As Robert Treat Paine urged audiences in the prologue to White's last play, "Be just Columbians, and assert your name/Avow your genius and protect your fame."[86] With the shifting tone in American drama during the early nineteenth century, audiences in the Jeffersonian theater could reflect on their Revolutionary heritage, pay homage to the men who had secured their liberty, express their disdain for aristocratic behavior, and ultimately relegate them to an apolitical zone in the past, or to an unspecified Arcadian land.

This strategy would prove relatively successful – at least for the early years of the new century. Though the elites who had initially sponsored the Boston and Philadelphia theaters had lost some of their influence in American society,[87] the theaters themselves were able to gain a more stable status within their communities. In 1802, Snelling Powell (brother of Charles Stuart Powell) secured the management of the Federal Street Theatre. A more efficient and cautious manager than his sibling, he was able to make a financial success of the venture. According to Clapp, he "conjured back into the Boxes the long absent taste and beauty of Boston," and the theater enjoyed a successful run under his management.[88] The same year that Powell took over the Federal Street house would prove the final year of operation for the Haymarket, which had limped along since 1799, with a few sporadic entertainments. It was sold in the spring of 1803 and torn down.[89] One of the last impediments to the Federal Street's undisputed claim to the Boston audience was removed in 1805, when the city passed an ordinance restricting performances to licensed spaces. This gave the Federal Street Theatre a virtual monopoly on theatrical entertainments, since it prohibited performances in exhibition rooms or museums. Thus, after 1805 the Boston theater enjoyed a relatively quiet and profitable period of development. The theater had come a long way from the object of Governor Hancock's persecution, to an institution protected by the laws of the Commonwealth.

When Chestnut Street manager Thomas Wignell died in 1803, it marked the end of an era for the Philadelphia theater. Happily, the management of the playhouse passed into the capable hands of William Warren, and then to the partnership of Warren and William B. Wood. Like Powell, Warren and Wood were able to revive the theater's fortunes and expand the company. The two sustained a thriving partnership until 1828.

The Park Theatre began the century in greater jeopardy. The political reversals of the 1800 election had toppled the Federalist might of the city and had further hindered efforts to create a stable, theater-going population in the city. In 1803, unwilling to support an expensive and unsuccessful venture, the theater's original proprietors allowed the theater to be sold at auction. Indeed, they seem, to some extent, to have relinquished interest in it even before that point. As Odell notes, "Dunlap attributed the thinness [of the audiences] to the constant attendance of 'our refined circles' at balls and card parties."[90] The critic Jonathan Oldstyle (Washington Irving) complained that the house was in such disrepair, so filthy and so poorly decorated that it had little to attract its wealthy patrons.[91]

The attitude of the Park Theatre's original proprietors appears markedly different from those of the Federal Street and Chestnut Street houses. Those men in Boston and Philadelphia, who had ordered the finest velvet curtains, the most expensive furnishings and trappings for their theaters, would hardly have tolerated mud-covered benches and floors ankle-deep in apple cores,

Figure 8. 1868 reprint (with names of audience members identified) of John Searle's 1822 watercolor, *Interior of the reconstructed Park Theatre*

peanut shells, and orange peels. Happily, however, for the Park Theatre, its new group of overseers, William Henderson, John C. Shaw, Daniel McCormick, John McVickar, Nicholas Low, and Joshua Waddington, seem to have seen the theater as at least a *potentially* vital component of New York's cultural development.[92] Indeed, the best-known interior portrait of the Park Theatre, painted by John Searle in 1822 (after the theater's destruction by fire and subsequent rebuilding under the patronage of John Jacob Astor and Dominick Lynch), is remarkable not for its depiction of the playhouse, but for its careful rendering of the *audience* – whose most important members are named and numbered in the borders of the work. Among those depicted are several members of the Livingston, Cruger, DeWitt Clinton, and Wilkes families, as well as the (still-living) proprietors, John Watts, William Bayard, and James Watson.[93] The New York theater had at last been given into the care of a group willing to ensure its continued presence in the city's cultural community.

Epilogue

"From an infant stage": the legacy of the early national theater

In 1798, Judith Sargent Murray predicted: "From an infant stage, I look for improvement. Gradually we shall progress ... In one word – the audience will refine the players and the players will refine the audience."[1] To what extent were Murray's speculations realized in the early national theater? How did the post-war playhouse shape the urban public sphere of the new nation? And how in turn did the nation mold the theater?

The period from 1783 to 1800 laid the foundation for the next century of America's theatrical progress. The founders of the Boston, New York, and Philadelphia theaters faced the task of establishing a worthy cultural product for a new nation: a process made more challenging by their desire to emulate the best European models, while simultaneously celebrating what was uniquely American in the new theater.

In constructing their theaters, the Boston, New York, and Philadelphia elite created a new construction of nationhood and of theater, pitting themselves against inherited ideas of republican virtue. In Boston and Philadelphia, they embedded their pro-theater rhetoric in patriotic language, thus transforming a "rational amusement" into a patriotic duty. In New York, they imagined their playhouse as a refuge from political debate. But in doing so, the theater's supporters placed an unfair burden on the theater, and developed unrealistic expectations of what playhouse entertainments might accomplish. Indeed, the disappointed reactions of each theater's trustees at the end of their first seasons suggest that their playhouses had failed to fulfill their cultural goals. Neither the founders nor the audiences could accept that their theaters were "works in progress" – which, like the nation, were in their infancy.

Moreover, the post-war elite, new to theater ownership, had difficulty reconciling the didactic function of their theaters with their concept of the playhouse as a money-making proposition. The tension between theatrical entertainment as a profit-oriented, private undertaking, versus a public "school of virtue," re-surfaced throughout the early national period, and complicated the relationship between the theaters' founders and their audiences. Should they sacrifice their mission to educate public taste in favor of box office considerations, or should they reform audience tastes by offering them "improving" theatrical fare? Though the founders never completely relinquished their hope that theater could educate its audience, they eventually acknowledged that box office realities demanded certain concessions to popular tastes.

To their surprise, the playhouse audience was far from the docile and respectful populace they had anticipated, and the audience's rebelliousness manifested itself in political demonstrations, as well as demands for popular drama. Inevitably, the novelty of a participatory democracy generated conflict over how those democratic principles should be applied (and by whom). Yet, the controversy that arose in the playhouse devastated the post-Revolutionary elite. They had envisioned their theaters as a "democracy of glee" – sites for reconciliation, not confrontation, failing to realize that the formation of national identity, or a national cultural product, would be an ongoing and negotiated process.

Yet as Royall Tyler commented in his prologue to *The Contrast*: "If ours the faults, the virtues too are ours."[2] For all the founders' shortcomings, they successfully established legitimate theatrical entertainments as an expression of American nationalism. Through their post-war economic and political maneuvering, the Boston, New York, and Philadelphia elites emerged as the *de facto* leaders of American culture, using their power to legitimize the theater as a tool of political and social control in the new nation. They created not an imagined culture, but an institutional one, centered around the concrete monuments to their might and achievement. The cultural product that they crafted reflected their attempts to shape American nationalism and symbolized their wish to create a society that would synthesize the old system of social deference with the benefits of Enlightenment rational thought. William Warland Clapp declared, "All honor is due to those who struggled manfully against the tide which opposed them, and through whose efforts that drama finally attained a firm position."[3]

Paradoxically, they were so successful in their demonstration of the power of theater to move and persuade its audience that they inspired their political and economic rivals to challenge them for supremacy in the playhouse. The invasion of political parties, and of the Philadelphia, Boston, and New

York mechanics, ironically, transformed the playhouse into a more genuine democracy than its founders had ever envisioned.

Thus the early national theater emerged as a cultural product of *conflicting* ideas of American nationalism. Ultimately, the greatest contribution that the theaters' founders and their rivals made to America's cultural progress was to educate the American audience – not to appreciate one particular author or aesthetic in the playhouse, but rather to guard jealously their right to shape their own national identity.

Tables

Table 1   Boston – Federal Street Theatre Founders

Tontine: Trustee/founder of the Boston Tontine Association
Union Bank: Trustee/founder of the Union Bank
Theatre: Theatre Trustee (note that a "?" by a name indicates that the individual may have signed pro-theater petitions or voted "yes" on the theater resolutions in the House, but that the exact level of their involvement cannot be determined)
Fed./Anti.: Federalist or Anti-Federalist (Republican) political allegiance where known

Name/Occupation	Tontine	Union Bank	Theatre	Fed. or Anti.
Amory, Jonathan	YES		YES	
Austin, Benjamin	YES		?	Republican
Barrell, Joseph (Merchant)	YES		YES	
Blake, Joseph		YES	?	
Codman, John, Jr. (Merchant)	YES		YES	
Coolidge, Joseph		YES	YES	
Davis, Caleb (Merchant)	YES	YES	?	
Dawes, Thomas	YES		?	
Fellowes, Nathaniel (Merchant)	YES	YES	?	
Gardiner, John	YES		YES	
Geyer, Frederick W. (Merchant)	YES	YES	?	
Greene, David		YES	?	
Jackson, Gen. Henry	YES		YES	
Jarvis, Charles (Physician)	YES	YES	YES	Republican
Higginson, Stephen (Merchant)	YES	YES	YES	Federalist
Hubbard, Daniel		YES	?	
Morton, Perez (Lawyer)	YES	YES	YES	Republican

(cont.)

Table 1   (*cont.*)

Name/Occupation	Tontine	Union Bank	Theatre	Fed. or Anti.
Phillips, William (Merchant)	YES		?	Federalist
Russell, Jos., Jr. (Merchant)	YES		YES	
Sewall, Samuel		YES	?	
Storer, Ebenezer (Merchant)	YES		YES	
Tudor, Wm. (Lawyer)	YES	YES	YES	Republican
Wedgery, William		YES	?	
Wendell, Oliver (Merchant)	YES	YES	?	

Table 2   Boston – Haymarket Theatre Founders

Names listed are drawn from the list of subscribers and shareholders found in the Annie Haven Thwing Card Catalog Collection at the Massachusetts Historical Society.

MCMA: Massachusetts Charitable Mechanics Association
AHA: Ancient and Honorable Artillery Company
Theatre: Shareholder in the original Haymarket (note that shares were sold or traded with some frequency in 1797–1799)
Fed./Anti.: Federalist or Anti-Federalist (Republican) political allegiance where known

Name/Occupation	MCMA	AHA	Theatre	Fed. or Anti.
Barnes, Jotham (Housewright)	YES		YES	
Baylis, William (Auctioneer)			YES	
Bicker, Martin (Merchant)	YES		YES	
Blake, George (Lawyer)			YES	
Blake, Nathaniel (Merchant)			YES	
Bolter, James (Housewright)	YES		YES	
Bradley, Samuel (Merchant)		YES		
Brailsford, Norton (Glazier)			YES	
Brown, John (Merchant)			YES	
Bullen, Bela (Merchant)			YES	
Chapman, Henry (Shipchandler)			YES	
Cooper, Samuel (Merchant)			YES	
Gardner, Lemuel (Cooper)	YES	YES	YES	
Gardner, Nathaniel (Merchant)			YES	
Green, Peter (Merchant)		YES	YES	
Eaton, Wm. Barnard (Trader)			YES	
Harris, Jonathan (Merchant)			YES	

(*cont.*)

Table 2   (*cont.*)

Name/Occupation	MCMA	AHA	Theatre	Fed. or Anti.
Hastings, Samuel (Merchant)		YES	YES	
Hatch, Israel (Gentleman)			YES	
Herring, Ebenezer (Bricklayer)			YES	
Holbrook, Asa (Trader)			YES	
Homer, Michael (Bricklayer)	YES	YES	YES	
Jarvis, Benjamin (Merchant)			YES	
Jarvis, Charles (Physician)			YES	Republican
Kelley, Gad (Merchant)			YES	
Merril, John H. (Furrier)			YES	
Messinger, Daniel (Hatter)	YES	YES	YES	Federalist
Osborne, John (Merchant)		YES	YES	
Osgood, Peter (Bricklayer)	YES	YES	YES	
Patten, Charles (Blacksmith)	YES		YES	
Penniman, Amos (Merchant)			YES	
Piper, Nathan (Merchant)			YES	
Richards, Samuel (Merchant)			YES	
Roby, Joseph (Tinman)			YES	
Russell, Benjamin (Printer)	YES	YES	YES	Federalist
Scudder, Daniel (Merchant)			YES	
Sommes, John (Merchant)			YES	
Stimpson, Caleb (Merchant)			YES	
Stoddard, Edward (Merchant)			YES	
Summer, Elisha (Wharfinger)			YES	
Thompson, William (Merchant)			YES	
Townshend, David (Jeweler)			YES	
Tubbs, William (Merchant)			YES	
Valentine, Nathaniel (Merchant)			YES	
Wade, Simeon (Housewright)	YES		YES	
Warren, Aaron (Merchant)			YES	
West, David (Bookseller)	YES		YES	
Whiting, John (Merchant)			YES	
Winship, Abiel (Merchant)			YES	

Out of 49 proprietors, 10 can be identified as dues-paying members of the Massachusetts Charitable Mechanics Association (membership shifted frequently due to non-payment of dues); 10 are members of the Ancient and Honorable Artillery Company. Only 18 of the original subscribers belong to professions considered as "artisan," while 28 are "smaller" merchants whose average property values were estimated at less than $6,000. Among the Mechanics, the highest estimated property value is attributed to David West, at $5,000. The smallest amount (among those who own property to be assessed) belongs to Ebenezer Herring, at $200.

Table 3   Philadelphia – Chestnut Street Theatre Founders

Land Co.: Involvement in at least *one* of the following land speculation ventures: Asylum Land Company, North American Land Company, Pennsylvania Land Company, Pennsylvania Population Company
Dancing Assembly: Listed as a member of the City Dancing Assembly
Bank: Director or shareholder in the Bank of North America or the Bank of Pennsylvania
Theatre: Members of the original Dramatic Association marked with an (*); all others joined post-1791.
Fed./Anti.: Federalist or Anti-Federalist (a.k.a. Republican or Democratic-Republican) political allegiance where known

Name/Occupation	Land Co.	Dancing Assembly	Bank	Theatre	Fed. or Anti.
Alexander, *Miss* C. (by John Wiliams)				YES	
Anderson, John				YES	
Anthony, Thomas P.				YES	
Ashley, John	YES			YES	
Barclay, John (Merchant)	YES		YES	YES*	
Barge, Jacob		YES		YES*	
Bass, Robert (Physician)				YES*	
Bingham, William (Merchant)	YES	YES	YES	YES	Federalist
Blight, Peter				YES	
Bordley, Elizabeth (by Beale Bordley)				YES	
Brown, John	YES			YES	
Buchanan, Robert				YES	
Bukely, R. S.				YES	
Carradine, Thomas				YES	
Cay, David (Merchant)				YES	
Claypoole, D. (Editor)				YES	
Clow, Andrew (Merchant)	YES			YES	
Crammond, Joseph (?)				YES	
Crammond, William (Merchant)	YES	YES		YES	
Crawford, James		YES		YES*	
Dallas, Alexander (Lawyer)	YES			YES	Republican

(cont.)

Table 3   *(cont.)*

Name/Occupation	Land Co.	Dancing Assembly	Bank	Theatre	Fed. or Anti.
Duffield, John (Merchant)				YES	
Dunlap, John (Editor)				YES	
Evans, Griffith		YES		YES	
Febiger, Christian	YES			YES	Republican
Franklin, Wm. T. (Secretary)	YES			YES*	Anti-Fed.
Franks, David (Merchant)	YES	YES		YES	Loyalist
Glentworth, James	YES			YES	
Goyoux de la Roche, J.				YES	
Hamillen (full name illegible)				YES	
Harrison, John				YES	
Hays, Samuel				YES	
Hill, Henry (Merchant)	YES			YES	Republican
Hunt, Pearson				YES	
Kean, John				YES	
Kepple, George (Merchant)				YES	
Killand, J.				YES	
Kingston, Stephen	YES	YES		YES	
Lawrence, John				YES	Loyalist
Leamey, John (Merchant)	YES		YES	YES	
Lyle, James	YES			YES	
Mackie (full name illegible)				YES	
McConnell, Maj. Mathew	YES			YES	
McKenzie, William				YES	
Meade, George				YES	
Miller, William				YES	
Minis, R.				YES	
Mitchell, John				YES	
Moore, R. (?)				YES	
Moore, Maj. Thomas	YES			YES*	
Morris, Robert	YES	YES	YES	YES	Federalist
Nicholson, John	YES	YES		YES	Republican
Palyart, Eugenio				YES	
Parker, William	YES			YES	
Patton, Capt. Robert				YES	
Penn, John				YES	

(cont.)

Table 3   (cont.)

Name/Occupation	Land Co.	Dancing Assembly	Bank	Theatre	Fed. or Anti.
Petit, Charles (Merchant)	YES	YES	YES	YES	Anti-Federalist
Pinkerton, David				YES	
Plumstead, Edward				YES	
Porter, Robert	YES			YES	
Prager, Michael				YES	
Pulaski, Charles				YES	
Pulaski, Hannah				YES	
Rainey, Robert				YES	
Ravano (Ravara?), Joseph				YES	
Read, John	YES			YES	
Redman, Joseph (Physician)		YES		YES*	
Richmond, C.				YES	
Ringold (full name illegible)				YES	
Sadler (full name illegible)				YES	
Smith, Thomas				YES	
Spence, Andrew				YES	
Stewart, Gen. Walter	YES		YES	YES*	
Stiles, William				YES	
Summers, Andrew				YES	
Swanwick, John (Lawyer)	YES	YES	YES	YES	Republican
Swire, John (d. 1795)				YES	
Taylor, George	YES			YES	
Thox, Edward				YES	
Travis, John	YES	YES		YES	
Tudor, George (Broker)			YES	YES	
Vaughan, John (Lawyer)	YES		YES	YES	
West, Francis	YES	YES		YES	
West, John				YES	
Westcott, Robert				YES	
Wollery (full name illegible)				YES	

Out of 90 original subscribers (1792), 14 can be identified as members of the City Dancing Assembly; 29 can be identified as land company investors; 8 were members of the original Dramatic Association (1788); and 9 were Trustees or Directors of the Bank of North America or the Bank of Pennsylvania.

Table 4 New York – Park Theatre Founders

Names listed are those involved in Park Theatre (names are drawn from *The Intimate Life of Alexander Hamilton*; the Diaries of William Dunlap; and *A History of the American Theatre*).

Bank: Involvement as a founder/shareholder in The Bank of New York
Tonine: Listed as shareholders in *Constitution of the Subscribers to the Tontine Coffee House*
Land: Involved in Black River or Yazoo Land speculations
Theatre: Shareholder in original Park Theatre
Fed./Anti.: Federalist or Anti-Federalist political allegiance (where known)

Name/Occupation	Bank	Tontine	Land	Theatre	Fed. or Anti.
Bayard, Wm. (Merchant)	YES	YES	YES	YES	(Loyalist)
Clinton, DeWitt		YES		YES	Federalist
Constable, Wm. (Merchant)		YES	YES	YES	Federalist
Cruger, Nicholas		YES		YES	Federalist
Dunlap, Wm. (Theatre Manager)				YES	
Fish, Nathaniel (Lawyer)		YES		YES	
Gouverneur, Isaac				YES	
Henderson, Wm. (Merchant)	YES	YES	YES	YES	
Hicks, Elias	YES			YES	
Hodgkinson, John (Actor)				YES	
Hoffman, Josiah Ogden		YES	YES	YES	Federalist
Kemble, Robert S. (Merchant)	YES	YES	YES	YES	
Kettletas, Gerret	YES			YES	
King, Rufus (Lawyer)	YES	YES		YES	
Lispensard, Thomas				YES	
Livingston, Brockholst (Lawyer)	YES	YES		YES	Anti-Fed.
Livingston, Edward (Lawyer)		YES		YES	Anti-Fed.
Low, Nicholas		YES	YES	YES	Federalist
Ludlow, Julian (Merchant)		YES		YES	
Lynch, Dominick (Merchant)	YES	YES		YES	
Morton, Jacob				YES	
Pollock, Carlisle	YES		YES	YES	
Prime, Nathaniel				YES	
Sands, Comfort (Lawyer)	YES	YES	YES	YES	
Scriba, George (Merchant)		YES	YES	YES	
Smith, Pascal N. (Merchant)		YES		YES	
Ten Eyck, Phillip				YES	
Tillinghast, Stephen (Merchant)				YES	
Van Rensselaer, Stephen (Lieut.-Gov.)				YES	

(*cont.*)

Table 4   (*cont.*)

Name/Occupation	Bank	Tontine	Land	Theatre	Fed. or Anti.
Verplanck, Gulian (Merchant)	YES	YES		YES	FED (Loyalist)
Waddington, Joshua	YES	YES		YES	FED (Loyalist)
Watson, James (Merchant)	YES	YES	YES	YES	
Watts, John (Lawyer?)		YES	YES	YES	
Wilkes, Charles	YES			YES	

Out of 32 original founders (not including William Dunlap, the theater manager, or John Hodgkinson, the actor), 21 were subscribers to the Tontine, 14 had ties to The Bank of New York, and 11 were involved in the Black River or Yazoo Land speculations.

Notes

Introduction

1 William Dunlap, *History of the American Theatre* (New York: Burt Franklin, 1963), vol. I, p. 133.

2 In this study, I use the phrase "elite" to describe a section of the wealthy members of Boston, New York, and Philadelphia society, linked to their respective groups by social and familial ties. I adopt this construction of the term from Peter Dobkin Hall, *The Organization of American Culture, 1700–1900: Private Institutions, Elites, and the Origins of American Nationality* (New York: New York University Press, 1982). Also see Stephen Brobeck, "Changes in the Composition and Structure of Philadelphia Elite Groups, 1756–1790," Ph.D. dissertation, University of Pennsylvania, 1973.

3 Susanne K. Sherman (edited posthumously by Lucy B. Pilkinton), *Comedies Useful: Southern Theatre History, 1775–1812* (Williamsburg, VA: Celest Press, 1998). Sherman's work (published posthumously) provides very detailed accounts of performances, as well as very useful appendices on the number of performances given in the major southern cities on a yearly basis.

4 William H. Pease and Jane H. Pease, *The Web of Progress: Private Values and Public Styles in Boston and Charleston, 1828–1843* (Athens, GA: University of Georgia Press, 1991).

5 Dunlap, *History of the American Theatre* (the Burt Franklin reprint of Dunlap's *History* contains Hodgkinson's own version of events in *A narrative of his connection with the Old American Company, 1792–1797*).

6 See George C. Odell, *Annals of the New York Stage* (New York: Columbia University Press, 1927–1949) and Joseph N. Ireland, *Records of the New York Stage, 1750–1860* (New York: B. Blom, 1966). Both of these chronicles offer detailed repertoire and cast list information.

7 I have deliberately shied away from textual analysis except in the cases where I believe an examination of an author's work or reception can shed light on the way in which the theaters' managers or proprietors marketed their cultural product.

1 Extravagance and dissipation

1 New York had a much less embattled history of pre-Revolutionary theater.

2 E. Digby Baltzell, *Puritan Boston and Quaker Philadelphia: Two Protestant Ethics*

and the Spirit of Class Authority and Leadership (New York: Macmillan Publishing Co., 1979).

3 Harrold C. Shiffler, "Religious Opposition to the Eighteenth-Century Philadelphia Stage," *Educational Theatre Journal* 14 (October 1962), p. 215. Also see William Dye, "Pennsylvania *versus* the Theatre," *Pennsylvania Magazine of History and Biography* 55 (1931), pp. 333–373.

4 Shiffler, "Religious Opposition," p. 215.

5 Thomas Clark Pollock, *The Philadelphia Theatre in the Eighteenth Century, Together with the Day Book of the Same Period* (New York: Greenwood Press, 1968), p. 5.

6 Gary Nash, *The Urban Crucible: The Northern Seaports and the Origins of the American Revolution* (Cambridge, MA: Harvard University Press, 1986), p. 63.

7 *Pennsylvania Archives*, VII, pp. 75–78.

8 Gary Nash, *Quakers and Politics; Pennsylvania 1681–1726*, new edition (Boston: Northeastern University Press, 1993), p. 341.

9 Between 1730 and 1750, roughly 70,000 German and Scots-Irish immigrants poured into Pennsylvania. Many moved out to the western portion of the state, but a sizable number settled in the Philadelphia area. See Nash, *Urban Crucible*, pp. 66–67.

10 Pollock, *Philadelphia Theatre*, p. 7. This theater was built to replace the one built on the city limits in 1723, and used sporadically as a site for strolling players and puppet shows.

11 Shiffler, "Religious Opposition," p. 218.

12 Richard Stine, "The Philadelphia Theater, 1682–1829: Its Growth as a Cultural Institution," Ph.D. dissertation, University of Pennsylvania, 1951, p. 28.

13 Shiffler, "Religious Opposition," p. 219.

14 Stephen Rosswurm, "Class Relations, Political Economy, and Society in Philadelphia," in Catherine E. Hutchins, ed., *Shaping a National Culture: The Philadelphia Experience, 1750–1800* (Winterthur, DE: Winterthur Museum, 1994), p. 47.

15 Brobeck, "Changes," p. 174.

16 In his study of the transformation of the Philadelphia elite in the pre- and post-war period, Brobeck has located thirty-six men, whom he identifies as the "core" group of the non-Quaker elite of the pre-war period. Among these men, thirteen were members of the Dancing Assembly, and eleven belonged to St. John's Lodge. Those numbers jumped dramatically by 1770, though the "core group" only increased by nine members during that fourteen-year period. For example, by 1770, twenty-six out of the forty-five core members had joined the Dancing Assembly.

17 Lynn Matluck Brooks, "The Philadelphia Dancing Assembly in the Eighteenth Century," *Dance Research Journal*, 21/1 (Spring 1989), p. 1.

18 Ibid.

19 Lynn Matluck Brooks, "Emblem of Gaiety, Love, and Legislation: Dance in Eighteenth-Century Philadelphia," *Pennsylvania Magazine of History and Biography* 115 (January 1991), pp. 63–89.

20 Richard Bushman, *The Refinement of America: Persons, Houses, Cities* (New York: Random House, 1992), p. 403.

21 Dunlap, *History of the American Theatre*, p. 28.

22 Pollock, *Philadelphia Theatre*, pp. 11–12.

23 Brooks McNamara, *The American Playhouse in the Eighteenth Century* (Cambridge, MA: Harvard University Press, 1969), pp. 53–55.

24 Ibid., pp. 62–65.

25 For day-by-day information on which plays were performed in Philadelphia, see Pollock, *Philadelphia Theatre*. For more information about the development of the stage and other fashionable entertainments in eighteenth-century London, see John Brewer, *Pleasures of the Imagination: English Culture in the Eighteenth Century* (New York: Farrar, Straus, & Giroux, 1997).

26 *Pennsylvania Gazette*, January 22, 1767.

27 Peter A. Davis, "Puritan mercantilism and the politics of anti-theatrical legislation in colonial America," in Ron Engle and Tice Miller, eds., *The American Stage: Social and economic issues from the colonial period to the present* (Cambridge: Cambridge University Press, 1993), p. 25.

28 For an account of this incident, see Pollock, *Philadelphia Theatre*, pp. 22–23.

29 Land banks were popular in rural regions, where currency could be issued and distributed on an "as-needed" basis. Private banks were much more popular among the merchant elite. I will discuss the banking system of the early national period in greater detail in chapters 2 and 3.

30 The Quakers and the Scots-Irish were not traditional allies; however, common concerns drew them together over the issue of the theater and opposition to the rising urban elite. For more on this topic see the following: Robert J. Gough, "Toward a Theory of Class and Social Conflict: A Social History of Wealthy Philadelphians, 1775 and 1800," Ph.D. dissertation, University of Pennsylvania; Kevin M. Sweeney, "High Style Vernacular: Lifestyles of the Colonial Elite," in Cary Carson, Ronald Hoffman, and Peter J. Albert, eds., *Of Consuming Interest: The Style of Life in the Eighteenth Century*, Charlottesville, VA: University Press of Virginia, 1994; Billy G. Smith, "Inequality in Late Colonial Philadelphia: A Note on Its Nature and Growth," *William and Mary Quarterly*, 3rd series, 41/4 (October 1984), pp. 629–645; Mary McKinney Schweitzer, "The Economy of Philadelphia and Its Hinterland," in Catherine E. Hutchins, ed., *Shaping a National Culture: The Philadelphia Experience, 1750–1800* (Winterthur, DE: Winterthur Museum, 1994).

31 William Warland Clapp, Jr., *A Record of the Boston Stage* (New York: Benjamin Blom, 1968), p. 1.

32 Cited in Kenneth Silverman, *A Cultural History of the American Revolution* (New York: Thomas Y. Crowell & Co., 1976), p. 66.

33 Jean-Christophe Agnew, *Worlds Apart: Theatre and the Marketplace in Anglo-American Thought, 1550–1750* (Cambridge: Cambridge University Press, 1986), p. 113.

34 Ibid., p. 151.

35 From 1 Corinthians 12:14; cited in Hall, *Organization of American Culture*, p. 23.

36 A centralized system would have allowed greater individual agency among the wealthiest merchants, while simultaneously eliminating smaller competitors.

37 Nash, *Urban Crucible*, p. 81.

38 Robert E. Wright, *Origins of Commercial Banking in America, 1750–1800* (Lanham, MD: Rowman and Littlefield, 2001). See chapter 1, "Colonial Finance and the Lack of Liquidity, 1750–1775."

39 Nash, *Urban Crucible*, pp. 80–83.
40 Margaret E. Newell, "A Revolution in Economic Thought: Currency and Development in Eighteenth-Century Massachusetts," in Conrad Edick Wright and Katheryn P. Viens, eds., *Entrepreneurs: the Boston Business Community, 1700–1850* (Boston: Massachusetts Historical Society and Northeastern University Press, 1997).
41 Bushman, *Refinement of America*, p. 187.
42 Clapp, Jr., *Boston Stage*, p. 2.
43 Cited in Davis, "Puritan mercantilism," p. 21.
44 Ibid.
45 Ibid., pp. 21–22.
46 Ibid., p. 22.
47 Nash, *Urban Crucible*, p. 132.
48 See Frank Lambert, *Pedlar in Divinity: George Whitfield and the Transatlantic Revivals, 1737–1770* (Princeton, NJ: Princeton University Press, 1994). Also see John E. Smith, *Jonathan Edwards: Puritan, Preacher, and Philosopher* (South Bend., IN: Notre Dame University Press, 1992).
49 Wright, *Origins of Commercial Banking*, p. 20.
50 Richard E. Brown, *Middle-Class Democracy and the Revolution in Massachusetts, 1691–1780* (Ithaca: Cornell University Press, 1955).
51 Rosalind Remer has observed that the Great Awakening underscored the economic divisions within Massachusetts, as well as the political and spiritual ones. She notes that (in general) members of New Light churches were allied with the Land Bank system, while those who supported the Silver Bank (or specie) system were primarily members of Anglican or Old Light churches. Rosalind Remer, "Old Lights and New Money: A Note on Religion, Economics, and the Social Order in 1740 Boston," *William and Mary Quarterly*, 3rd series, 47/4 (October 1990), pp. 566–573.
52 T. H. Breen, "'Baubles of Britain': The American and Consumer Revolutions of the Eighteenth Century," *Past and Present* 119 (May 1996), p. 90.
53 Diaries of John Rowe, Massachusetts Historical Society. Also see article on Rowe, "Diary of John Rowe," *Proceedings of the Massachusetts Historical Society*, second series, 10 (1896). The article notes that "Rowe was a leader in all social affairs... As a merchant, Mason, member of clubs, an officer of Trinity Church... he knew everyone in town," p. 30. Rowe also records seeing David Douglass perform the "Lecture on Heads" at a local tavern on July 31, 1769. The "Lecture on Heads" was a popular, flexible, one-man performance that actors often used either between seasons or when no theater space was readily available. Its text could also be adapted to satirize local politicians or social figures.
54 David W. Conroy, *In Public Houses: Drink and the Revolution of Authority in Colonial Massachusetts* (Chapel Hill, NC: University of North Carolina Press, 1995), pp. 89–95.
55 Cited in Barry Witham, ed., *Theatre in the Colonies and United States, 1750–1915, a Documentary History* (Cambridge: Cambridge University Press, 1996), p. 18.
56 For more information about pre-Revolutionary demonstrations, see Peter Shaw, *American Patriots and the Rituals of Revolution* (Cambridge, MA: Harvard University Press, 1981). Shaw discusses the transformation of traditional celebratory events, such as Pope Day, into rituals which legitimized the American rebellion.

57 In his *History of Massachusetts, from 1764 to July 1775*, Alden Bradford suggests that there were "repeated" attempts made to revoke Massachusetts's anti-theatrical legislation during 1767, and that the renewal of the law was a response to this effort. Neither Bradford nor Clapp mentions the individuals or groups who initiated the request. It is possible that David Douglass was making a further effort to extend his touring circuit into Boston, yet he remained in Philadelphia from November of 1766 through August of 1767. However, the anti-theater flurry does coincide with the arrival of actor John Henry in the colonies. Henry was to become Hallam's partner after the war, and to visit Boston as an emissary for the theater in 1790. It is possible he was engaged in a similar mission at this time. Alden Bradford, *History of Massachusetts, from 1764 to July 1775* (Boston: Richardson and Lord, 1822), p. 116.

58 See Baltzell, *Puritan Boston* and Rhys Isaacs, *The Transformation of Virginia, 1740–1790* (Chapel Hill, NC: University of North Carolina Press, 1982).

59 Jack P. Greene, *Pursuits of Happiness: The Social Development of Early Modern British Colonies and the Formation of American Culture* (Chapel Hill, NC: University of North Carolina Press, 1988). It should be noted that other colonies – most notably Virginia – also manifested a wide disparity between the wealthy and the poorer classes. However, its lack of adherence to either a centralized system of colonial power or a dominant religion helps to distinguish its pattern of development in the pre-Revolutionary period.

60 It is worth noting that the system of "patroonships" remained part of New York's economic and social structure well into the nineteenth century. Historian David Grimsted is currently developing a study of the "down-renters'" struggle to abolish the patroon system in the 1840s.

61 Edwin Burrows and Mike Wallace chronicle the disintegrating relationship between the colony's settlers and traders and their Indian neighbors. Over a forty-year period, white settlers and fur traders grew increasingly exploitative in their treatment of their former Indian allies, often provoking violent retaliation. See Edwin G. Burrows and Mike Wallace, *Gotham: A History of New York City to 1898* (New York: Oxford University Press, 1999), pp. 22–24, 37–40.

62 Nash, *Urban Crucible*, pp. 24–25.

63 Ibid., pp. 40–45

64 Greene, *Pursuits of Happiness*, p. 124.

65 Burrows and Wallace, *Gotham*, pp. 118–137. It should be noted that in addition to the opportunities for economic growth, the early years of the eighteenth century brought serious internal challenges to the colony in the form of slave uprisings and racial unrest. Just under one-fifth of the city's population were black slaves. An uprising in 1712, led by roughly two dozen slaves, led to both a violent backlash on the part of the white citizens (who tortured to death many of those involved in the incident) and to increasingly stringent slave laws that essentially drove the free black population off the island of Manhattan. See ibid., pp. 148–149.

66 Greene, *Pursuits of Happiness*, p. 125.

67 Burrows and Wallace, *Gotham*, p. 136.

68 See Greene, *Pursuits of Happiness*, pp. 125–127. Unlike New Jersey and Pennsylvania, expansion across New York's hinterlands was curtailed by the French and the Great

Lakes Indian tribes who occupied much of the western territory. The royal government distributed much of the open land that remained, creating roughly thirty "great
baronial estates," much like the early Dutch patroonships.

69 Arthur Hornblow, *A History of the Theatre in America: From Its Beginnings to the
Present Time*, vol. I (Philadelphia: J. B. Lippincott Company, 1919), p. 43. Also see
Thomas Allston Brown, *A History of the American Stage, containing biographical sketches
of nearly every member of the profession that has appeared on the American Stage from
1733–1870* (New York: Burt Franklin, 1969).

70 Hornblow, *Theatre in America*, pp. 42–43.

71 Ibid., p. 43.

72 Burrows and Wallace, *Gotham*, p. 144.

73 Nash, *Urban Crucible*, p. 76.

74 Ibid., p. 77.

75 Ibid., pp. 78–79.

76 Burrows and Wallace, *Gotham*, p. 151.

77 Nash, *Urban Crucible*, pp. 88–89.

78 The title Prime Minister was not official at this point, and quotation marks are used
around Walpole's unofficially conferred but popularly used moniker.

79 Burrows and Wallace, *Gotham*, p. 152.

80 Nash, *Urban Crucible*, p. 92.

81 This event is cited in both Ireland's *Records of the New York Stage* and in McNamara's
American Playhouse.

82 Brooks McNamara notes that there is some disagreement about whether the Murray-
Kean Company used the *same* site as the theater of 1732, or whether there were two
separate theater sites, both owned by Van Dam, the first at Pearl Street, and the
second at Nassau Street. See McNamara, *American Playhouse*, p. 29.

83 McNamara is careful to note that whether these were structural changes or divisions
created by rail barriers between the different sections remains unclear. See ibid.,
p. 31.

84 Ibid., p. 43.

85 Matthew Clarkson, July 17, 1753, Misc. Mss. Clarkson, Matthew, New-York Historical Society.

86 Cited in McNamara, *American Playhouse*, p. 43.

87 Ibid., p. 45.

88 Leopold Launitz-Schurer, *Loyal Whigs and Revolutionaries: The Making of the Revolution in New York, 1765–1776* (New York: New York University Press, 1980), p. 14.

89 Ibid., pp. 12–13.

90 See Ireland, *Records*, p. 28. Ireland cites a letter from Douglass in which Douglass
claims to have engaged the building on Cruger's Wharf "before we had any reason to
apprehend denial." Douglass's letter suggests that the refusal to allow performances
was probably also a surprise to Cruger.

91 Cited in Witham, *Theatre in the Colonies*, p. 18.

92 *Weyman's New York Gazette*, May 12, 1766.

93 Launitz-Schurer, *Loyal Whigs and Revolutionaries*, p. 23.

94 Ibid., p. 25.

95 See Nash's discussion of the Stamp Act in *Urban Crucible*, especially p. 132.
96 Cited in Ann Fairfax Withington, *Toward a More Perfect Union: Virtue and the Formation of American Republics* (New York: Oxford University Press, 1991), pp. 27–28.
97 *New-York Journal*, January 7, 1768. Also see Withington, *Toward a More Perfect Union*, pp. 41–42.
98 Withington, *Toward a More Perfect Union*, p. 36.
99 Ireland, *Records*, p. 55.
100 Launitz-Schurer, *Loyal Whigs and Revolutionaries*, p. 78.
101 Ibid., p. 82.
102 Nash, *Urban Crucible*, p. 237.
103 Burrows and Wallace, *Gotham*, p. 223. This group later became known as the Committee of One Hundred.

2 Revolutionary transformations

1 Cited in Witham, *Theatre in the Colonies*, p. 20.
2 Withington, *Toward a More Perfect Union*, p. 46.
3 Ibid., p. 24.
4 Cited in Silverman, *Cultural History*, p. 334.
5 Jared Brown, *Theatre in America During the Revolution* (Cambridge: Cambridge University Press, 1995), p. 131.
6 Rowe Diary. See entries for December 29, 1775, January 22, 1776, and February 24, 1776. The January 22, 1776 performance included a production of *The Blockade of Boston*, a play which satirizes the American Army in general and George Washington in particular. Hardly conciliatory material.
7 Cited in Paul Leicester Ford, *Washington and the Theatre* (New York: Burt Franklin, 1970), pp. 26–27.
8 Samuel Adams to Samuel P. Savage, October 17, 1778, Samuel P. Savage Papers, Massachusetts Historical Society.
9 See Jared Brown, *Theatre in America*, pp. 54–55. Also see "Commonplace Book," *c.* 1780, given to Dr. I. T. Sharpless in 1828, Historical Society of Pennsylvania. The Commonplace Book contains an account of the Meschianza, a notorious British celebration held on a loyalist estate on the outskirts of Philadelphia. This entertainment most nearly resembled a court masque in the lavishness of its design. It involved a number of British officers, as well as the daughters of several prominent Philadelphia loyalists.
10 Wayne Bockelman and Owen Ireland, "The Internal Revolution in Pennsylvania; an Ethnic-Religious Interpretation," *Pennsylvania History* 41/2 (April 1974), p. 141.
11 Ibid., p. 147.
12 Gordon S. Wood, *The Creation of the American Republic, 1776–1787* (New York: W. W. Norton & Co., 1993 edn.), pp. 226–227.
13 Bockelman and Ireland, "Internal Revolution," pp. 155–156.

14 Douglas M. Arnold, *A Republican Revolution: Ideology and Politics in Pennsylvania, 1776–1790* (New York: Garland Publishing, 1989), pp. 43–52.

15 See the appendices of Stephen Brobeck's dissertation, which trace the diminution of the Quaker elite population in pre-war Philadelphia.

16 For more on the ideological mission of the State Constitutionalists, see Wood, *Creation of the American Republic*, pp. 226–233, and Arnold, *Republican Revolution*, pp. 188–193.

17 Cited in Wood, *Creation of the American Republic*, p. 226.

18 Gregory H. Nobles, " 'Yet the Old Republicans Still Persevere': Samuel Adams, John Hancock, and the Crisis of Popular Leadership in Revolutionary Massachusetts, 1775–1790," in Ronald Hoffman and Peter J. Albert, eds., *The Transforming Hand of Revolution* (Charlottesville, VA: University Press of Virginia, 1995), pp. 259–260.

19 Ibid., pp. 260–261.

20 See Stephen E. Patterson, *Political Parties in Revolutionary Massachusetts* (Madison, WI: University of Wisconsin Press, 1973). Especially see chapter 1, "Antipartisan Theory and Partisan Reality," pp. 3–32.

21 Richard E. Brown, *Middle-Class Democracy*, p. 393.

22 See Nobles, " 'Yet the Old Republicans Still Persevere' "; see also Ronald Formisano, *The Transformation of Political Culture: Massachusetts Parties, 1790s–1840s* (New York: Oxford University Press, 1983).

23 See Nobles, " 'Yet the Old Republicans Still Persevere'," for excerpts of Warren's comments on Hancock.

24 See Jared Brown, *Theatre in America*, p. 131, and Burrows and Wallace, *Gotham*, p. 227.

25 Janice Potter-MacKinnon, *The Liberty We Seek: Loyalist Ideology in Colonial New York and Massachusetts* (Cambridge, MA: Harvard University Press, 1983), p. viii.

26 Philip Ranlet, *The New York Loyalists* (Knoxville, TN: University of Tennessee Press, 1986), pp. 158–159.

27 Ibid., p. 150.

28 Odell, *Annals*, vol. 1, p. 232.

29 Ibid., pp. 232–235.

30 *Loudon's Packet*, October 10, 1785. Cited in ibid., p. 236.

31 Hugh Rankin, *The Theatre in Colonial America* (Chapel Hill, NC: University of North Carolina Press, 1965), p. 196.

32 Weldon B. Durham, ed., *American Theatre Companies, 1749–1887* (New York: Greenwood Press, 1986), pp. 14–15.

33 As early as 1791, Wignell approached General Henry Knox (then in Philadelphia) in an effort to secure his support for a new theater in Pennsylvania. Knox declined. See letter from Henry Knox to Thomas Wignell and Alexander Reinagle, September 26, 1791, Henry Knox Papers.

34 According to Odell, Miss Tuke had little talent as a performer. He cites New York papers that dismiss her as "lifeless and uninteresting," and suggest that her preferment is due to "a manager's [Hallam's] partiality." See Odell, *Annals*, vol. 1, p. 253.

35 Rankin, *Theatre in Colonial America*, pp. 196–197.

36 *Pennsylvania Packet*, February 17, 1789.

37 General Henry Jackson to General Henry Knox, January 26, 1794, Henry Knox Papers.

38 Maier, p. 272. For more on the concept of the world stage in the Revolutionary era, see Jeffrey H. Richards, *Theatre Enough: American Culture and the Metaphor of the World Stage, 1607–1789* (Durham, NC: Duke University Press, 1991). See also Stanley Elkins and Eric McKitrick, "The Founding Fathers: Young Men of the Revolution," *Political Science Quarterly* 76 (June 1961), pp. 181–216. Elkins and McKitrick note that many of the key Federalists who campaigned for the establishment of the Constitution and who promoted a vision of national over local interests were under the age of forty-five, and had "made their careers" in the war, thus they truly *did* comprise a "new" generation, even though they occasionally allied with members of the pre-war elite (or their descendants).

39 Benedict Anderson, *Imagined Communities: Reflections on the Origin and Spread of Nationalism* (London: Verso Editions, 1983), p. 129.

40 This phrase recurs with some frequency in Philadelphia's *Freeman's Journal*, and targets the wealthy cabal that the *Journal* feared would swallow up Philadelphia society. For an example, see the attack on the Federal Constitution, described as the "foundation upon which the well-born mean to build up their schemes of profit and aggrandizement." *The Freeman's Journal*, October 29, 1788.

41 Gordon S. Wood, *The Radicalism of the American Revolution* (New York: Alfred A. Knopf, 1992), p. 191. See also Elkins and McKitrick, "Founding Fathers."

42 Dunlap, *History of the American Theatre*, vol. i, p. 107.

43 Petition submitted by Lewis Hallam, November 9, 1788, Historical Society of Pennsylvania. Also see *Pennsylvania Archives*, first series, x, pp. 141–143.

44 Christopher Marshall, February 18, 1784, Diary, Historical Society of Pennsylvania. Marshall's diary records the door-to-door campaign that the Quakers staged to get signatures on their anti-theater petition. For other Quaker comments on this issue, see the Pemberton Papers, November 28, 1783, Historical Society of Pennsylvania. James Pemberton writes to his brother John about the need for the "Friends to manifest their disapprobation of the attempt of a company of stage players to introduce themselves into this city."

45 Letter from Hallam to the "Friends of the Drama," *Pennsylvania Packet*, February 21, 1784.

46 From 1783 to 1788, while Hallam was trying to secure a repeal of the anti-theater law, he maintained a correspondence with Philadelphia printer Thomas Bradford. Bradford appears to have been Hallam's source of local information while Hallam toured out of state with the Old American Company. For letters between Hallam and Bradford (some of which hint that Hallam hoped to keep his plans for the theater a secret) see the Bradford Collection at the Historical Society of Pennsylvania, 1785–1786.

47 *Statutes at Large of Pennsylvania*, chapter 1248, vol. xii.

48 *Independent Gazetteer*, January 31, 1787.

49 It is important to note that while Hallam continued to stage performances at the Southwark Theatre, the Quakers continued their protests. For an example, see a signed letter of remonstrance from the Quaker community against theatrical entertainments in the *Independent Gazetteer*, December 10, 1785. For more information on Hallam's illegal entertainments see Pollock, *Philadelphia Theatre*.

50 Some members of the post-war elite in Philadelphia, such as Thomas Willing, had also formed part of the pre-war Anglican elite, yet in the post-war period they were forced to re-establish their authority under the State Constitutionalists, and to assimilate "new men" who had acquired wartime fortunes, and who shared their political goals. In Boston many members of the rising post-war elite, such as William Tudor and Charles Jarvis, were only in their mid-twenties during the war, and were only beginning to enter into their professions in the 1780s.

51 Formisano, *Transformation of Political Culture*, pp. 10–13. Also see Edward Shil, *Center and Periphery: Essays in Macrosociology* (Chicago: University of Chicago Press, 1975).

52 Formisano, *Transformation of Political Culture*, pp. 85–88. Also see Withington, *Toward a More Perfect Union*; David Waldstreicher, *In the Midst of Perpetual Fetes: The Making of American Nationalism, 1776–1820* (Chapel Hill, NC: University of North Carolina Press, 1997); and Simon P. Newman, *Parades, and the Politics of the Street: Festive Culture in the Early American Republic* (Philadelphia: University of Pennsylvania Press, 1997).

53 George Washington to the Continental Congress, requesting funds for the army.

54 Rosswurm, "Class Relations," p. 45.

55 For a discussion of the State Constitutionalists' motivations, see Wood, *Creation of the American Republic*, pp. 226–233. Also see Arnold, *Republican Revolution*, pp. 188–193.

56 Examples of State Constitutionalists' initiatives during this period are the Test Acts of 1777/1779, the anti-theatrical legislation of 1779, the attack on the charter of the College of Philadelphia, and the revocation of the charter of the First Presbyterian Church in 1786. Paradoxically, these acts undermined the basis of the State Constitutionalists' authority, and allowed the Federalists to challenge them for possession of the Revolutionary Center, on the grounds that the State Constitutionalists had violated the same Revolutionary principles that they were sworn to uphold.

57 "Legions," in *Independent Gazetteer*, February 21, 1784.

58 Janet Wilson, "The Bank of North America and Pennsylvania Politics, 1781–1787," in *Pennsylvania Magazine of History and Biography*, 66/1 (January 1942), pp. 3–4.

59 Bray Hammond, *Banks and Politics in America from the Revolution to the Civil War* (Princeton: Princeton University Press, 1957), p. 51. The Bank initially issued 1,000 shares, 600 of which were held by the United States and 400 of which were in the hands of private stockholders. Twelve of the private shareholders, including Thomas Willing, James Wilson, William Bingham, and Thomas Fitzsimmons, remained on the Bank's board for almost a decade.

60 *Independent Gazetteer*, March 13, 1784.

61 The Bank's first directors included the following men: Thomas Willing (father of Ann Willing Bingham and father-in-law to William Bingham), Thomas Fitzsimmons, John Maxwell Nesbitt, Henry Hill (future theater overseer), James Wilson, Samuel Osgood, Cadwalader Morris, Andrew Caladwell, Samuel Ingles, Samuel Meredith, William Bingham, and Timothy Matlock. Its opponents, who signed an anti-Bank petition, included James Pearson, Robert Smith, William Graham, John Barker, John Kling, George Leib, Levi Budd, Frederick Heimberger, Robert Lollar (or Loller),

and John Smilie. For a complete voting list on the Bank issue, see Mathew Carey's account of the Bank debates listed below.

62 Wilson, "The Bank of North America," pp. 16–17.

63 Wright, *Origins of Commercial Banking*, pp. 80–82.

64 For example, the Bank initially excluded Quakers from membership in the Bank, perhaps as punishment for their failure to support the war effort. The Bank's managers were ultimately forced to admit Quakers to the Bank in 1784, when the Quakers threatened to start their own bank. See Hammond, *Banks and Politics*, p. 52.

65 Ibid., p. 57.

66 The term "federal government" may seem premature in the period 1783–1788, but I suggest that for the Federalists, a crucial part of establishing the government's legitimacy lay in defending its authority to enter into legal contracts, as in the case of the Bank charter.

67 Mathew Carey, *Debates and Proceedings of the General Assembly of Pennsylvania on the Memorials Praying for a Repeal or Suspension of the Law Annulling the Charter of the Bank* (Philadelphia: Carey, 1786), pp. 9–10. Carey also explicitly linked the State Constitutionalists' attacks on the Bank with their similar attack on the College of Philadelphia (another elite, Federalist sponsored institution).

68 Thomas Paine, *Dissertations on Government, The Affairs of the Bank and Paper Money* (Philadelphia, 1786), p. 22.

69 Cited in Carey, *Debates and Proceedings*, pp. 19–31.

70 Cited in Hammond, *Banks and Politics*, p. 63.

71 Reported in the *Independent Gazetteer*, December 15, 1786. The actual vote was taken on December 13, 1786, but was not officially approved until March, 1787.

72 For a discussion of this period, see Owen Ireland, "The People's Triumph: The Federalist Majority in Pennsylvania, 1787–1788," *Pennsylvania History*, 56/2, 1989, pp. 93–113.

73 See the "Letter to the Mechanics" in the *Independent Gazetteer*, October 10, 1786.

74 See the letter from "Centinel" in *The Freeman's Journal*, October 28, 1788.

75 Though no complete list of members for the Dramatic Association survives, the following men are known to have been members because they signed petitions from the Dramatic Association submitted to the General Assembly: General Walter Stewart, Major Thomas L. Moore, William Temple Franklin, Dr. Robert Bass, John Barclay, Jacob Barge, Dr. Joseph Redman, and John West. Stephen Brobeck's dissertation lists members of the "core group" of the Philadelphia elite during the late 1780s. The members include Robert Morris, George Clymer, Samuel Meredith, Henry Hill, John Nixon, William Bingham, Thomas Willing, Samuel Powell, and Thomas Mifflin. Of these men, Morris, Hill, Bingham, Willing, Clymer, and Nixon were theater supporters.

76 *Pennsylvania Packet*, January 7, 1789.

77 Petition of the Dramatic Association to the General Assembly, *Minutes of the General Assembly*, February 16, 1789; see also *Pennsylvania Packet*, February 17, 1789.

78 *Pennsylvania Packet*, February 16, 1789.

79 Petition of the Dramatic Association to the General Assembly, *Minutes of the General Assembly*, February 16, 1789; see also *Pennsylvania Packet*, February 17, 1789.

80 These were acts which effectively disenfranchised the Quaker population and prohibited their involvement in state government unless they swore an oath of allegiance to the Commonwealth – something Quakers are expressly forbidden
   to do.

81 *Pennsylvania Museum* 5 (1789), pp. 187–190.

82 *Independent Gazetteer*, March 7, 1789.

83 This information is drawn from roll-call votes printed in Carey's work on the Bank
   of North America, 1786; Owen Ireland's tabulations of Federalist/anti-Federalist
   counties in *Religion, Ethnicity, and Politics: Ratifying the Constitution in Pennsylvania*
   (Pennsylvania: Penn State University Press, 1995), pp. 191–194; and reports on the
   theater votes in the General Assembly in the *Independent Gazetteer*, March 7, 1789.
   Though the representatives changed during this five-year period, patterns of voting
   remained roughly similar.

84 *Independent Gazetteer*, March 7, 1789.

85 Henry Knox of Philadelphia to Samuel Breck of Boston, July 16, 1789, Henry Knox
   Papers.

86 Patterson, *Political Parties*. For Hancock's involvement in the 1767 law, see *Journal
   of the House of Representatives of Massachusetts, 1767–1768* (Boston: Massachusetts
   Historical Society, 1975). For Adams's comments on wartime theatricals see Samuel
   Adams to Samuel P. Savage, October 17, 1778, Samuel P. Savage Papers, Massachusetts
   Historical Society.

87 Hall, *Organization of American Culture*, pp. 65–66.

88 Tamara Plakins Thornton, *Cultivating Gentlemen: The Meaning of Country Life
   Among the Boston Elite, 1785–1860* (New Haven: Yale University Press, 1989), p. 58.

89 Ibid., p. 46.

90 Bushman, *Refinement of America*, p. 191.

91 Handwritten notes in copies of *Sans souci* in the archives at the Boston Atheneum
   and the American Antiquarian Society make tentative identifications of the Boston
   figures represented in the play, who were members of the real-life Sans Souci Club.
   Among those listed are Perez Morton and Harrison Gray Otis (future theater supporters).

92 Mercy Otis Warren, *Sans souci, alias, Free and easy, or, An evening's peep into a
   polite circle* (Boston: Warden and Russell, 1785). p. 4. It should be noted that
   Warren's authorship of the play is disputed, and that she herself disclaimed it, say-
   ing, "I hope I shall never write anything I should be so much ashamed to avow
   as that little indigested farago," cited in Charles Warren, "Samuel Adams and the
   Sans Souci Club in 1785," *Proceedings of the Massachusetts Historical Society* 60 (1927),
   p. 343.

93 Warren, *Sans souci*, p. 7.

94 Charles Warren, "Samuel Adams," p. 342. It may seem contradictory for Mercy Otis
   Warren to object to public entertainments, when she had written several plays herself.
   However, I would suggest that her anti-theater stance in the immediate post-war
   period had its roots in her strong apprehensions about the use that a frivolous and
   seemingly un-republican society would make of a public playhouse.

95 Waldstreicher, *Perpetual Fetes*, p. 81. Also see Charles Warren, "Samuel Adams."

96 *Massachusetts Magazine*, June, 1789. The magazine also contains an allusion to Perez Morton, one of the chief sponsors of the theater, the Boston Tontine Association, and the Union Bank. Morton was, in many ways, a less than savory character. The son of a Boston tavern-keeper, he managed to secure a Harvard education and marry well. However, he had an affair with his wife's sister, which ended in her suicide after she discovered she was carrying his child. See the suicide note written by Francesca Theodora Apthorp Thornton, Miscellaneous Manuscripts, Massachusetts Historical Society. Also see the portrait of Morton's long-suffering wife at the Worcester Museum in Worcester, MA.

97 Charles Warren, "Samuel Adams," p. 321.

98 Theodore Sedgewick, January 9, 1791, Sedgewick Collection, Massachusetts Historical Society.

99 Walter Muir Whitehill discusses the movement of Boston's merchants into increasingly new and grand neighborhoods, largely planned by architect Charles Bulfinch. Bulfinch translated his European, neoclassical inspired designs into private mansions and public buildings, transforming the look of Boston architecture. See Walter Muir Whitehill, *Boston: A Topographical History*, 2nd edition, enlarged (Cambridge, MA: Belknap Press of Harvard University Press, 1968), chapter 3, "The Boston of Bulfinch." Also see Harold and James Kirker, *Bulfinch's Boston, 1787–1817* (New York: Oxford University Press, 1964).

100 Hall, *Organization of American Culture*, p. 181.

101 *Constitution of the Boston Tontine Association* (Boston: Benjamin Russell, 1791).

102 Pauline Maier, "The Debate Over Incorporations: Massachusetts in the Early Republic," in Conrad Edick Wright, ed., *Massachusetts and the New Nation* (Boston: Massachusetts Historical Society and Northeastern University Press, 1992), p. 74.

103 *Constitution of the Boston Tontine Association.*

104 To trace the progress of the Tontiners' petitions, see the Journals of the House of Representatives and Journals of the Senate, 1791–1793, in the Massachusetts State House Special Collections as well as newspapers of the time, such as the *Independent Chronicle and Daily Advertiser*, and the *American Apollo*.

105 Paul Goodman, *The Democratic-Republicans of Massachusetts: Politics in a Young Republic* (Cambridge, MA: Harvard University Press, 1964), p. 42.

106 John W. Tyler, "Persistence and Change within the Boston Business Community," in Conrad Edick Wright and Katheryn P. Viens, eds., *Entrepreneurs: The Boston Business Community, 1700–1850* (Boston: Northeastern University Press, 1997), pp. 97–119.

107 For opposition to the Tontine, see *Independent Chronicle and Universal Daily Advertiser*, February 9, 1792, which offers an account of the proceedings of the House. Also see John C. Howard to Elizabeth Wainwright, December 6, 1791, Elizabeth Wainwright Papers, Massachusetts Historical Society. Howard, writing of planned civic improvements, notes that "*pro bono publico* ought to be the maxim for everyone."

108 Clapp, Jr., *Boston Stage*, p. 5.

109 "Petition for a clause for a theater," October 8, 1791, Miscellaneous Manuscripts, Massachusetts Historical Society.

110 Journal of the House of Representatives, January 20, 1792, and January 26, 1792, vol. I, May 1791–March 1792 session, Massachusetts State House Special Collections.

111 *Argus*, November 8, 1791. I am grateful to Seth Cotlar who first drew my attention to Abraham Bishop while we were in residence at the McNeil Center for Early American Studies.

112 Goodman, *Democratic-Republicans of Massachusetts*, p. 40.

113 *Independent Chronicle and Universal Daily Advertiser*, January 26, 1792.

114 Ibid., February 2, 1792.

115 "Petition for a clause for a theater."

116 John Gardiner, *The Speech of John Gardiner* (Boston: Apollo Press, 1792), p. 3. Gardiner's speech addresses more than an ancient prejudice against the theater – it speaks to the transformation of the post-Revolutionary society as a whole.

117 Philo Dramaticus, *The Rights of the Drama* (Boston, 1792).

118 William Haliburton, "Effects of the Stage on the Manners of the People: and the Propriety of Encouraging and Establishing a Virtuous Theater: By a Bostonian" (Boston: Young & Etheridge, 1792).

119 Hancock may have had a more *personal* motive for blocking the interests of the Tontiners. In February and March of 1789, Stephen Higginson, a wealthy Essex merchant and affiliate of the Tontiners, had published a series of scathing editorials on Hancock in the *Massachusetts Centinel*, entitled "The Writings of Laco," in which he derided Hancock as vain, arrogant, and ignorant. Higginson observed, "I never could learn of any extraordinary merit or services of his . . . he has shared largely in the reputation and laurels acquired by others." Higginson added, "He has become so vain of the reputation he has fortuitously enjoyed, and has been so flattered and pampered by his dependants, that he cannot brook anything like independence in others . . . and hence it is that we find him so averse to associate with men of real respectability." See Stephen Higginson, *The Writings of Laco* (Boston, 1789), pp. 13–14. Small wonder that Hancock would bear a grudge against a man who had so slandered his reputation (or that he would extend that grudge against his friends).

120 By 1792, the Tontine included such men as Dr. Charles Jarvis, Joseph Barrell, General Henry Jackson, Perez Morton, and John Gardiner.

121 The signers of the Bank petition represent eleven out of the original twenty-one Tontine subscribers, and among those *not* named in the "Act to Incorporate sundry persons by the name of the President and Directors of the Union Bank" are two other Tontiners, Samuel Blodget, Jr., and Benjamin Greene, who appear as Bank directors in 1793. See *Fleet's Pocket Almanack* (Boston: 1793).

122 Cited in Goodman, *Democratic-Republicans of Massachusetts*, p. 41.

123 This information is drawn from votes recorded in the Journals of the House and Senate 1791–1793. Of the three related initiatives, the Union Bank is the only vote that is more evenly distributed – which is not surprising, considering it is the only one of the three acts that passed. Resistance was concentrated in Worcester County, the northern part of Middlesex County, and the southern section of Norfolk County. Support for these initiatives was strongest in Suffolk and Essex Counties. As Pauline Maier notes in her essay "The Debate Over Incorporations," to the general public, acts of incorporation seemed potentially dangerous tools which could transform

a democratic body into one governed by an elite. See the *Journal of the House of Representatives*, May 1791–March 1792 session, Massachusetts State House Special Collections.

124 Naomi R. Lamoreaux, *Insider Lending: Banks, personal connections, and economic development in industrial New England* (Cambridge: Cambridge University Press, 1994), p. 4.

125 John Watson, *Annals of Philadelphia and Pennsylvania* (Philadelphia: Leary, Stuart, and Company, 1909), vol. 1, p. 140.

126 Charles Durang, *The Philadelphia Stage: From 1749 to 1821*, Series I, in the *Philadelphia Sunday Dispatch*, May 7, 1854 to June 29, 1854, vol. xv.

127 Ann Willing Bingham was the wife of William Bingham, one of the wealthiest men in America. She was recognized as one of the leaders of the "Republican Court," Philadelphia's elite social circle. Ann Bingham had spent the early part of the 1780s in Europe, where she absorbed the social traditions and elegance of court circles that she tried to re-create back in the United States. Durang claims that she was one of the prime movers behind the formation of the Dramatic Association. I have not yet found any information that either supports or disproves this claim.

128 John Harold Herr, "Thomas Wignell and the Chesnut Street Theatre," Ph.D. dissertation, Department of Theater, Michigan State University, 1969, p. 30. Note that Herr's spelling of "Chesnut" is an accepted version of the theater's name, not an error.

129 *Federal Gazette and Philadelphia Daily Advertiser*, February 11, 1791. The "Friends of the Drama" also expressed their outrage that Hallam had neglected to recruit a group of "seven or eight good [British] actors . . . who came to America for the avowed purpose of joining your company."

130 It is interesting to note that the "Friends of the Drama" do not seem to have objected to the *content* of the plays being presented by Hallam's Company, which included such old favorites as *School for Scandal*, *Richard III*, *Rosina, or the Reapers*, *The West Indian*, and *The Beaux' Stratagem*. These plays, despite their identification with British culture, remained staples of the American theatre throughout the 1790s. See Pollock, *Philadelphia Theatre*, pp. 161–162 for a list of performances during the time of Hallam's dispute with the "Friends of the Drama."

131 *Federal Gazette and Philadelphia Daily Advertiser*, February 15, 1791.

132 Cited in Herr, "Thomas Wignell," p. 51.

133 Note that these men are members of the "core group" of elite that Stephen Brobeck discusses, with the exception of Pettit, who belonged to what Brobeck defines as the "radical subgroup" of the Philadelphia elite. All of these men had ties to the Bank of North America, and to the Federalist agenda (though there were changes in their political views as the 1790s progressed). Herr suggests that Reinagle's partnership with Wignell was instrumental in attracting members of the Philadelphia elite to the new project. Herr suggests that the elite were already familiar with Reinagle through his concerts at the City Tavern, and that Reinagle gave the project a more "refined" tone. See Herr, "Thomas Wignell," pp. 42–46. Subscribers to the new theater included many members of the Philadelphia elite, men who had defended the theater to the General Assembly, and men who had formed part of the Dramatic

Association. The list of the original fifty-eight subscribers can be found in the Society Collection at the Historical Society of Pennsylvania. Funds for the theater were kept at the Bank of North America. For more information on the accounts of the theater, see the Account Book in the Chestnut Street Theatre Collection at the Historical Society of Pennsylvania and the Henry Hill Collection at the Library Company of Philadelphia.

134 Mary McKinney Schweitzer, "The Spatial Organization of Federalist Philadelphia, 1790," *Journal of Interdisciplinary History* 24/1 (Summer 1993), p. 37.

135 Thompson Westcott, *The Historic Mansions and Buildings of Philadelphia, with Some Notice of their Owners and Occupants* (Philadelphia: Porter and Coates, 1877).

136 "Proposals by Messieurs Wignell and Reinagle for Erecting a New Theater in Philadelphia," June 22, 1792, Society Collection, Historical Society of Pennsylvania.

137 *Dunlap's American Daily Advertiser*, September 12, 1791. There is some suggestion of a subterfuge being used in buying lots for the theater. Due to the public outcry from the theater's opponents, Wignell, Reinagle, and the theater subscribers arranged the transaction for the theater land through a third party, a lawyer named John Dickinson, who purchased the land in his own name and then leased it to the theater managers. This version of events is recounted in McNamara, *American Playhouse*, p. 105. John Dickinson was indeed the owner of the land upon which the theater was built – in fact, he tried to foreclose on the managers in 1799.

138 For more information on property transactions in Boston during this period see Annie Haven Thwing, *The Crooked and Narrow Streets of Boston, 1630–1822* (Boston: Marshal Jones Company, 1920); also see Annie Haven Thwing, *Inhabitants and Estates of the Town of Boston, 1630–1800* (Boston: New England Historic Genealogical Society, 2001). For information on property development as perceived by a resident of Boston during the 1790s, see the Thomas Wallcut Papers, Massachusetts Historical Society. In a handwritten essay entitled "Hints as to Widening Streets," Wallcutt praises the Tontiners for their "disinterested Public Spirit" in contributing to the renovation of the Ward 10 area.

139 Nathaniel Cutting, September 18, 1792, cited in "Extracts from the Diary of Nathaniel Cutting," *Proceedings of the Massachusetts Historical Society* 12 (1873), p. 63.

140 *Boston Gazette and Country Journal*, September 3, 1792.

141 Cited in Clapp, Jr., *Boston Stage*, p. 9.

142 *Boston Gazette and Country Journal*, November 26, 1792.

143 See advertisements in the *Independent Chronicle and Universal Daily Advertiser* and the *Boston Gazette and Country Journal*, Fall, 1792.

144 *Boston Gazette and Country Journal*, November 12, 1792.

145 See Clapp, Jr., *Boston Stage*, p. 12. Also see the *American Apollo*, December 7, 1792. The *Apollo* was supported by members of the Tontine, and gives an account of the incident weighted in their favor.

146 A sarcastic letter appeared in the *Boston Gazette and Country Journal* on December 24, 1792, just a few weeks after the Board Alley incident, suggesting that the theater's supporters offer "the gift of a piece of land . . . sufficiently spacious and conveniently situated to build a State House," as a "strong inducement for the House of

Representatives at their next session to accommodate [the] injured persons with a repeal of the law prohibiting stage plays." The letter is particularly interesting, since it seems to suggest that the Tontiners were not above a kind of *quid pro quo* offer to the government, and, moreover, that the government's objections to the theater were not based on moral issues, but self-interest.

147 See the Journals of the House of Representatives and Journals of the Senate, May 1792–March 1793. The vote was taken on March 26, 1793. Also see *Independent Chronicle and Universal Daily Advertiser*, April 12, 1793, for a list of which initiatives were approved and which were not approved.

148 For a complete list of the original theater subscribers, see the Record Book in the Federal Street Theatre Collection at the Boston Public Library. There were fifty-five original subscribers. It is interesting to note that the Record Book records the intention of the subscribers to "wait upon his excellency Governor Hancock," in order that "he may have the opportunity of being a subscriber." Given Hancock's long-standing opposition to the theater and the Tontiners, this was certainly a bold move – and one that was apparently rejected by Hancock.

149 Gardiner tried to rally support for the Boston theater by appealing to Boston's competitive spirit, noting that "strangers complain much for a want of resort [in Boston] . . . and they leave us for New York or Philadelphia." See Gardiner's speech on the theater, pp. 15–16. Gardiner and Morris also emphasized the fact that every polished civilization from the Greeks to the Elizabethans had maintained a permanent theater.

150 The Federal Street Theatre was designed and built by Charles Bulfinch, with the aid of the Tontine Construction Company. The architect of the Chestnut Street Theatre remains in dispute, partly because final construction on the building was not completed until 1805 and various alterations in the design took place during that time. For a detailed account of the evolution of the Chestnut Street Theatre's design, see McNamara, *American Playhouse*, pp. 104–112.

151 For an engraving which depicts both the Tontine Crescent and the Federal Street Theatre, see Douglass Shand-Tucci, *Built in Boston: City and Suburb, 1800–1950* (Amherst: University of Massachusetts Press, 1988), p. 6.

152 Walter Muir Whitehill described the Tontine Crescent as a "spectacular innovation," having "an elegance reminiscent of the Adam brothers in London, or the dignified symmetries of Bath." The Tontine Crescent consisted of sixteen three-story houses. See Whitehill, *Boston*, pp. 52–53. Also see Kirker, *Bulfinch's Boston*.

153 Federal Street Theatre Collection, Boston Public Library.

154 *Dunlap's American Daily Advertiser*, February 4, 1793.

155 See Pollock, *Philadelphia Theatre*, for activities of small theater companies in Philadelphia during this period. See the Federal Street Theatre Collection at the Boston Public Library for correspondence between Morton and Wignell.

156 Abby Hamilton to Sarah Bache, November 25, 1792, Hamilton Collection, Historical Society of Pennsylvania.

157 Henry Jackson to Henry Knox, January 26, 1794, Henry Knox Papers.

158 McNamara, *American Playhouse*, p. 108. Note that McNamara's figure is from 1820, by which time the theater had undergone substantial renovations. From correspondence

among Wignell, Reinagle, and the theater trustees, it seems that the land on which the theater was built cost approximately $20,000, and that the theater building itself cost substantially more. When the theater finally opened in February, 1794, after a delay due to the yellow fever epidemic, Wignell and Reinagle were in debt for an additional $20,000 to $35,000. This estimate is based on accounts for the theater, which do not specify which debts are ongoing and which are new. See account records for the theater dated October 24 and 28, 1794 in the Henry Hill Collection, Library Company of Philadelphia.

159 *Dunlap's Daily Advertiser*, February 15, 1793.
160 See Karen Weyler, "A Speculating Spirit: Trade, Speculation, and Gambling in Early American Fiction," *Early American Literature*, 31/3(1996), p. 207. Weyler argues that the 1790s saw a transition from selflessness to selfishness, in terms of profit-making and speculation. This certainly seems to have been the case in both Boston and Philadelphia. Members of the wealthiest classes in both cities became heavily invested in private land speculation and turnpike deals during the first years of the 1790s. Also see *Dunlap's Daily Advertiser*, February 28, 1793.
161 *Dunlap's Daily Advertiser*, March 1, 1793.
162 Ibid., March 15, 1793 (Supplement).
163 Because of the fever, Wignell took the company to New Jersey for a truncated season. The Chestnut Street house lost approximately six months' revenue in the fever disaster, and accrued an additional $20,000 in debts.
164 Martin S. Pernick, "Parties, Politics, and Pestilence: Epidemic Yellow Fever in Philadelphia and the Rise of the First Party System," in *A Melancholy Scene of Devastation: The Public Response to the 1793 Philadelphia Yellow Fever Epidemic* (Philadelphia: Science History Publications, 1997), p. 119.
165 Increase Sumner to the Honorable William Cushing, February 14, 1794, Cushing Family Papers, 1650–1840, Massachusetts Historical Society.

3 "A democracy of glee"

1 Clapp, Jr., *Boston Stage*, p. 5.
2 *Columbian Centinel*, January 29, 1794.
3 Ibid.
4 Reference made to the Board Alley Theatre, Nathaniel Cutting, September 18, 1792, cited in "Extracts from the Diary of Nathaniel Cutting," p. 63.
5 Clapp, Jr., *Boston Stage*, pp. 19–20. Also see McNamara, *American Playhouse*, pp. 121–123.
6 Clapp, Jr., *Boston Stage*, pp. 19–20; McNamara, *American Playhouse*, pp. 121–123.
7 Cited in McNamara, *American Playhouse*, pp. 115–116.
8 For more information about recorded impressions of foreign travelers, see William Pencak, "In Search of the American Character: French Travelers in Eighteenth Century Pennsylvania," *Pennsylvania History* 55/1 (January 1988), pp. 2–30.
9 McNamara, *American Playhouse*, pp. 115–116.
10 Perez Morton to Alexander Reinagle, October 17, 1793, Federal Street Theatre Collection, Boston Public Library.

11 Clapp, Jr., *Boston Stage*, pp. 22–23. Powell initially had a partner in the management of the Federal Street house, by the name of Baker. He and Baker quarreled a few months after the theater's opening and Baker left the company. Neither Clapp's nor Dunlap's histories offer much personal background on Powell, and he has left little correspondence, beyond his interactions with the Federal Street Trustees, and public materials related to the Haymarket Theatre, which appeared in the Boston newspapers.

12 Dunlap, *History of the American Theatre*, vol. 1, p. 176.

13 Henry Brooke, *Gustavus Vasa, or The deliverer of his country*, with alterations and amendments as performed at the New Theatre in Boston (Boston: John West, 1794), p. 30.

14 Ibid., p. 62.

15 Faye E. Dudden, *Women in the American Theatre: Actresses and Audiences, 1790–1870* (New Haven: Yale University Press, 1994), p. 18.

16 Judith Sargent Murray, *The Gleaner, A Miscellaneous Production in three volumes* (Boston: I. Thomas Andrews and E. T. Andrews, 1798), pp. 225–240, section xxiv on the theater. Note that the work was originally published under the pseudonym "Constantina." Faye Dudden offers a brief, but interesting, discussion of Murray as an "early feminist author." See Dudden, *Women in the American Theatre*, pp. 18–19.

17 William Dunlap, cited in Odell, *Annals*, vol. ii, p. 346.

18 Ibid., pp. 345–346.

19 *General Advertiser*, February 24, 1794.

20 Typical lyrics from *The Castle of Andalusia* include: "Love, gay illusion/Pleasing delusion/What sweet intrusion/Possesses the mind!" Hardly the stuff of republican heroism. See *The Songs in the Castle of Andalusia, a Comic Opera, as Performed at the New Theatre, Chesnut Street* (Philadelphia: Mathew Carey, 1794), p. 9. Library Company of Philadelphia.

21 Sporadic reviews of plays appear in both Boston and Philadelphia papers throughout the 1790s. I have tried to include what I feel to be the most pertinent information from the early reviews (in this case, information that relates to the plays as reflective of American culture/character). The reviews are often entertaining, such as the May 12, 1794, Boston *Independent Chronicle and Universal Daily Advertiser* comments on Charles Stuart Powell's performance as Richard III, which recommends that Powell "lay aside his guttural mode of pronouncing Tragedy," and observes that the "impropriety" of the costumes in the production "was too glaring to pass without censure." However, since they are the opinion of only a limited number of individuals, they should not be accepted as a general consensus on the quality of the theater.

22 *General Advertiser*, March 24, 1794.

23 Ibid., February 24, 1794.

24 Ibid., February 25, 1794.

25 Wood, *Creation of the American Republic*, pp. 471–519.

26 Thornton, *Cultivating Gentlemen*, p. 18.

27 For more information on the bank controversy, see Hammond, *Banks and Politics*, p. 115.

28 See John L. Brooke, "Ancient Lodges and Self-Created Societies: Voluntary Association and the Public Sphere in the Early Republic," in Ronald Hoffman and Peter J.
   Albert, eds., *Launching the Extended Republic: The Federalist Era* (Charlottesville, VA:
   University Press of Virginia, 1996), pp. 273–377. Brooke notes that "voluntary societies
   stood at the epicenter of efforts to define and redefine the public arena in the new nation; all through the 1790s they provided both vehicle and issue for republican strife,"
   p. 276. Philadelphians Peter DuPonceau and John Swanwick (theater shareholders)
   were among the most vocal new members of Pennsylvania's Democratic-Republican
   Society. For more information on the activities of the Democratic-Republican Society of Pennsylvania and their pro-French policies, see the minutes of the society for
   1793–1794, located at the Historical Society of Pennsylvania.
29 Tontiners William Tudor, Perez Morton, and Charles Jarvis were members of
   Boston's Constitutional Society. While they seemed to have moved away from allegiance to the Federalist cause, it should be noted that they continued to work and
   interact with some of Massachusetts's most powerful Federalist families. See Paul
   Goodman, *Democratic-Republicans of Massachusetts*, pp. 99–100. For information on
   William Tudor's political allegiance, see Charles Warren, *Jacobin and Junto; or, Early
   American Politics as Viewed in the Diary of Dr. Nathaniel Ames, 1758–1822* (Cambridge,
   MA: Harvard University Press, 1931).
30 I have summarized the rise of party conflict in the early national period, including only the most relevant information that affected incidents in the playhouse.
   For more information on the rise of popular parties in the early national period, and responses to the French Revolution, see Waldstreicher, *Perpetual Fetes*,
   and Newman, *Parades*. For more information on the growth of political parties in Massachusetts see Goodman, *Democratic-Republicans of Massachusetts*; for
   material on party controversy in Pennsylvania see Harry Marlin Tinkcom, *The Republicans and Federalists in Pennsylvania, 1790–1801* (Harrisburg: Pennsylvania Historical and Museum Commission, 1950). Ethel E. Ramusson discusses the bitterness between Federalists and their former allies, turned Republican, in her article,
   "Democratic Environment: Aristocratic Aspiration," *Pennsylvania Magazine of History and Biography*, 90/2 (April 1966), pp. 155–182. In particular, she notes that after
   John Swanwick's defection from the Federalist parties, many of his former friends
   "threatened to kick him in the streets if he says a word in favor of democracy,"
   p. 177.
31 *Independent Chronicle and Universal Daily Advertiser*, January 23, 1794.
32 Ibid., January 30, 1794. It is interesting to note that the author observes that there
   are few "American" tunes/cultural manufactures available to fill the theater, and that
   America's art is essentially a European import!
33 Sarah L. Flucker to Lucy Knox, February 15, 1794, Henry Knox Papers. The Flucker
   family was Federalist in its political leanings.
34 Including Tontiner and theater founder Charles Jarvis.
35 Increase Sumner to the Hon. William Cushing, February 14, 1794, Cushing Family
   Papers, 1650–1840, Massachusetts Historical Society.
36 William Cushing to Increase Sumner, February 24, 1794, Cushing Family Papers,
   1650–1840, Massachusetts Historical Society.

37 *Columbian Centinel*, February 22, 1794.

38 *Federal Orrery*, January 14, 1796.

39 See the *General Advertiser*, February 19, 1794, February 25, 1794, February 26, 1794, February 28, 1794, and May 7, 1794 for mention of the audience demands for "Ça Ira." It is interesting to note that after March 3, 1794, the theater managers stopped running the statement which proclaimed that audience song requests would not be accommodated.

40 Ibid., February 19, 1794.

41 Ibid., February 28, 1794.

42 Liam Riordan, "'O dear, what can the matter be?': Political Culture and Popular Song in Benjamin Carr's *Federal Overture*," unpublished paper, December 1995. I am grateful to Liam for sharing his research with me at the McNeil Center for Early American Studies.

43 See letters from Sarah L. Flucker to Lucy Knox, February 15, 1794, Henry Knox Papers, and letters from Increase Sumner to William Cushing, February 14, 1794, Cushing Family Papers, 1650–1840, Massachusetts Historical Society. Note that Clapp's *Boston Stage* denies that any Boston theater riots took place in 1794 – he does, however, allude to one in Philadelphia, but does not provide additional details. Clapp, Jr., *Boston Stage*, p. 23.

44 See Faye Dudden's interesting interpretation of Rowson's career as a strategic balance between political activist, feminist, and capitalist. Dudden, *Women in the American Theatre*, pp. 9–11.

45 Susanna Rowson, "America, Commerce, Freedom" (Philadelphia, 1794), New York Public Library.

46 Clapp, Jr., *Boston Stage*, p. 22.

47 *Columbian Centinel*, February 5, 1794.

48 Ibid., February 12, 1794.

49 Theatrical prologues of the period were, in many ways, analogous to the formal toasts that accompanied almost every public occasion during this period (and which were printed in the newspapers). David Waldstreicher's *Perpetual Fetes* offers an extensive discussion of toasts, their content, and symbolic meaning.

50 Susanna Rowson, *Slaves in Algiers* (Philadelphia: Wrigley and Berriman, 1794), prologue.

51 Rowson came under attack by William Cobbett, the arch-Federalist Philadelphia editor better known as "Peter Porcupine." Cobbett objected to the "feminist" tone of Rowson's writings, deeming it improbable that the heroine of *Slaves in Algiers* should be the only rational voice of republican thought. See William Cobbett, *A Kick for a Bite; or Review upon Review; with a Critical Essay on the Works of Mrs. Rowson*, 2nd edition (Philadelphia: Thomas Bradford, 1796). See also Amelia Howe Kritzer, "Playing with Republican Motherhood: self-representation in plays by Susanna Haswell Rowson and Judith Sargent Murray," *Early American Literature* 31/2 (1966), pp. 150–166.

52 By 1795, Philadelphian barber-cum-playwright John Murdock was *demanding* that the Chestnut Street managers stage his works, claiming that he had as much right as any British author or member of the gentry to express his views in the theater. Also

in 1795, Boston mechanics took their first tentative steps towards the formation of a mechanics association, a society intended to sponsor the same type of lavish social entertainments that had been the province of the Boston elite. This development will be discussed in chapter 4.

53 "The Glass, or Speculation: A Poem Containing an Account of the Ancient and Genius of the Modern, Speculators" (New York, 1791), p. 1.

54 *Dunlap's Daily Advertiser*, February 15, 1793.

55 Weyler, "Speculating Spirit," p. 207.

56 The first of these corporations, the Asylum Company, was founded by Robert Morris and John Nicholson in 1794 (though in fact Morris and Nicholson had been acquiring property for the company as early as 1792). The Asylum Company controlled approximately six million acres of land in western Pennsylvania, which it planned to sell to French immigrants fleeing the revolution. The venture gave Morris and his associates control over a sizable portion of Luzerne, Northumberland, and Northampton Counties, and would permit them to have a substantial voice in how the land was settled and developed. For information about the structure of the company, see the *Articles of Agreement, Asylum Company* (Philadelphia: Poulson, August 26, 1794). Also see *Plan of the Association of the Asylum Company* (Philadelphia: Aitken and Son, 1795). This edition contains improvements and changes made to the original 1794 agreement.

57 This information is compiled from lists of members/subscribers to each of the four land companies, housed at the Historical Society of Pennsylvania, and from the list of original subscribers to the Chestnut Street Theatre in the Chestnut Street Theatre Collection at the Historical Society of Pennsylvania. It should be noted that some of the names on the original subscribers' list for the Theatre are either illegible or undecipherable, so I have not been able to match those names to ones which might appear in the land company lists.

58 *Independent Chronicle and Universal Daily Advertiser*, March 10, 1794 and March 13, 1794.

59 *Philadelphia General Advertiser*, February 24, 1794.

60 For material related to *The Contrast* and early American drama, see Jeffrey Richards's excellent bibliography and prefatory comments in Jeffrey H. Richards, ed., *Early American Drama*, New York: Penguin Group, 1997); Lucy Elizabeth Rinehart, "A Nation's 'Noble Spectacle': Royall Tyler's *The Contrast* as Metatheatrical Commentary," *American Drama*, 3/2 (1994), pp. 29–52; John Evelev; "*The Contrast*: The Problem of Theatricality and Political and Social Crisis in Postrevolutionary America," *Early American Literature* 31/1 (1996), pp. 74–97; Jürgen C. Wolter, ed., *The Dawning of American Drama: American Dramatic Criticism, 1746–1915* (Westport, CT: Greenwood Press, 1993).

61 A limited run does not necessarily indicate that a play was unpopular. Because the audience "pool" of the time was relatively limited, managers did their best to offer a constantly rotating menu of plays. Therefore, a play could be extremely successful, and still only have one or two showings over a several year period. Tyler's *The Contrast* debuted in a December 1, 1787 reading by Thomas Wignell at the City Tavern. For more information about early performances, see Pollock, *Philadelphia Theatre*, p. 407.

62 *General Advertiser*, April 1, 1794.

63 Ruth Harsha McKenzie, "Organization, Production, and Management at the Chestnut Street Theatre, Philadelphia from 1791 to 1820," Ph.D. dissertation, Stanford University, 1952. McKenzie offers a line-by-line analysis of selected scripts used at the Chestnut Street Theatre, altered by Thomas Wignell. I have compared McKenzie's cuts with my own readings of the scripts. All further citations from the Chestnut Street promptbooks are based on my own readings.

64 It should be noted that theaters did occasionally publish versions of scripts with the prompter's changes. One example is Henry Brooke's *Gustavus Vasa, or The deliverer of his country*, published "with alterations and amendments as performed at the New Theatre in Boston," printed by John West, Boston, 1794.

65 Pollock, *Philadelphia Theatre*. See index for list of dates and years of performance.

66 See the outstanding promptbook collection at the Library Company of Philadelphia for more information. The Library Company's copy of *Rosina* contains one humorous note handwritten by the prompter on the front inside page of the script: "I foresee what will happen to this orchestra with a Dutch leader knowing no English."

67 Richard Cumberland, *The Carmelite*, Promptbook Collection, Library Company of Philadelphia.

68 Richard Cumberland, *The Box Lobby Challenge*, Promptbook Collection, Library Company of Philadelphia.

69 *Pennsylvania Gazette*, September 10, 1794.

70 *Federal Orrery*, January 14, 1796. Hodgkinson retaliated against Paine by advertising an afterpiece called "The New Bow-Wow," which ran concurrently with cautions to Paine to stop his "barking" against Hodgkinson. I have not been able to locate a text for "The New Bow-Wow," unfortunately.

71 Waldstreicher, *Perpetual Fetes*, p. 92.

72 David R. Brigham, *Public Culture in the Early Republic: Peale's Museum and Its Audience* (Washington: Smithsonian Institution Press, 1995), pp. 1–16.

73 "At a General Meeting of Subscribers to the New Theatre," June 25, 1795, Chestnut Street Theatre Collection, Historical Society of Pennsylvania.

74 Letter from William Tudor to Charles Stuart Powell, March 4, 1795, Tudor Ice Co. Collection, Baker Library, Harvard Business School.

75 Ibid.

4 Butcher, baker, candlestick maker

1 Shils, "Center and Periphery," p. 15.

2 The evolution of the Tammany Society and its connection to the John Street Theatre and the New York elite will be discussed in chapter 5. It is important to note, however, that while the timeline for the building and opening of the Park Theatre does not correspond to those of the Chestnut and Federal Street playhouses, the timeline for rising mechanic discontent in each city is roughly synchronous. In each case, that unrest had an impact on the elites' ability to enjoy their theatrical entertainments.

3 An earlier version of John Murdock's struggle with the Chestnut Street Theatre appears in *The Journal of American Drama and Theatre*. See Heather S. Nathans,

"Trampling Native Genius: John Murdock *versus* The Chestnut Street Theatre," *Journal of American Drama and Theatre*, 14/1 (2002), pp. 29–43.

4 John Murdock, *The Beau Metamorphasized; or The Generous Maid* (Philadelphia: Joseph C. Charless, 1800).

5 Daniel F. Havens, *The Columbian Muse of Comedy: The Development of a Native Tradition in Early American Social Comedy, 1787–1845* (Carbondale: Southern Illinois University Press, 1973).

6 Ronald Schultz, *The Republic of Labor: Philadelphia Artisans and the Politics of Class, 1720–1830* (New York: Oxford University Press, 1993), p. 128.

7 Henry Simpson, *The Lives of Eminent Philadelphians, Now Deceased* (Philadelphia: William Brotherhead, 1859), p. 87.

8 It should be noted that a third event may also have factored into contemporary views on slavery: the 1793 slave uprising in Saint-Domingue led by Toussaint Louverture. Refugees from the rebellion streamed into the United States in 1793 (the character of George Friendly Jr. in Murdock's play is engaged to a refugee from the rebellion).

9 See Pernick, "Parties, Politics, and Pestilence."

10 *A Narrative of the Proceedings of the Black People During the Late Awful Calamity in Philadelphia* (Philadelphia, 1794), pp. 17–18. Note that Allen and Jones were refuting printer Mathew Carey's assertion that Philadelphia blacks had used the time of crisis to loot the white homes they visited. Allen and Jones reminded Carey that since he had *fled* the city during the fever, he was in no position to speak about the events that had taken place during his absence.

11 Tench Coxe Collection, Historical Society of Pennsylvania.

12 The Democratic-Republicans were not unanimously opposed to slavery. However, even those who still tacitly supported the system, like Thomas Jefferson, were deeply conflicted over its continuance in a supposedly democratic system.

13 *Address of a Convention of Delegates from the Abolition Society to the Citizens of the United States* (Philadelphia, 1794), p. 5.

14 See the list of subscribers for Murdock's 1795 printing of *The Triumphs of Love*.

15 Schultz, *Republic of Labor*, p. 128.

16 One of the chief attractions of Burk's *Bunker-Hill* was the realistic scene painting, which, according to some critics, attracted as much audience approval as the play's patriotic subject matter.

17 Playwrights such as John Daly Burk (an Irish immigrant and Boston newspaper editor), Royall Tyler (a Harvard graduate who had once aspired to marry John Adams's daughter), Robert Treat Paine (Boston newspaper editor and offspring of a well-connected Boston family), and William Dunlap (who had received formal training in the arts) had a better "claim" to genius than did a professional hairdresser. As the rise of literary magazines and "gentlemen playwrights," such as James Nelson Barker and Robert T. Conrad, in the early nineteenth century, suggests, for many Americans, the arts remained the province of the leisured and educated class.

18 Murdock offers an account of his efforts to stage his first play in the Introduction to *The Beau Metamorphasized*.

19 Jennifer Stiles offers a different interpretation of the George–Sambo relationship in her essay, "Import or Immigrant? The Representation of Blacks and Irish on the

American Stage from 1767–1856," *Journal of American Drama and Theatre* 12/2 (Spring 2000), pp. 38–54. Stiles places Murdock's treatment of black (and Irish) characters in the context of a broader survey of black/Irish stereotypes in the early national theatre.

20 See Billy G. Smith, *The "Lower Sort": Philadelphia's Laboring People, 1750–1800* (Ithaca: Cornell University Press, 1990) for a discussion of urban overcrowding, Irish immigration, and increased mortality rates in the post-war period.

21 John Murdock, *The Triumphs of Love, or Happy Reconciliation* (Philadelphia: R. Folwell, 1795), p. 22.

22 Ibid., p. 21.

23 Ibid., p. 22.

24 For more information on the Democratic-Republican societies of the early national period, see Philip S. Foner, ed., *The Democratic-Republican Societies, 1790–1800: A Documentary Sourcebook of Constitutions, Declarations, Addresses, Resolutions, and Toasts* (Westport, CT: Greenwood Press, 1976).

25 Royall Tyler, *The Contrast*, p. 60 in Arthur Hobson Quinn, ed., *Representative American Plays: From 1767 to the Present Day*, 6th edition (New York: Appleton-Century-Crofts, Inc., 1930).

26 The exclusivity and elitism of the Society of the Cincinnati provoked a strong negative response among many of the working-class males who had fought during the Revolution. The rise of the "Ancient and Honorable Artillery Company" was, in some measure, a response to the Cincinnati. Most of the members of the Ancient and Honorable companies were drawn from the artisan class.

27 Murdock, *Triumphs of Love*, pp. 19–20.

28 Schultz, *Republic of Labor*, p. 118.

29 Newman, *Parades*, p. 89.

30 *Philadelphia Gazette and Universal Daily Advertiser*, February 24, 1796.

31 *Aurora*, January 16, 1795.

32 Murdock did not name the "friends" who were able to compel production of his play, but his list of subscribers for the published version of the script includes some powerful members of Philadelphia's Democratic-Republican society, as well as some of the Pennsylvania delegates to the Abolition Society (Benjamin Rush and Tench Coxe among them).

33 *Philadelphia Gazette and Universal Daily Advertiser*, February 24, 1796.

34 *Aurora*, May 25, 1795.

35 *Philadelphia Gazette and Universal Daily Advertiser*, February 24, 1796.

36 *Aurora*, February 10, 1796.

37 *Philadelphia Gazette and Universal Daily Advertiser*, February 25, 1796. The critic also added that the managers had been fully justified in refusing to re-mount the production, since they were dependent on box office revenues for their support and the play would certainly fail to make a profit.

38 Petition of the Dramatic Association to the General Assembly, *Minutes of the General Assembly*, February 16, 1789. Also see *Pennsylvania Packet*, February 17, 1789.

39 Schultz, *Republic of Labor*, p. 133.

40 Report from the *Independent Gazetteer*, cited in Bache's *Aurora*, July 9, 1795.

41 It should be noted that in 1792, the Democratic-Republicans had created their own Dancing Assembly, to rival the City Dancing Assembly dominated by the post-war elite. The two assemblies sponsored rival celebrations of Washington's birthday. However, he compromised by attending *both* and by giving the same speech of thanks to each party. Information on the *second* Dancing Assembly is housed at the Historical Society of Pennsylvania. Unfortunately, the records are incomplete, and give little indication of the success or duration of the group. It should also be noted that the two dancing assemblies are "lumped together" under the heading "City Dancing Assembly," though they were clearly two separate and distinct organizations.

42 *Aurora*, January 16, 1795.

43 Ibid., November 2, 1795.

44 Ibid., October 5, 1795.

45 Ibid., November 23, 1795.

46 There is a historical marker on this site – though no marker exists for the Chestnut Street Theatre, which is now the site of an administrative building.

47 *Aurora*, February 21, 1795.

48 Ibid., November 4, 1795.

49 *Philadelphia Gazette and Universal Daily Advertiser*, January 14, 1796.

50 It should be remembered that members of the company and members of the orchestra were generally not American. Much of the acting company was from Britain, while the orchestra included British, French, and Dutch emigrés. The "American" audience at the Chestnut Street house may have resented the arrogance of a "foreign" orchestra in refusing to respond to their requests. For information on the composition of theater orchestras during this period, see Susan L. Porter, *With an Air Debonair: Musical Theatre in America, 1785–1815* (Washington: Smithsonian Institution Press, 1991). See especially chapter 9, "The Orchestra in the Theatre."

51 *Philadelphia Gazette and Universal Daily Advertiser*, February 22, 1796.

52 See listings of Ricketts's offerings in Pollock's *Philadelphia Theatre*.

53 *Philadelphia Gazette and Universal Daily Advertiser*, February 22, 1796.

54 Ibid., February 27, 1796. The reviewer may be protesting the more formal music favored by Reinagle (himself a gifted composer). Porter's *With an Air Debonair* discusses the evolving form of American musical theater during this period, but makes no specific mention of whether Scotch and Irish tunes indicated a particular *political* agenda.

55 Schultz, *Republic of Labor*, p. 142. I mentioned in chapter 3 that from 1792 to 1798 Pennsylvania was rife with land speculation companies, and that many of the wealthiest men in the state, including several prominent Federalist theater supporters such as Robert Morris and William Bingham, were heavily involved in these projects.

56 *Philadelphia Gazette and Universal Daily Advertiser*, March 4, 1796.

57 Thomas Sedgewick, a Federalist of Stockbridge, MA, wrote to his friend Ephraim Williams from Philadelphia concerning the rash of stock and speculation disasters, noting, "I am not sorry that the bubble of speculation has burst... Every moment's continuation of those vile causes would have given them a more malign influence." Sedgewick specifically mentions Morris and Nicholson as two men particularly hard-hit by the crisis. Thomas Sedgewick to Ephraim Williams, December 24, 1796, Sedgewick Family Papers, Massachusetts Historical Society.

58 *Philadelphia Gazette and Universal Daily Advertiser*, March 4, 1796.
59 *Aurora*, April 26, 1796.
60 See Tinkcom, *Republicans and Federalists*, pp. 159–162, for details on voting margins.
61 Ibid., pp. 168–172.
62 Pollock, *Philadelphia Theatre*, p. 59.
63 Ibid., p. 61.
64 An earlier discussion of the Federal Street Theatre's controversy with the Boston Mechanics appeared in the *New England Theatre Journal*. See Heather S. Nathans, "'All of the Federalist School?': Choosing Sides and Creating Identities in the Boston Theatre Wars," *New England Theatre Journal* 11 (2000), pp. 1–18.
65 *Polar Star*, October 6, 1796.
66 See Gary J. Kornblith, "Artisan Federalism: New England Mechanics and the Political Economy of the 1790s," in Ronald Hoffman and Peter J. Albert, eds., *Launching the Extended Republic: The Federalist Era* (Charlottesville, VA: University Press of Virginia, 1996).
67 See John Alden, "A Season in Federal Street: J. B. Williamson and the Boston Theatre, 1796–1797," *Proceedings of the American Antiquarian Society* 65 (1955), pp. 9–74. See also Richard Stoddard, "The Haymarket Theatre, Boston," *Educational Theatre Journal* (March 1975), pp. 63–70. Recently, Steve Wilmer and Ginger Strand have both described the theater wars in the early Republic as political showdowns between Federalists and Republicans. While this may apply in some cases, it was certainly not the case in the Federal Street/Haymarket struggle. See Ginger Strand's essay, "The Theater and the Republic: Defining Party on Boston's Early Rival Stages," in Jeffrey H. Mason and J. Ellen Gainor, eds., *Performing America: Cultural Nationalism in American Theatre* (Ann Arbor: University of Michigan Press, 1999), pp. 19–37. See also Steve Wilmer, "Partisan Theatre in the Early Years of the United States," *Theatre Survey* 40/2 (1999), pp. 1–25.

Interestingly, Charles Jarvis appears to have purchased one share in the Haymarket Theatre, though his name does not appear in any other connection with the playhouse. Jarvis had a stroke or seizure in 1796, and may have been unable to participate in overseeing the house for some period of time. In a letter to his wife, Thomas Dwight notes, "Dr. Jarvis rose from the table and was seized with a fit," which Dwight says was diagnosed as either epilepsy or apoplexy. Thomas Dwight to Hannah Dwight, February 4, 1796, Dwight-Howard Papers, Massachusetts Historical Society.
68 Clapp, Jr., *Boston Stage*, pp. 35–36.
69 Ibid., p. 6.
70 Thwing, *Inhabitants and Estates*, records the names and professions of the proprietors of the Haymarket Theatre.
71 It should be noted that the Tontiners encompassed both members of the Federalist Essex Junto (see below) and the Democratic-Republicans. Though these two factions were political opponents, they shared common financial goals through the Tontine.
72 The Ancient and Honorable Artillery company was, in many ways, similar to the Society of the Cincinnati. However, the Cincinnati was a brotherhood of former Revolutionary officers, while the Ancient and Honorable Artillery Company admitted men of lower military and social rank.

73 *Columbian Centinel*, January 29, 1794. Note that Benjamin Russell's *Centinel* praises the theater, perhaps in an attempt to generate curiosity and enthusiasm.

74 In a letter to the Federal Street Trustees in January, 1797, manager John Williamson noted that the Haymarket had begun as "the desperate efforts of spleen and ambition." See the Federal Street Theatre Collection, Boston Public Library.

75 The proprietors appointed Colonel John Steele Tyler, brother of playwright Royall Tyler, to the management of the theater. Colonel Tyler occasionally solicited his brother for prologues and new plays; however, so did the Haymarket Theatre! For more information on this connection, see G. Thomas Tanselle, *Royall Tyler* (Cambridge, MA: Harvard University Press, 1967).

76 *Massachusetts Mercury*, April 5, 1796.

77 Clapp, Jr., *Boston Stage*, p. 36.

78 Prologue to be spoken at the Theatre, written by Robert Treat Paine, *Federal Orrery*, November 9, 1795. Paine was at that time known as Thomas Paine. He officially changed his name in the early 1800s after the death of his older brother, R. T. Paine.

79 *Constitution of the Associated Mechanics of the Town of Boston*, cited in Joseph Tinker Buckingham's *Annals of the Massachusetts Charitable Mechanics Association* (Boston, 1853). The Constitution stipulates: "The Funds in this Association shall be appropriated in promoting the interests thereof... They shall be invested in the public stock at the discretion of the Trustees."

80 Buckingham, *Annals*, p. 15. The exact amount raised in 1795 is quoted as $211.00.

81 Among the merchants petitioned were the following Tontine/Bank/Theatre affiliates: Thomas Russell, John Coffin Jones, Stephen Higginson, John Codman, Nathaniel Fellowes, and Samuel Brown. Note that among these men, Fellowes and Brown were staunch Republicans.

82 Buckingham, *Annals*, pp. 16–17.

83 For a description of the Mechanics' events, see Buckingham's *Annals*.

84 Cited in ibid., p. 12. Interestingly, when the Mechanics petitioned for incorporation in 1799 (they petitioned each year from 1795 to 1806), they observed, "When your petitioners first solicited the attention of the Honorable Legislature... such was the state of political parties in our country that extreme jealousy was a virtue; – and associations of every description were considered as rallying points for sedition," adding, "unfortunately and very unjustly, the mechanic association incurred this suspicion." The mechanics informed the Massachusetts legislature that their activities for the past three years (1796 to 1799) had been completely apolitical, and that thus they deserved to be allowed to incorporate.

85 In reviewing the membership records now housed at the present-day Massachusetts Charitable Mechanics Association, there seems to have been a moderate amount of "turnover" in membership in the early years of the organization. This seems to have been related to the paying of dues (some members may have been dropped for non-payment).

86 Paul Revere, a local hero of the Revolution, is perhaps the *best*-known and most obvious member of the mechanic class. Indeed, he served as the first president of the Mechanics Association and his name appears on the original 1791 petition circulated by Perez Morton to repeal Massachusetts's anti-theatrical legislation.

However, since his name does not appear in connection with the Haymarket Theatre (as shareholder or supporter), and since I have not found discussion of the Haymarket among his correspondence at the Massachusetts Historical Society, I have not included him in my biographies of those mechanics connected to the rise of the Haymarket.

87 Buckingham, *Annals*, p. 29.

88 See Kornblith, "Artisan Federalism," pp. 251–252. Also see John Bixler Hench, "The Newspaper in a Republic: Boston's *Centinel* and *Chronicle*, 1784–1801," Ph.D. dissertation, Clark University, 1979.

89 Eugene Perry Link, *Democratic-Republican Societies, 1790–1800* (New York: Columbia University Press, 1942), p. 133. See Kornblith, "Artisan Federalism," p. 250. In 1792, Russell got into a dispute with Senator Benjamin Austin, in which Austin insulted Russell, claiming that he was not a "gentleman," and thus not fit to comment on a particular issue being introduced at the Boston town meeting. Russell retaliated by spitting on Austin. Austin sued him for damages and was awarded one pound in compensation.

90 Lisa B. Lubow, "From Carpenter to Capitalist: The Business of Building in Post-Revolutionary Boston," in Conrad Edick Wright and Katheryn P. Viens, eds., *Entrepreneurs: the Boston Business Community, 1700–1850* (Boston: Massachusetts Historical Society and Northeastern University Press, 1997), p. 181–183. See the Suffolk County Tax Records for incomes of individual members of the Tontine and the Mechanics.

91 I have reviewed the United States Direct Tax Records of 1798 for the proprietors of the Haymarket Theatre. Among the Mechanics who held stock in the Haymarket, the wealthiest were Lemuel Gardner, a cooper, who owned a wharf with three stores, valued at $4,500, and David West, a bookseller, whose shop and property were valued at $5,000. Other estates range in value from $200, owned by Ebenezer Herring, a bricklayer, to $2,500, owned by Charles Patten, blacksmith. This information was compiled by comparing the Tax Records with the list of shareholders in the Haymarket Theatre as given in Thwing, *Inhabitants and Estates*.

92 Kornblith, "Artisan Federalism," p. 255.

93 Ibid., p. 266.

94 See proposals for the new theater in the *Massachusetts Mercury*, April 9, 1796.

95 *Columbian Centinel*, November 19, 1796.

96 Ibid., December 14, 1796.

97 See descriptions in Dunlap, *History of the American Theatre*, vol. I, p. 141. Also see Stoddard, "The Haymarket Theatre, Boston," p. 65.

98 *Massachusetts Mercury*, April 15, 1796.

99 Dunlap, *History of the American Theatre*, vol. I, p. 140.

100 *Polar Star*, October 8, 1796.

101 Ibid., December 30, 1796.

102 Ibid., December 24, 1796.

103 Ibid., October 31, 1796.

104 Hannah Cowley, *The Belle's Stratagem* (Boston: Apollo Press, 1794), "with alterations and amendments as performed at the New Theatre, Boston . . . N.B. Those passages

marked with inverted commas are omitted in representation." The 1794 edition performed at Federal Street omits a line in which the French are referred to as "frog-eating dunderheads."

105 See advertisements for January 31, 1797 and February 1, 1797: the Haymarket Theatre had offered a successful production of *The Mountaineers* on January 30, and the Federal Street Theatre announced its own production for February 1. The Haymarket had offered *The Merchant of Venice* on January 27 and received good notices; and the Federal Street advertised a forthcoming production for February 3.

106 Thomas Dwight to Hannah Dwight, February 5, 1797, Dwight-Howard Papers, Massachusetts Historical Society.

107 *Polar Star*, December 27, 1796. It is worth noting that John Daly Burk, the editor of the *Polar Star*, author of *Bunker-Hill*, and future enemy of Federalist John Adams, maintained a relatively neutral tone when discussing both theaters.

108 *Columbian Centinel*, December 29, 1796.

109 Ibid., December 31, 1796.

110 Ibid., February 22, 1797.

111 Thomas Dwight to Hannah Dwight, February 23, 1796, Dwight-Howard Papers, Massachusetts Historical Society.

112 Ibid.

113 Samuel Hewes to Republican Society, Portland, Maine, cited in Foner, ed., *Democratic-Republican Societies*, p. 266.

114 Thomas Dwight to Hannah Dwight, January 22, 1796, January 26, 1796, and January 28, 1796, Dwight-Howard Papers, Massachusetts Historical Society.

115 Clapp, Jr., *Boston Stage*, p. 57. Also see the *Independent Chronicle and Universal Daily Advertiser*, February 24, 1797, for discussion of charity benefits for Algerian captives.

116 For more about Burk's life and works outside of Clapp and Dunlap, see: Charles Campbell, *Some Materials to Serve for a Brief Memoir of John Daly Burk* (Albany: J. Munsell, 1868); Edward Avery Wyatt, "John Daly Burk: Patriot, Playwright, Historian," in *Southern Sketches 7* (Charlottesville, VA: Historical Publishing Company, 1936).

117 Cited in Richard M. Moody, *Dramas for the American Theatre, 1762–1909* (Boston: Houghton Mifflin Company, 1969).

118 Dunlap attacks the play in both his diaries and his *History of the Theatre*. Yet he himself was reduced to including it in the repertoire for July Fourth celebrations. As Odell notes, "Dunlap staged a play against which his shafts of satire could not be sufficiently barbed in 1797 . . . *Bunker-Hill* . . . It matters hugely whose box office is at stake." See Odell, *Annals*, p. 102.

119 Samuel Parkman to William White, Sr., December 14, 1796, White Family Papers Collection, American Antiquarian Society.

120 D. Mumerl (writing unclear) to William White, Sr., December 12, 1796, White Family Papers Collection, American Antiquarian Society.

121 Ibid.

122 Samuel Parkman to William White, Sr., December 14, 1796, White Family Papers Collection, American Antiquarian Society.

123 *Polar Star*, December 17, 1796.

124 Bushman, *Refinement of America*, p. 193.

125 Ibid.

126 *Columbian Centinel* reprinting article from the New York *Argus*, January 14, 1797.

127 *Columbian Centinel*, March 8, 1797.

128 *Orlando; or, Parental persecution* (Boston: Printing by John Russell, 1797), p. 64, epilogue.

129 William Dunlap apparently had the opportunity to read a copy of *Orlando*. On November 25, 1797, he described it in his diary as an "attempt at a tragedy by a young man of the name of White, who attempted playing & has published with his drama a head of himself in the character of Orlando. It is poor stuff." See Diary of William Dunlap, p. 174.

130 *Columbian Centinel*, March 11, 1797.

131 William Augustus of Charlestown to William Charles White, July 6, 1798, White Family Papers Collection.

132 White did make one brief return to the stage. In desperate need of money, he joined New York's Park Theatre for the 1800–1801 season.

133 Michael Warner, *The Letters of the Republic: Publication and the Public Sphere in Eighteenth-Century America* (Cambridge, MA: Harvard University Press, 1990), pp. 120–121.

134 Ibid., p. 121.

135 White wrote two successful plays in the early nineteenth century, before his untimely death at age thirty-eight. I will mention those plays (which differ substantially from *Orlando* in both theme and content) in chapter 6.

136 Federal Street Theatre Collection, Boston Public Library, and *Independent Chronicle and Universal Daily Advertiser*, March 6, 1797.

137 John B. Williamson to the Federal Street Trustees, January, 1797 (writing of date unclear), Federal Street Theatre Collection, Boston Public Library.

138 John Hodgkinson to the Federal Street Trustees, December 27, 1797, Federal Street Theatre Collection, Boston Public Library.

139 Thomas Dwight to Hannah Dwight, February 11, 1798, Dwight-Howard Papers, Massachusetts Historical Society.

140 Clapp, Jr., *Boston Stage*, p. 59.

141 In a letter to the Trustees, dated March 10, 1798, Charles Bulfinch says that he is disappointed at the "present unfinished state" of the theater, which he didn't feel justified the expense of $125,000 already charged to the Trustees. Charles Bulfinch to the Federal Street Trustees, March 10, 1798, Federal Street Theatre Collection, Boston Public Library.

142 Ibid.

143 John Hodgkinson to William Tudor, February 15, 1798, Federal Street Theatre Collection, Boston Public Library.

144 John Hodgkinson to William Tudor, December 8, 1798, Federal Street Theatre Collection, Boston Public Library.

145 See Conrad Edick Wright, *The Transformation of Charity in Postrevolutionary New England* (Boston: Northeastern University Press, 1992). In Appendix Two, Wright

charts the changes in tax assessments among members of the Mechanics Association.

146 John Hodgkinson to the Trustees of the Federal Street Theatre, December 11, 1798, Federal Street Theatre Collection, Boston Public Library.

5 A commercial community

1 Allan Nevins, *History of the Bank of New York and Trust Company, 1784–1934* (New York: Arno Press, 1976), p. 2.

2 Linda Grant DePauw, *The Eleventh Pillar: New York State and the Federal Constitution* (Ithaca, NY: Cornell University Press, 1966).

3 E. Wilder Spaulding, *New York in the Critical Period, 1783–1789* (New York: Columbia University Press, 1932), p. 10. It is important to recognize that while the yeomanry and mechanic population may have encouraged their representatives to vote against ratification, such protests did not automatically or permanently class them with the anti-Federalists.

4 Ibid., pp. 7–9.

5 Ibid., p. 97.

6 Ibid., p. 98.

7 Ibid., p. 101.

8 Ibid., p. 103.

9 Julius Goebel, ed., *The Law Practice of Alexander Hamilton, documents and commentary* (New York: Columbia University Press, 1964–1981), vol. I, p. 215.

10 Spaulding's work in particular contains a helpful collection of maps which trace votes of the New York Assembly between 1785 and 1788. Spaulding, *New York*, pp. 276–279.

11 *Pennsylvania Gazette*, March 3, 1784.

12 *Minutes of the Common Council, volume I, February 10, 1784–April 2, 1793* (City of New York, 1917), p. 178.

13 See Joseph N. Ireland, *Records*, p. 72. Ireland suggests that some citizens petitioned the New York government between 1785 and 1786 to protest the re-opening of the theater.

14 Cited in ibid., p. 69.

15 Edith Wharton, *The Age of Innocence* (Mineola, NY: Dover Publications, 1997 reprint), p. 31.

16 Ibid.

17 Allan McLane Hamilton, *The Intimate Life of Alexander Hamilton, based chiefly on original family letters and documents, many of which have never been published* (New York: C. Scribner's Sons, 1910), p. 172. I am greatly indebted to Christine McKay, the archivist at The Bank of New York who first drew my attention to McLane Hamilton's biography, and thus to the list of subscribers.

18 *Diary of William Dunlap (1766–1839) the memoirs of a dramatist, theatrical manager, painter, critic, novelist, and historian* (New York: Printed for the New-York Historical Society, 1930), vol. I. Dunlap mentions Sands, Henderson, Pollock, Ten Eyck, Livingston, Morton, and Hodgkinson at various points throughout his entries.

19 *Daily Advertiser*, March 12, 1794.

20 *New York Packet*, April 25, 1783.

21 Spaulding, *New York*, p. 84.

22 Nevins, *Bank of New York*, p. 3.

23 Cathy Matson, "Public Vices, Private Benefit: William Duer and His Circle, 1776–1792," in William Pencak and Conrad Edick Wright, eds., *New York and the Rise of American Capitalism: Economic Development and the Social and Political History of an American State, 1780–1870* (New York: New-York Historical Society, 1989), p. 97.

24 Ibid.

25 Nevins, *Bank of New York*, p. 4–5.

26 Ibid., p. 4.

27 Matson, "Public Vices," p. 98.

28 Ibid., p. 107.

29 Henrietta Maria Colden to John Laurance, April 11, 1792, John Laurance Papers, New-York Historical Society.

30 Burrows and Wallace, *Gotham*, p. 301.

31 See ibid. Also see Rufus Wilmont Griswold, *The Republican Court, Or American Society in the Days of Washington* (New York: D. Appleton and Company, 1855) for a description of lifestyles among the post-war rich and famous.

32 See the Print Collections of the American Antiquarian Society.

33 Burrows and Wallace, *Gotham*, p. 306.

34 *New-York Journal*, January 18, 1792.

35 See the Tontine Coffee House Collection, 1789–1823, at the New-York Historical Society. Also see the *Constitution and Nominations of the Subscribers to the Tontine Coffee House* (New York, 1796), New-York Historical Society.

36 Alfred F. Young, *The Democratic-Republicans of New York: The Origins, 1763–1797* (Chapel Hill, NC: University of North Carolina Press, 1967). Young notes: "The large operators [in New York's economy] with one or two exceptions, were Federalists." See p. 171.

37 On July 31, 1793, the *New-York Journal* complained about the "aristocratic junto" in the city, conspiring with the British. As early as 1792, groups with different political affiliations and class allegiances had begun to hold separate Independence Day celebrations. For example, in his astoundingly comprehensive chronicle of the city's history, Isaac N. Stokes describes the various Fourth of July festivities taking place in the city: "The Gentlemen Merchants" dined at the Tontine Coffee House; the officers of the Society of the Cincinnati dined at the City Tavern; the officers of the militia dined in the lower rooms of the Coffee House; and the members of the Tammany Society celebrated at "Corre's" (a tavern). Stokes also notes that "Republicans of every class" were invited to "Mr. Avery's at Belvidere House," although the "members" will dine above stairs and all others will dine below. See Isaac N. Stokes, *The Iconography of Manhattan Island, 1498–1909* (Union, NJ: Lawbook Exchange; Mansfield Centre, CT: Martino Fine Books, 1998), vol. I, p. 1298.

38 Josiah Ogden Hoffman to Stephen Van Rensselaer, June 20, 1792, Misc. Mss. Hoffman, Josiah Ogden, New-York Historical Society.

39 Young, *Democratic-Republicans*, p. 202.

40 The *Columbian Gazetteer*, May 12, 1794 offers a description of the Sons of Tammany wearing "bucktails" in their hats. For a description of the early years of the Tammany Society, see Morris Robert Werner, *Tammany Hall* (New York: Doubleday, Doran & Company, 1928). In its early days, the Tammany Society included a fairly wide range of members, among them Josiah Ogden Hoffman, a noted "eastern Federalist." See Werner, p. 320. On May 7, 1792, the Gates Papers at the New-York Historical Society contain an invitation from Hoffman to Gates to attend the Society's festivities. See Josiah Ogden Hoffman to General Gates, May 7, 1792, Gates Papers, New-York Historical Society.

41 Werner, *Tammany Hall*, p. 12.

42 Stokes, *Iconography of Manhattan Island*, vol. I, p. 1285. See also Werner, *Tammany Hall*, pp. 11–12. Stokes notes that the Tammany Society tries to raise the funds to erect a new Tammany Hall, but are unable to gather enough money. They have to wait until 1811 to build their new building. See Stokes, pp. 1286–1287. See also the "Plan of the New York Tammanial Tontine Association," New-York Historical Society.

43 *Daily Advertiser*, June 6, 1792.

44 Werner, *Tammany Hall*, p. 16.

45 Stokes, *Iconography of Manhattan Island*, vol. I, p. 1296.

46 *Columbian Gazetteer*, December 21, 1793.

47 Diary of John Anderson, BV Anderson, John, New-York Historical Society.

48 Don B. Wilmeth and Christopher Bigsby, eds., *The Cambridge History of American Theatre, Volume I: Beginnings to 1870* (Cambridge: Cambridge University Press, 1998), p. 135.

49 *Daily Advertiser*, March 3, 1794.

50 Ibid., March 6, 1794.

51 See both the *Daily Advertiser*, March 7, 1794 and the *New York Journal*, March 12, 1794.

52 Ann Julia Hatton enjoyed a somewhat strange career both in the United States and in her native Great Britain. She was the eighth child in the immensely talented Kemble acting family. She assumed a variety of names during her career, some self-designated and some by marriage (she was known variously as Ann Curtis, Ann Julia Hatton, and Ann of Swansea). Information about her time in America is somewhat sketchy and contradictory. Some sources, including the Quinn Collection at the New-York Historical Society, suggest that she may have been married to an American tavern-keeper named Hatton (which would certainly account for her intimacy with members of the Tammany Society). Other accounts suggest that Hatton was a musician/performer. Percy Fitzgerald's *The Kembles* depicts her as the bane of her elder siblings (and perhaps mentally unstable). According to Fitzgerald, before her sojourn in America, she published letters in the London papers begging for funds because her wealthy family refused to contribute to her support. Although she gave public lectures on a variety of topics, she "could not conform to modesty," and remained an embarrassment to her family. Her lack of success in England may have prompted her to try her fortunes in America, and she did enjoy between three and four years of profitable work in New York through her affiliation with the Tammany Society.

Ultimately she returned to England, where her sister Sarah Siddons offered her a pension to agree to stay at least 150 miles away from her at all times. She ended her career as an author, writing novels under the name "Ann of Swansea." See Percy Fitzgerald, *The Kembles, Volume Two* (New York: Benjamin Blom, 1969), pp. 98–107.

In his diary, William Dunlap reflects on her strange career: "Mrs. Hatton is perhaps still alive. She was lame when she was here – became afterward enormously fat . . . In England [she] published novels &c under the application of Anne of Swansey [*sic*], the place of her residence." *Diary of William Dunlap*, p. 714.

53 Stokes, *Iconography of Manhattan Island*, vol. I, p. 1308.

54 *Daily Advertiser*, August 17, 1794.

55 Burrows and Wallace note that Greenwich Street (future site of the Greenwich Theatre) was "home to numerous artisans and shopkeepers as well as a small population of free blacks . . . Some merchants, professionals, and prosperous master artisans [began] to drift a bit further north." See Burrows and Wallace, *Gotham*, pp. 373–374.

56 Elizabeth Blackmar, *Manhattan for Rent, 1785–1850* (Ithaca, NY: Cornell University Press, 1989), p. 78.

57 Mary C. Henderson, *City and the Theatre: New York Playhouses from Bowling Green to Times Square* (Clifton, NJ: James T. White & Co., 1975), p. 50.

58 Blackmar, *Manhattan for Rent*, p. 78.

59 Journal of Henry Wansey, June 30, 1784, cited in Stokes, *Iconography of Manhattan Island*, vol. I, p. 1310.

60 Diary of William Strickland, BV Strickland, September 25, 1794, New-York Historical Society.

61 John Anderson comments on the building of the church in *his* diary, noting on January 1, 1794 that it is "nearly finished." Diary of John Anderson, New-York Historical Society.

62 Diary of William Strickland, September 28, 1794, New-York Historical Society.

63 Young, *Democratic-Republicans*, p. 469.

64 *Daily Advertiser*, August 19, 1794. See also Stokes, *Iconography of Manhattan Island*, vol. I, p. 1312.

65 *American Minerva*, August 29, 1794.

66 Cited in Stokes, *Iconography of Manhattan Island*, vol. I, p. 1313.

67 See the Register of Deeds at the New York City Register's Office. The Register's Office has Deeds Books and Conveyance Books that record property transactions from the pre-war period through 1915.

68 Blackmar, *Manhattan for Rent*, p. 77.

69 See the City Register of Deeds and the *New York Directory and Registry for the Year 1794* (New York: William Duncan, 1794), at the New-York Historical Society.

70 See the City Register of Deeds. It should be noted that the Registry listings sometimes make confusing jumps in terminology, between the designations of "lots" and "blocks."

71 *Votes and Proceedings of the Senate, October 1784–April 1785: Journal of the Senate of the State of New York.* (New York: S. Loudon, Printer to the State, 1785), p. 21.

72 Stokes, *Iconography of Manhattan Island*, vol. I, p. 457. Also see Griswold, *Republican Court*, pp. 13–16.

73 Griswold, *Republican Court*, p. 13.
74 See Stokes, *Iconography of Manhattan Island*, vol. I, pp. 155–156. Also see the plan for "The Vineyards" by James Willson in the Bancker Collection Box B-F, folder C, New York Public Library.
75 See the records of shareholders for The Bank of New York. Ann White is listed as holding ten shares in the Bank. Archives of The Bank of New York. I am grateful to The Bank of New York's archivist, Christine McKay, who took an interest in the quest for Ann White and did a great deal of hunting among the archives on my behalf.
76 Theatre Collection, Park Street, Museum of the City of New York. The Collection contains an artist's drawing of the cornerstone laid in 1795.
77 Stokes, *Iconography of Manhattan Island*, vol. I, p. 457. See the view of New York from Long Island, drawn in 1796 by Archibald Robinson.
78 Ibid., vol. I, p. 443. Stokes cites a letter written by Walter Rutherford, October 2, 1796, which describes the progress of the theater building.
79 See Joseph N. Ireland, *Records*, p. 128. Ireland notes when yellow fever returns to the city between 1795 and 1796. Also see the Diary of William Laight, July 13–20 and August 21, 22, 23, 1796. Laight notes where the fever appeared in the city. Diary of William Laight, BV Laight, New-York Historical Society.
80 The proprietors of both the Boston and Philadelphia theaters also fell prey to the lure of land speculation. Fortunately for them, their theaters had already been established when their financial crises struck.
81 Various loans to Henderson and Sands (two of the biggest investors in the various land deals) are recorded in the account books of The Bank of New York between 1796 and 1798. It should be noted that the surviving bank books are divided into Profit and Loss Statements, Balance Sheets, and Account Ledgers. See Archives of The Bank of New York.
82 In Goebel's records of *The Law Practice of Alexander Hamilton*, the defendants' outstanding debts are listed in the accounts of their cases. See Goebel, vol. IV, pp. 228–232, 388, 372.
83 Depositors' Accounts, May, 1795–May, 1796, Archives of The Bank of New York.
84 List of Balances from Ledger, June 12, 1797, Archives of The Bank of New York.
85 Ibid. Also see Balance Sheet beginning June 12, 1797 and ending April 9, 1798, Archives of The Bank of New York.
86 *Mott and Hurton's New York Weekly Chronicle*, January 22, 1795.
87 *Daily Advertiser*, January 21, 1795.
88 James E. Cronin, ed., *Diary of Elihu Hubbard Smith, 1771–1798* (Philadelphia: American Philosophical Society, 1973), p. 157.
89 *Argus*, November 16, 1797.
90 *American Minerva*, June 13, 1796.
91 For more information on Ricketts's efforts to compete with the John Street Theatre, see James S. Moy, "The Greenwich Street Theatre, 1797–1799," *Theatre Survey*, vol. XX, no. 2, 1979, pp. 15–26. According to Moy, the site, while initially intended as one of Ricketts's touring houses for his east coast circuit, was rapidly abandoned after two short seasons. Thereafter it was used by various touring companies from 1798 to 1799, when it was sold and eventually torn down.

92 See sampling of advertisements in the *Daily Advertiser*, 1795 for notices on Mrs. Hatton, and for descriptions of other amusements on offer.

93 See the *Daily Advertiser*, March 14–March 18, 1795 for a complaint from a citizen concerned about the prospect of two theaters in the city. The writer suggests that such a plan "would be opposed by the citizens generally." Ricketts used this "concern" as an excuse for not loaning his theatre to Wignell and Reinagle's visiting company.

94 Diary of John Anderson, New-York Historical Society.

95 *Daily Advertiser*, September 12, 1797. Also see James S. Moy, "The Greenwich Street Theatre, 1797–1799," *Theatre Survey*, vol. xx, no. 2, November 1979, pp. 15–26.

96 *Argus*, April 3, 1797.

97 Diary of William Dunlap, p. 205, New-York Historical Society.

98 Ibid., pp. 203–206.

99 See Cronin, ed., *Diary of Elihu Hubbard Smith*, p. 344, entry on January 30, 1798.

100 While Dunlap's idealistic rhetoric may seem to echo the words of the Boston and Philadelphia theater founders, what seems most compelling and individual about Dunlap's vision for the theater is his lifelong commitment to promoting the arts in America, to chronicling their history, and to establishing an American cultural aesthetic. Though often forced to concede high-flown democratic principles to box office necessity, he remained deeply invested in the development of the drama in the new nation, as his diaries attest.

101 Cited in Witham, *Theatre in the Colonies*, pp. 67–68.

102 A number of Dunlap's most successful plays, including *The Father, or American Shandyism* (1789), *Darby's Return* (1789), *André* (1798), *The Glory of Columbia* (1803), and *A Trip to Niagara* (1828) tried to define the "American" character for the national audience. Dunlap also translated numerous plays, many by the prolific German author Kotzebue, including *The Stranger* (1798), *False Shame* (1799) and *Pizarro in Peru* (1800). Kotzebue's work reflected the sentimental themes gaining popularity in early nineteenth-century American literature, vaunting the power of emotion and feeling over intellect and reason.

     In addition to his passion for the arts, Dunlap also demonstrated a strong interest in political and humanitarian causes – especially that of the abolitionists. Born in Perth Amboy, New Jersey, he grew up surrounded by slave-owning families (including his own): an experience that led him to join the New York Abolition Society, serving as its Secretary for a number of years. He was also a trustee of the African School in New York and drew up a memorial for Congress against the slave trade. Upon his father's death, he freed his family's slaves. For more information on Dunlap's career and writings, see: Robert H. Canary, *William Dunlap* (New York: Twayne, 1970); Oral Sumner Coad, *William Dunlap: A Study of his Life and Works and His Place in Contemporary Culture* (New York: Russell and Russell, 1962).

103 Diary of William Laight, January 29, 1798, New-York Historical Society.

104 *Daily Advertiser*, January 31, 1798. The opening night plays included *All in a Bustle*, *As You Like It*, and *The Purse, or an American Tar*.

105 William Milns, *All in a Bustle; or The New House* (New York: Literary Printing Office, 1798), p. 14.

106 See Joseph N. Ireland, *Records*, p. 175. Receipts from the first night totaled $1,232; receipts from the second night totaled $513; and receipts from the third

night totaled $265. During the next week, the box office totals averaged $333 per night.

107 Dunlap, *History of the American Theatre*, vol. II, p. 17.

108 The John Street Theatre was sold and torn down in 1799. The Park Theatre proprietors had been farsighted enough to make a contractual agreement with Hallam, Dunlap, Hodgkinson, et al. that would prohibit them opening a theater in competition with the Park Street house (perhaps they had learned from the disaster in Boston!).

6 Into the hands of the people

1 Clapp, Jr., *Boston Stage*, p. 26. Italics original to Clapp's text.

2 William Dunlap, 1797, cited in Witham, *Theatre in the Colonies*, p. 68.

3 William Dunlap, 1797, cited ibid.

4 "Hail Columbia," cited in *Porcupine's Gazette*, April 28, 1798. No mere ten days' wonder, "Hail Columbia" rapidly made its way into the lexicon of American musical and theatrical entertainment, and remained a byword in the theater well into the first decades of the nineteenth century.

5 For more information on the XYZ Affair, see Stanley Elkins and Eric McKitrick, *The Age of Federalism: The Early American Republic, 1788–1800* (New York: Oxford University Press, 1993), pp. 582–588. Also see Richard Buel, Jr., *Securing the Revolution: Ideology and American Politics, 1789–1815* (Ithaca: Cornell University Press, 1972).

6 Elkins and McKitrick, *Age of Federalism*, p. 588.

7 *Porcupine's Gazette*, April 24, 1798. The "sacrilegious hymn" is a reference to the pro-French tune, "Ça Ira."

8 Stewart Mitchell, ed., *New Letters of Abigail Adams, 1788–1801* (Boston: Houghton Mifflin Company, 1947), pp. 164–165.

9 *Aurora*, April 26, 1798, also cited in *Porcupine's Gazette*, April 27, 1798.

10 Mitchell, ed., *New Letters of Abigail Adams*, p. 166.

11 Waldstreicher, *Perpetual Fetes*, p. 163.

12 Ibid., p. 164.

13 Buel, *Securing the Revolution*, p. 182.

14 Ultimately, it was the conflict over how the party should manage the government and the nation's relations with France that produced a schism in the Federalist party, and allowed the Republicans to win the national election of 1800.

15 During the spring of 1798, the Chestnut Street house lost three of its strongest male performers: John Moreton died, James Fennell left the stage (temporarily) to pursue a career in salt manufacture, and Thomas Cooper joined New York's John Street Company. See Gresdna Ann Doty, *The Career of Mrs. Anne Brunton Merry in the American Theatre* (Baton Rouge: Louisiana State University Press, 1971), p. 67.

16 From the *Philadelphia Gazette*, February 23, 1799, cited in Pollock, *Philadelphia Theatre*, p. 64.

17 Ricketts's Circus burned down on December 17, 1799.

18 "Resolutions and articles of agreement entered into and adopted by the proprietors of the building and lots of the New Theatre in Philadelphia," Philadelphia, 1799, Sterling Memorial Library, Yale University.

19 Eleanor Young, *Forgotten Patriot: Robert Morris* (New York: Macmillan Company, 1950), p. 219.

20 Ironically, the marble masks of Comedy and Tragedy made to adorn Morris's new home were removed after his bankruptcy and sent to the Chestnut Street Theatre!

21 The house is still standing in the western part of city, near the Schuylkill River. The estate is now known as Lemon Hill, but was known as "The Hills" when Morris owned it.

22 William B. Wood, *Personal Recollections of the Stage* (Philadelphia: Henry Carey Baird, 1855), p. 39.

23 Baltzell, *Puritan Boston*, p. 30. Other members of the Philadelphia elite *did* found important families – but not in Philadelphia. For example, the Binghams left Philadelphia in 1800 when Ann Willing Bingham became seriously ill with "lung fever." The family traveled to Madeira, hoping that the climate would help her recover, but she died en route at age thirty-seven. William Bingham moved to upstate New York, where he owned a sizable portion of land. His family remained influential in the area (Binghamton!) for several generations. By 1806, the fabulous Bingham mansion in Philadelphia had been converted into a hotel.

24 Tamara Plakins Thornton and Robert F. Dalzell have both written outstanding studies of the fates of late eighteenth- and early nineteenth-century members of the Boston elite who founded Boston's reigning families. Yet in neither of these books do the Tontiners play any significant role. See Thornton, *Cultivating Gentlemen*, and Robert F. Dalzell, Jr., *Enterprising Elite: The Boston Associates and the World They Made* (Cambridge, MA: Harvard University Press, 1987).

25 *Federal Gazette and Daily Advertiser*, February 6, 1798.

26 Goodman, *Democratic-Republicans of Massachusetts*, p. 102.

27 Ibid., p. 105.

28 Ibid., p. 101.

29 John Coffin Jones Collection, January 2, 1798, Baker Business Library, Harvard University.

30 *Massachusetts Mercury*, February 20, 1798.

31 Clapp, Jr., *Boston Stage*, p. 59.

32 Ibid.

33 Thomas Dwight to Hannah Dwight, February 2, 1798, Dwight-Howard Collection, Massachusetts Historical Society.

34 Thomas Dwight to Hannah Dwight, February 6, 1798, Dwight-Howard Collection, Massachusetts Historical Society.

35 The Bostonian Society has a fascinating watercolor by an unknown artist depicting the burning theater in the background, while the lower part of the picture shows three groups of figures: a Pan standing on the masks of Comedy and Tragedy, a mourning muse leaning on a broken column, and, in the right-hand corner, a triumphant muse and three cherubs, holding an engraving of plans for a *new* theater building, surmounted by an American eagle. The painting is obviously a reference to the

Tontiners' plans to rebuild the playhouse. A reproduction of the painting appears in Harold and James Kirker, *Bulfinch's Boston*, plate 7.

36 John Hodgkinson to Thomas Bartlett, March 13, 1798, Federal Street Theatre Collection, Boston Public Library. Hodgkinson's use of the word "party" is intriguing. I have already suggested that the schism between the Federal Street and Haymarket seemed due less to political than class rivalry. Hodgkinson's suggestion that the proprietors of the Haymarket were no longer able to *afford* to maintain the theater seems to support this contention.

37 The refusal of the Tontiners to buy the Haymarket is especially strange in light of the fact that by 1798, the Haymarket and the Federal Street had been forced into an uneasy alliance. Realizing that they could not successfully compete, they agreed to divide the theatrical season, with the Federal Street operating in the winter months and the Haymarket reserving the summer season. The burning of the Federal Street house meant that the season shifted quickly to the Haymarket.

38 *Federal Gazette and Daily Advertiser*, February 22, 1798.

39 It also offered a boon to other improvised performance sites, such as Mr. Dearborn's Exhibition Room, which offered performances by Charles and Snelling Powell. Seats were sold for the "Pit, Box, and Gallery," suggesting some type of hastily created theatrical space. See *Federal Gazette and Daily Advertiser*, February 17, 1798. Snelling Powell and J. B. Barker (manager of the Haymarket Hotel) also circulated a proposal for building a Columbian Vauxhall, as "an elegant resort of fashionable entertainment." Ibid., March 8, 1798. The project never got off the ground, perhaps because it lacked the sponsorship of the Boston elite who would have the leisure to use it.

40 "The Launch: a federal song," Newburyport, MA (?), 1798 (?), American Antiquarian Society.

41 *Boston Gazette*, July 23, 1798. "Adams and Liberty" was written by Robert Treat Paine (a.k.a. Thomas Paine), longtime supporter of the theater and firm Federalist. Although Federalist spirit was running high during this period, the Jacobins still posed a threat to their success. As Federalist Fisher Ames noted, "Jacobinism in the vicinity of Boston is not yet dead; it sleepeth." Cited in Warren, *Jacobin or Junto*, p. 74.

42 Clapp, Jr., *Boston Stage*, p. 67. It should be noted that while "formal" theater in Boston suffered, popular entertainments flourished. Pinchbeck's Pig of Knowledge and The Knowing Dog proved profitable shows during this period, as did Ricketts's Circus, which traveled to Boston in the summer of 1798. The financial success of the learned animal shows is easy to understand, since they do not require large or permanent performing spaces, but can be adapted to fit available playing areas. Nor do they require substantial expense to maintain. David Brett Mizelle has done a fascinating study of learned animal shows of the eighteenth century and their connection to notions of learning and self-fashioning. I appreciated the opportunity to discuss his work with him at the McNeil Center for Early American Studies.

43 *Massachusetts Mercury*, November 6, 1798. Also cited in Warren, *Jacobin or Junto*, p. 77.

44 *Constitutional Telegraph*, November 20, 1799.

45 Hodgkinson made an interesting attempt to break his contract with the Boston theaters. As of 1799, the law against theatrical entertainments had still not been formally
repealed (since Hancock never signed the act into law in 1793). Thus Hodgkinson
tried to assert that since theatrical entertainments were still technically illegal, his
contract with the theater could not be binding. See Dunlap's *History of the American
Theatre*, p. 114. After Hodgkinson left, a succession of managers tried to take over the
theater, each failing within a season. See Clapp's *Boston Stage* for more information.
46 Playwright and newspaper editor, John Daly Burk (*Bunker-Hill*) was prosecuted by
John Adams under the Alien and Sedition Acts for his anti-Federalist rhetoric.
47 Cited in Alfred Young, *Democratic-Republicans*, p. 478.
48 Cited ibid., p. 479.
49 See ibid., p. 495. Young notes that the "Affair of the Ferrymen" had such far-reaching
consequences that some attributed the Federalist downfall of 1800 to the incident.
50 Ibid., pp. 399–405.
51 Werner, *Tammany Hall*, pp. 22–23.
52 Richards, ed., *Early American Drama*, p. 60.
53 Lucy Rinehart, "'Manly Exercises': Post-Revolutionary Performances of Authority
in the Theatrical Career of William Dunlap," *Early American Literature*, 36/2 (2001),
pp. 263–293.
54 Odell, *Annals*, vol. 2, p. 17.
55 Ibid., p. 19.
56 Richards, ed., *Early American Drama*, p. 61.
57 Rinehart, "'Manly Exercises'," pp. 264–266.
58 William Dunlap, *André*, in Richards, ed., *Early American Drama*, p. 94.
59 Rinehart, "'Manly Exercises'," p. 277.
60 Smith died of yellow fever in 1798.
61 Fredrika J. Teute, "Sensibility in the Forest: Elihu Hubbard Smith's *Edwin and
Angelina; or The Banditti*," unpublished version of paper presented at the Second Biennial Conference of the Society of Early Americanists, 2001. My thanks to Professor
Teute for sharing a copy of her essay with me.
62 Ibid., p. 3.
63 Cronin, ed., *Diary of Elihu Hubbard Smith*, pp. 415–416.
64 Sadly, Smith died in the yellow fever epidemic of 1798, and so we are deprived of his
further insights into the evolution of the early national theater.
65 Thomas Dwight to Hannah Dwight, January 31, 1799, Dwight-Howard Papers, Massachusetts Historical Society. See Len Travers, *Celebrating the Fourth: Independence
Day and the Rites of Nationalism in the Early Republic* (Amherst: University of Massachusetts Press, 1997), p. 124. Travers mentions a Fourth of July performance at the
Haymarket in 1799, which included a three-act piece entitled "Washington," as well
as other afterpieces, including a "savage dance." Even this type of attention-getting
display could not rescue the failing theater.
66 Clapp, Jr., *Boston Stage*, p. 69.
67 Ibid., p. 70.
68 Ibid., p. 71.
69 *Constitutional Telegraph*, January 10, 1800.

70 Odell, *Annals*, vol. II, pp. 77–78. Odell also notes a somewhat humorous episode attached to the Park Theatre's efforts to honor Washington. Actor Thomas Abthorpe Cooper (apparently noted for his inattention to memorizing his lines) tried to deliver a monody on Washington's death and had to be repeatedly prompted. His disgraceful behavior earned him a public rebuke in several newspapers. See ibid.

71 Petition of the Dramatic Association to the General Assembly, *Minutes of the General Assembly*, February 16, 1789.

72 Formisano, *Transformation of Political Culture*, pp. 57–83.

73 Lance Banning, *The Jeffersonian Persuasion: Evolution of a Party Ideology* (Ithaca: Cornell University Press, 1978), p. 273.

74 Kotzebue's plays had been gaining popularity in the states towards the end of the eighteenth century, as advertisements in various papers suggest. However, his popularity appears to have increased rapidly after 1800. Dunlap translated six of his works for production at the Park Street Theatre in New York. See Frank Pierce Hill, *American Plays, printed 1714–1830: A Bibliographical Record* (New York: Burt Franklin, 1972). See also David Grimsted, *Melodrama Unveiled: American Theater and Culture, 1800–1850* (Berkeley: University of California Press, 1968), pp. 10–15.

75 Grimsted, *Melodrama Unveiled*, p. 11.

76 Banning has argued that the "Revolution of 1800" was perhaps not as sweeping as it first appeared, in terms of affecting instant changes in law and policy. He argues that Jefferson's innovations were made gradually and with a number of compromises along the way. However, the *ideological* change his administration ushered in certainly appeared revolutionary. Robert Wiebe has suggested that ultimately the controversy between Federalists and Republicans could be seen as "a struggle over the interior design of the same ideological house." Robert H. Wiebe, *The Opening of American Society: From the Adoption of the Constitution to the Eve of Disunion* (New York: Random House, 1984), p. xiii.

77 See Appendix 2 in Grimsted's *Melodrama Unveiled*, for percentages of foreign *versus* "native" plays produced in America between 1800 and 1850.

78 Hill, *American Plays*, pp. 138–145. I have not included "Dramatic dialogues" in this list.

79 Gary A. Richardson, "Plays and Playwrights, 1800–1865," in Don B. Wilmeth and Christopher Bigsby, eds., *The Cambridge History of American Theatre, Volume I: Beginnings to 1870* (Cambridge: Cambridge University Press, 1998), p. 251.

80 J. H. Nichols, *The Essex junto, or, Quixotic guardian*: a comedy in four acts by a citizen of Massachusetts (Salem, MA: Printed by Nathaniel Coverly, Jun.), 1802.

81 J. H. Nichols, *Jefferson and liberty; or, a Celebration of the fourth of March*. A patriotic tragedy: a picture of the perfidy of corrupt administration, in five acts (Boston: Sold at the Print-Office, Temple Street), 1801.

82 Richardson, "Plays and Playwrights," p. 263.

83 William Charles White, *The Clergyman's Daughter* (Boston: Joshua Belcher, 1810), p. 80.

84 Jay Fliegelman, *Declaring Independence: Jefferson, Natural Language, and the Culture of Performance* (Stanford: Stanford University Press, 1993), pp. 23–24, 189.

85 William Charles White, *Avowals of a Republican* (Worcester: Isaac Sturtevant, 1813), p. v.

86 Robert Treat Paine, prologue to William Charles White, *The Poor Lodger* (Boston: Joshua Belcher, 1811), p. 1.
87 Though Tudor, Jarvis, Morton and their associates gained political positions during the first decade of the nineteenth century, they had lost much of their financial clout. In a letter from February 14, 1805, William Tudor apologizes to his friend Henry Knox for having to demand repayment of a loan. But he claims that he needs the money to help launch his son's new business. His son, Frederic Tudor, became known as the "Ice King," for his successful ice importing business. See William Tudor to Henry Knox, February 14, 1805, Henry Knox Papers.
88 Clapp, Jr., *Boston Stage*, p. 79.
89 Though their theater ultimately failed, the Boston Mechanics continued to grow and thrive as an organization, finally receiving permission to incorporate in 1806. For more information see *The Quiet Philanthropy*, Massachusetts Charitable Mechanics Association, 1995.
90 Odell, *Annals*, vol. II, p. 172.
91 Ibid.
92 These men all have connections to the New York Tontine and The Bank of New York, suggesting that the patterns of affiliation created in the eighteenth century still persisted, even though the groups may have re-aligned themselves or self-selected out those unable or unwilling to participate.
93 See John Searle, *Interior of the reconstructed Park Theatre*, 1822. The version of the painting with the identifying names is taken from the original picture, owned by William Bayard (one of the original theater supporters), and published as a reprint by Elias Dexter, New York, 1868. See the J. Clarence Davies Collection at the Museum of the City of New York.

Epilogue: "From an infant stage"

1 Judith Sargent Murray, *The Gleaner*, section XXIV.
2 Cited in Don B. Wilmeth, *Staging the Nation: Plays from the American Theater, 1787–1909* (Boston: Bedford Books, 1998), p. 538.
3 Clapp, Jr., *Boston Stage*, p. 76.

Bibliography

Primary sources

Newspapers and journals

American Apollo (Boston)
American Minerva (New York)
Argus (Boston)
Argus (New York)
Aurora (Philadelphia)
Boston Gazette
Boston Gazette and Country Journal
Columbian Centinel (Boston)
Columbian Gazetteer (New York)
Constitutional Telegraph (Boston)
Courier (Boston)
Daily Advertiser (New York)
Dunlap's American Daily Advertiser (Philadelphia)
Federal Gazette and Daily Advertiser (Boston)
Federal Gazette and Philadelphia Daily Advertiser
Federal Orrery (Boston)
Fleet's Pocket Almanack (Boston)
The Freeman's Journal (Pennsylvania)
General Advertiser (Boston)
Independent Chronicle and Universal Daily Advertiser (Boston)
Independent Gazetteer (Pennsylvania)
Loudon's New-York Packet
Massachusetts Magazine
Massachusetts Mercury
Mott and Hurton's New York Weekly Chronicle
National Gazette
New-York Journal
New York Packet
Pennsylvania Gazette

Pennsylvania Museum
Pennsylvania Packet
Philadelphia Gazette and Universal Daily Advertiser
Philadelphia General Advertiser
Philadelphia Minerva
Polar Star (Boston)
Porcupine's Gazette (Philadelphia)
Republican Gazetteer (Boston)
Russell's Gazette (Boston)
Weyman's New York Gazette

Correspondence, business, and state records

Archives of The Bank of New York
Bancker Collection, New York Public Library
Bradford Collection, Historical Society of Pennsylvania
Chestnut Street Theatre Collection, Historical Society of Pennsylvania
City Dancing Assembly Collection, Historical Society of Pennsylvania
Clymer Papers, Cadwalader Collection, Historical Society of Pennsylvania
"Commonplace Book," *c.* 1780, Historical Society of Pennsylvania
Cushing Family Papers, Massachusetts Historical Society
Dwight-Howard Papers, Massachusetts Historical Society
Federal Street Theatre Collection, Boston Public Library
Gates Papers, New-York Historical Society
Hamilton Collection, Historical Society of Pennsylvania
Henry Hill Collection, Library Company of Philadelphia
Henry Knox Papers
John Coffin Jones Collection, Baker Business Library, Harvard University
John Laurance Papers, New-York Historical Society
Diary of John Anderson, BV Anderson, John, New-York Historical Society
Diary of William Laight, BV Laight, New-York Historical Society
Diary of Christopher Marshall, Historical Society of Pennsylvania
Diary of William Strickland, BV Strickland, New-York Historical Society
Elizabeth Wainwright Papers, Massachusetts Historical Society
Harrison G. Otis Papers, Massachusetts Historical Society
Journals of the House of Representatives, Massachusetts State House Special Collections
Journals of the Senate, Massachusetts State House Special Collections
Minutes of the Democratic-Republican Society of Pennsylvania, 1793–1794, Historical Society of Pennsylvania
Miscellaneous Manuscripts, Massachusetts Historical Society
Miscellaneous Manuscript Collection, New-York Historical Society
Pemberton Papers, Historical Society of Pennsylvania
Petition for a Clause for a Theater, Miscellaneous Documents Collection, Massachusetts Historical Society
Petition submitted by Lewis Hallam, November 9, 1788, Historical Society of Pennsylvania

"Plan of the New York Tammanial Tontine Association," New-York Historical Society
Print Collections of the American Antiquarian Society
Promptbook Collection, Library Company of Philadelphia
"Resolutions and articles of agreement entered into and adopted by the proprietors of the building and lots of the New Theatre in Philadelphia." Philadelphia, 1799, Sterling Memorial Library, Yale University.
Rowe, John. Diaries, 1764–1779. John Rowe Diaries, Massachusetts Historical Society.
Samuel P. Savage Papers, Massachusetts Historical Society
Sedgewick Family Papers, Massachusetts Historical Society
Society Collection, Historical Society of Pennsylvania
Tench Coxe Collection, Historical Society of Pennsylvania
Theatre Collection, Park Street, Museum of the City of New York
Thomas Wallcut Papers, Massachusetts Historical Society
Tontine Coffee House Collection, New-York Historical Society
Tudor Ice Co. Collection, Harvard Business School
White Family Papers Collection, American Antiquarian Society

Texts and documents

Acts and Resolves, Public and Private of the Province of Massachusetts Bay. Boston: Wright and Potter Printing Company, 1910.
Address of a Convention of Delegates from the Abolition Society to the Citizens of the United States. Philadelphia, 1794.
Address and Petition of a Number of the Clergy of Various Denominations in the City of Philadelphia to the Senate and House of Representatives of the State of Pennsylvania, Relative to the Passing of a Law Against Vice and Immorality, To which are Subjoined Some Considerations in Favor of Said Petition, So far as it Relates to the Prohibition of Theatrical Exhibitions. Philadelphia: William Young, 1793.
Allen, Richard and Absalom Jones. *A Narrative of the Proceedings of the Black People During the Late Awful Calamity in Philadelphia*. Philadelphia, 1794.
Articles of Agreement, Asylum Company. Philadelphia: Poulson, 1794.
Brooke, Henry. *Gustavus Vasa, A Tragedy in Five Acts*. Boston: John West, 1794.
Burk, John Daly. *Bunker-Hill, or, The death of General Warren*. Baltimore, MD: Printed by Richard D. Rider, 1808.
Carey, Mathew. *Debates and Proceedings of the General Assembly of Pennsylvania on Memorials Praying for a Repeal or Suspension of the Law Annulling the Charter of the Bank*. Philadelphia: Carey, 1786.
City of Boston Report of Joint Standing Committee on Ordinances of the Nomenclature of Streets. Boston: E. Thwing, 1880, Massachusetts Historical Society.
Cobbett, William. *A Kick for a Bite; or Review upon Review; with a Critical Essay on the Works of Mrs. Rowson*. 2nd edition. Philadelphia: Thomas Bradford, 1796.
Colman, George. *The Mountaineers, A Comic Opera*. Boston: Joseph Press, 1795.
Constitution of the Boston Tontine Association. Boston: Benjamin Russell, 1791.
Constitution and Nominations of the Subscribers to the Tontine Coffee House. New York, 1796.

Cowley, Hannah. *The Belle's Stratagem.* Boston: Apollo Press, 1794.

Who's the Dupe? New York: David Longworth, 1807.

Diary of William Dunlap (1766–1839) the memoirs of a dramatist, theatrical manager, painter, critic, novelist, and historian. 3 vols. New York: Printed for the New-York Historical Society, 1930.

"Diary of John Rowe." *Proceedings of the Massachusetts Historical Society.* Second series, 10 (1896).

Dunlap, William. *André.* New York: T. & J. Swords, 1789.

"Extracts from the Diary of Nathaniel Cutting." *Proceedings of the Massachusetts Historical Society* 12 (1873).

Gardiner, John. *The Speech of John Gardiner.* Boston: Apollo Press, 1792.

"The Glass, or Speculation: A Poem Containing an Account of the Ancient and Genius of the Modern, Speculators." New York, 1791.

Haliburton, William. "Effects of the Stage on the Manners of the People: and the Propriety of Encouraging and Establishing a Virtuous Theater: By a Bostonian." Boston: Young & Etheridge, 1792.

Higginson, Stephen. *The Writings of Laco.* Boston, 1789.

Journal of the House of Representatives of Massachusetts, 1767–1768. Boston: Massachusetts Historical Society, 1975.

"The Launch: a federal song." Newburyport, MA (?), 1798 (?).

Minutes of the Common Council, Volume I, February 10, 1784–April 2, 1793. City of New York, 1917.

Minutes of the General Assembly, 1789. Pennsylvania: Zacariah Poulson, 1790.

Martin, Alexander. *Play of Columbus.* Philadelphia: Benjamin Franklin Bache, 1798.

Milns, William. *All in a Bustle; or The New House.* New York: Literary Printing Office, 1798.

Murdock, John. *The Triumphs of Love, or Happy Reconciliation.* Philadelphia: R. Folwell, 1795.

The Politicians, or A State of Things. Philadelphia, 1798.

The Beau Metamorphasized, or The Generous Maid. Philadelphia: Joseph C. Charless, 1800.

Murphy, Arthur. *The Way to Keep Him.* New York: David Longworth, 1817.

Murray, Judith Sargent. *The Gleaner, A Miscellaneous Production in three volumes.* Boston: I. Thomas Andrews and E. T. Andrews, 1798.

Murray, Lindley. *Extracts from the Writings of Divers Eminent Authors of Different Denominations and at Various Periods of Time, Representing the Evils and Pernicious Effects of Stage Plays.* Philadelphia: Benjamin and Jacob Johnson, 1799.

New York Directory and Registry for the Year 1794. New York: William Duncan, 1794.

Nichols, J. H. *Jefferson and liberty; or, Celebration of the fourth of March.* A patriotic tragedy: a picture of the perfidy of corrupt administration, in five acts. Boston: Sold at the Print-Office, Temple Street, 1801.

The Essex junto, or, Quixotic guardian: a comedy, in four acts by a citizen of Massachusetts. Salem, MA: Printed by Nathaniel Coverly, Jun., 1802.

O'Hara, Kane. *Midas, A Burletta in Two Acts.* Boston: Apollo Press, 1794.

O'Keefe, John. *The Poor Soldier: A Comic Opera in Two Acts*. Philadelphia: Henry Taylor, 1791.

The Agreeable Surprise: A Comic Opera in Two Acts. Boston: Apollo Press, 1794.

Paine, Robert Treat. "The Green Mountain Farmer, A New Patriotic Song." Boston: Mr. Linley, 1798.

"Adams and Liberty." Boston, 1798.

Paine, Thomas. *Dissertations on Government, the Affairs of the Bank and Paper Money*. Philadelphia, 1786.

Pennsylvania Archives. Philadelphia: J. Severns and Company, 1852–1856.

Philo Dramaticus, *The Rights of the Drama*. Boston, 1792.

Plan of the Association of the Asylum Company. Philadelphia: Aitken and Son, 1795.

Plan of Association of the North American Land Company. Philadelphia, 1795.

Plan of Association of the Pennsylvania Land Company. Philadelphia, 1797.

Plan of Association of the Pennsylvania Property Company. Philadelphia, 1797.

Plan of Association of the Territorial Company. Philadelphia, 1795.

A Record of the Streets, Alleys, Places, etc. in the City of Boston. Boston: City of Boston Printing Department, 1910.

Register of Deeds. New York City Register's Office.

Roll of Members of the Ancient and Honorable Artillery Company of Massachusetts. Boston, 1895.

Rowe, John. "Diary of John Rowe." *Proceedings of the Massachusetts Historical Society*, Second Series, 10 (1896).

Rowson, Susanna. "America, Commerce, Freedom." Philadelphia, 1794.

Slaves in Algiers. Philadelphia: Wrigley and Berriman, 1794.

Russell, Benjamin. "Address Delivered Before the Massachusetts Charitable Mechanics Association." Boston, 1809.

Songs in the Castle of Andalusia, A Comic Opera, as Performed at the New Theatre, Chesnut Street. Philadelphia: Mathew Carey, 1794. Library Company of Philadelphia.

Statutes at Large of Pennsylvania from 1682–1809. Harrisburg, J. M. Busche, 1869–1915.

"Theatre." (Pamphlet.) Boston, 1794.

Twenty-Second Report of the Record Commissioners United States Direct Tax of 1798, United States Census of 1790, for Boston only. Massachusetts Historical Society.

Tyler, Royall. *The Contrast: A Comedy in Five Acts (published under an Assignment of the Copyright by Thomas Wignell)*. Philadelphia: Prichard and Hall, 1790.

Votes and Proceedings of the Senate, October 1784–April 1785: Journal of the Senate of the State of New York. New York: S. Loudon, Printer to the State, 1785.

Warren, Mercy Otis. *Sans souci, alias, Free and easy, or, An evening's peep into a polite circle*. Boston: Warden and Russell, 1785.

White, William Charles. *Orlando; or, Parental persecution*. Boston: Printing by John Russell, 1797.

The Clergyman's Daughter. Boston: Joshua Belcher, 1810.

The Poor Lodger. Boston: Joshua Belcher, 1811.

Avowals of a Republican. Worcester: Isaac Sturtevant, 1813.

Wilson, James. *Considerations on the Bank of North America*. Philadelphia: Hall and Sellers, 1785.

Secondary sources

Agnew, Jean-Christophe. *Worlds Apart: Theatre and the Marketplace in Anglo-American Thought, 1550–1750*. Cambridge: Cambridge University Press, 1986.

Alden, John. "A Season in Federal Street: J.B. Williamson and the Boston Theatre, 1796–1797." *Proceedings of the American Antiquarian Society* 65 (1955): 9–74.

Anderson, Benedict. *Imagined Communities: Reflections on the Origins and Spread of Nationalism*. London: Verso Editions, 1983.

Arbuckle, Robert D. *Pennsylvania Speculator and Patriot: The Entrepreneurial John Nicholson, 1757–1800*. University Park: Pennsylvania State University Press, 1975.

Arnold, Douglas M. *A Republican Revolution: Ideology and Politics in Pennsylvania, 1776–1790*. New York: Garland Publishing, 1989.

Baltzell, E. Digby. *Puritan Boston and Quaker Philadelphia: Two Protestant Ethics and the Spirit of Class Authority and Leadership*. New York: Macmillan Publishing Co., 1979.

Banner, Jr., James M. *To the Hartford Convention: The Federalists and the Origins of Party Politics in Massachusetts, 1789–1815*. New York: Alfred A. Knopf, 1970.

Banning, Lance. *The Jeffersonian Persuasion: Evolution of a Party Ideology*. Ithaca: Cornell University Press, 1978.

Bercovitch, Sacvan. *Rites of Assent: Transformations in the Symbolic Construction of America*. New York: Routledge, 1993.

Berthoff, Rowland. "Independence and Attachment, Virtue and Interest: From Republican Citizen to Free Enterprise, 1787–1837," in *Uprooted Americans: Essays to Honor Oscar Handlin*. Boston: Little, Brown, and Company, 1979.

Blackmar, Elizabeth. *Manhattan for Rent, 1785–1850*. Ithaca, NY: Cornell University Press, 1989.

Bockelman, Wayne and Owen Ireland. "The Internal Revolution in Pennsylvania; an Ethnic-Religious Interpretation." *Pennsylvania History* 41/2 (April 1974): 125–161.

Bradford, Alden. *History of Massachusetts, from 1764 to July 1775*. Boston: Richardson and Lord, 1822.

Breen, T. H. " 'Baubles of Britain': The American and Consumer Revolutions of the Eighteenth Century." *Past and Present* 119 (May 1996): 73–104.

Brewer, John. *Pleasures of the Imagination: English Culture in the Eighteenth Century*. New York: Farrar, Straus, & Giroux, 1997.

Brigham, Clarence S. *History and Bibliography of American Newspapers, 1690–1820*, 2 vols. Cambridge, MA: Harvard University Printing Office, 1947.

Brigham, David R. *Public Culture in the Early Republic: Peale's Museum and Its Audience*. Washington: Smithsonian Institution Press, 1995.

Brobeck, Stephen. "Changes in the Composition and Structure of Philadelphia Elite Groups, 1765–1790." Ph.D. dissertation, University of Pennsylvania, 1973.

Brooke, John L. "Ancient Lodges and Self-Created Societies: Voluntary Association and the Public Sphere in the Early Republic," in Ronald Hoffman and Peter J. Albert, eds., *Launching the Extended Republic: The Federalist Era*. Charlottesville, VA: University Press of Virginia, 1996.

Brooks, Lynn Matluck. "The Philadelphia Dancing Assembly in the Early Eighteenth Century." *Dance Research Journal* 21/1 (Spring 1989): 1–6.

"Emblem of Gaiety, Love and Legislation: Dance in Eighteenth-Century Philadelphia." *Pennsylvania Magazine of History and Biography* 115 (January 1991): 63–89.

Brown, Jared. *Theatre in America During the Revolution.* Cambridge: Cambridge University Press, 1995.

Brown, Richard E. *Middle-Class Democracy and the Revolution in Massachusetts, 1691–1780.* Ithaca: Cornell University Press, 1955.

Brown, Thomas Allston. *A History of the American Stage, containing biographical sketches of nearly every member of the profession that has appeared on the American Stage from 1733–1870.* New York: Burt Franklin, 1969.

Bryan, George B. *American Theatrical Regulation, 1607–1900.* Metuchen, NJ: Scarecrow Press, 1993.

Buckingham, Joseph Tinker. *Annals of the Massachusetts Charitable Mechanics Association.* Boston, 1853.

Buel, Jr., Richard. *Securing the Revolution: Ideology and American Politics, 1789–1815.* Ithaca: Cornell University Press, 1972.

Burrows, Edwin G. and Mike Wallace. *Gotham: A History of New York City to 1898.* New York: Oxford University Press, 1999.

Bushman, Richard L. *The Refinement of America: Persons, Houses, Cities.* New York: Random House, 1992.

Campbell, Charles. *Some Materials to Serve for a Brief Memoir of John Daly Burk.* Albany: J. Munsell, 1868.

Canary, Robert H. *William Dunlap.* New York: Twayne, 1970.

Clapp, Jr., William Warland. *A Record of the Boston Stage.* New York: Benjamin Blom, 1968.

Coad, Oral Sumner. *William Dunlap: A Study of His Life and Works and His Place in Contemporary Culture.* New York: Russell and Russell, 1962.

Conroy, David W. *In Public Houses: Drink and the Revolution of Authority in Colonial Massachusetts.* Chapel Hill, NC: University of North Carolina Press, 1995.

Cronin, James E., ed. *Diary of Elihu Hubbard Smith, 1771–1798,* Philadelphia: American Philosophical Society, 1973.

Dalzell, Jr., Robert F. *Enterprising Elite: The Boston Associates and the World They Made.* Cambridge, MA: Harvard University Press, 1987.

Davis, Peter A. "Puritan mercantilism and the politics of anti-theatrical legislation in colonial America," in Ron Engle and Tice Miller, eds., *The American Stage: Social and economic issues from the colonial period to the present.* Cambridge: Cambridge University Press, 1993.

DePauw, Linda Grant. *The Eleventh Pillar: New York State and the Federal Constitution.* Ithaca, NY: Cornell University Press, 1966.

Doerflinger, Thomas M. *A Vigorous Spirit of Enterprise: Merchants and Economic Development in Revolutionary Philadelphia.* Chapel Hill, NC: University of North Carolina Press, 1986.

Dictionary of American Biography, s.v. Austin, Belknap, Blodget, Codman, Higginson, Phillips, Russell, Smith, Tudor. Boston: J. R. Osgood and Company, 1872.

Doty, Gresdna Ann. *The Career of Mrs. Anne Brunton Merry in the American Theatre.* Baton Rouge: Louisiana State University Press, 1971.

Dudden, Faye E. *Women in the American Theatre: Actresses and Audiences, 1790–1870*. New Haven: Yale University Press, 1994.

Dunlap, William. *History of the American Theatre*. 3 vols. in 1. New York: Burt Franklin, 1963.

Durang, Charles. *The Philadelphia Stage: From 1749 to 1821*, Series I, in the *Philadelphia Sunday Dispatch*, May 7, 1854 to June 29, 1854.

Durham, Weldon B., ed. *American Theatre Companies, 1749–1887*. New York: Greenwood Press, 1986.

Dye, William. "Pennsylvania *versus* the Theatre," *Pennsylvania Magazine of History and Biography* 55 (1931): 333–373.

Elkins, Stanley and Eric McKitrick. "The Founding Fathers: Young Men of the Revolution." *Political Science Quarterly* 76 (June 1961): 181–216.

The Age of Federalism: The Early American Republic, 1788–1800. New York: Oxford University Press, 1993.

Ellis, Joseph J. *After the Revolution: Profiles of Early American Culture*. New York: W. W. Norton and Company, 1979.

Evelev, John. "*The Contrast*: The Problem of Theatricality and Political and Social Crisis in Postrevolutionary America." *Early American Literature* 31/1 (1996): 74–97.

Fitzgerald, Percy. *The Kembles, Volume Two*. New York: Benjamin Blom, 1969.

Fliegelman, Jay. *Declaring Independence: Jefferson, Natural Language, and the Culture of Performance*. Stanford: Stanford University Press, 1993.

Foner, Philip S., ed. *The Democratic-Republican Societies, 1790–1800: A Documentary Sourcebook of Constitutions, Declarations, Addresses, Resolutions, and Toasts*. Westport, CT: Greenwood Press, 1976.

Ford, Paul Leicester. *Washington and the Theatre*. New York: Burt Franklin, 1970.

Formisano, Ronald. *The Transformation of Political Culture: Massachusetts Parties, 1790s–1840s*. New York: Oxford University Press, 1983.

Goebel, Julius, ed. *The Law Practice of Alexander Hamilton, documents and commentary*. 5 vols. New York: Columbia University Press, 1964–1981.

Goodman, Paul. *The Democratic-Republicans of Massachusetts: Politics in a Young Republic*. Cambridge, MA: Harvard University Press, 1964.

Gough, Robert J. "Toward a Theory of Class and Social Conflict: A Social History of Wealthy Philadelphians, 1775 and 1800." Ph.D. dissertation, University of Pennsylvania.

Greene, Jack P. *Pursuits of Happiness: The Social Development of Early Modern British Colonies and the Formation of American Culture*. Chapel Hill, NC: University of North Carolina Press, 1988.

Grimsted, David. *Melodrama Unveiled: American Theater and Culture, 1800–1850*. Berkeley: University of California Press, 1968.

Griswold, Rufus Wilmont. *The Republican Court, Or American Society in the Days of Washington*. New York: D. Appleton and Company, 1855.

Hall, Peter Dobkin. *The Organization of American Culture, 1700–1900: Private Institutions, Elites, and the Origins of American Nationality*. New York: New York University Press, 1982.

Hall, Van Beck. *Politics Without Parties, Massachusetts, 1780–1791*. Pittsburgh: University of Pittsburgh Press, 1972.

Hamilton, Allan McLane. *The Intimate Life of Alexander Hamilton, based chiefly on original family letters and documents, many of which have never been published*. New York: C. Scribner's Sons, 1910.

Hammond, Bray. *Banks and Politics in America from the Revolution to the Civil War*. Princeton: Princeton University Press, 1957.

Havens, Daniel F. *The Columbian Muse of Comedy: The Development of a Native Tradition in Early American Social Comedy, 1787–1845*. Carbondale: Southern Illinois University Press, 1973.

Hench, John Bixler. "The Newspaper in a Republic: Boston's *Centinel* and *Chronicle*, 1784–1801". Ph.D. dissertation, Clark University, 1979.

Henderson, Mary C. *City and the Theatre: New York Playhouses from Bowling Green to Times Square*. Clifton, NJ: James T. White & Co., 1975.

Herr, John Harold. "Thomas Wignell and the Chesnut Street Theatre." Ph.D. dissertation, Michigan State University, 1969.

Hill, Frank Pierce. *American Plays, printed 1714–1830: A Bibliographical Record*. New York: Burt Franklin, 1972.

Hornblow, Arthur. *A History of the Theatre in America: From Its Beginnings to the Present Time*, vol. I. Philadelphia: J. B. Lippincott Company, 1919.

Ireland, Joseph N. *Records of the New York Stage, 1750–1860*. New York: B. Blom, 1966.

Ireland, Owen. "The Ethnic-Religious Dimension of Pennsylvania Politics, 1778–1779." *William and Mary Quarterly*, 3rd series, 30/3 (July 1973): 423–449.

"The Crux of Politics: Religion and Party in Pennsylvania, 1778–1789." *William and Mary Quarterly*, 3rd series, 42/4 (October 1985): 453–476.

"The People's Triumph: The Federalist Majority in Pennsylvania, 1787–1788." *Pennsylvania History*, 56/2 (1989): 93–113.

Religion, Ethnicity, and Politics: Ratifying the Constitution in Pennsylvania. University Park: Pennsylvania State University Press, 1995.

Isaacs, Rhys. *The Transformation of Virginia, 1740–1790*. Chapel Hill, NC: Published by the Institute of Early American History and Culture, Williamsburg, VA, by the University of North Carolina Press, 1982.

Kay, Jane Holtz. *Lost Boston*. Boston: Houghton Mifflin Company, 1980.

Kerber, Linda K. *Federalists in Dissent: Imagery and Ideology in Jeffersonian America*. Ithaca: Cornell University Press, 1970.

Kirker, Harold and James. *Bulfinch's Boston, 1787–1817*. New York: Oxford University Press, 1964.

Kornblith, Gary, J. "Artisan Federalism: New England Mechanics and the Political Economy of the 1790s," in Ronald Hoffman and Peter J. Albert, eds., *Launching the Extended Republic: The Federalist Era*. Charlottesville, VA: University Press of Virginia, 1996.

Kritzer, Amelia Howe. "Playing with Republican Motherhood: self-representation in plays by Susanna Haswell Rowson and Judith Sargent Murray." *Early American Literature* 31/2 (1966): 150–166.

Lair, Meredith. "Red Coat Theater: Negotiating Identity in Occupied Philadelphia, 1777–1778." Unpublished paper, Pennsylvania State University History Department, 1997.

Lambert, Frank. *Pedlar in Divinity: George Whitfield and the Transatlantic Revivals, 1737–1770*. Princeton, NJ: Princeton University Press, 1994.

Lamoreaux, Naomi R. *Insider Lending: Banks, personal connections, and economic development in industrial New England*. Cambridge: Cambridge University Press, 1994.

Launitz-Schurer, Leopold. *Loyal Whigs and Revolutionaries: The Making of the Revolution in New York, 1765–1766*. New York: New York University Press, 1980.

Link, Eugene Perry. *Democratic-Republican Societies, 1790–1800*. New York: Columbia University Press, 1942.

Lubow, Lisa B. "From Carpenter to Capitalist: The Business of Building in Post-Revolutionary Boston," in Conrad Edick Wright and Katheryn P. Viens, eds., *Entrepreneurs: the Boston Business Community, 1700–1850*. Boston: Massachusetts Historical Society and Northeastern University Press, 1997.

McKenzie, Ruth Harsha. "Organization, Production, and Management at the Chestnut Street Theatre, Philadelphia from 1791 to 1820." Ph.D. dissertation, Stanford University, 1952.

McNamara, Brooks. *The American Playhouse in the Eighteenth Century*. Cambridge, MA: Harvard University Press, 1969.

Maier, Pauline. *The Old Revolutionaries: Political Lives in the Time of Samuel Adams*. New York: Knopf, distributed by Random House, 1980.

"The Debate Over Incorporations: Massachusetts in the Early Republic," in Conrad Edick Wright, ed., *Massachusetts and the New Nation*. Boston: Massachusetts Historical Society and Northeastern University Press, 1992.

Main, Jackson Turner. *The Anti-Federalists: Critics of the Constitution, 1781–1788*. New York: W. W. Norton and Company, 1961.

Mason, Jeffrey H. and J. Ellen Gainor, eds. *Performing America: Cultural Nationalism in American Theater*. Ann Arbor, MI: University of Michigan Press, 1999.

Matson, Cathy. "Public Vices, Private Benefit: William Duer and His Circle, 1776–1792," in William Pencak and Conrad Edick Wright, eds., *New York and the Rise of American Capitalism: Economic Development and the Social and Political History of an American State, 1780–1870*. New York: New-York Historical Society, 1989.

Meserve, Walter J. and William R. Reardon, eds. *Satiric Comedies*. Bloomington: Indiana University Press, 1969.

Mitchell, Stewart, ed. *New Letters of Abigail Adams, 1788–1801*. Boston: Houghton Mifflin Company, 1947.

Moody, Richard M. *Dramas for the American Theatre, 1762–1909*. Boston: Houghton Mifflin Company, 1969.

Moy, James S. "The Greenwich Street Theatre, 1797–1799," *Theatre Survey* 20/2 (November 1979): 15–26.

Nash, Gary B. *The Urban Crucible: The Northern Seaports and the Origins of the American Revolution*. Cambridge, MA: Harvard University Press, 1986.

Quakers and Politics; Pennsylvania 1681–1726, new edition. Boston: Northeastern University Press, 1993.

Nathans, Heather S. "'All of the Federalist School?': Choosing Sides and Creating Identities in the Boston Theatre Wars." *New England Theatre Journal* 11 (2000): 1–18.

———. "Trampling Native Genius: John Murdock *Versus* The Chestnut Street Theatre." *Journal of American Drama and Theatre*, 14/1 (2002): 29–43.

Nevins, Allan. *History of the Bank of New York and Trust Company, 1784–1934*. New York: Arno Press, 1976.

Newell, Margaret E. "A Revolution in Economic Thought: Currency and Development in Eighteenth-Century Massachusetts," in Conrad Edick Wright and Katheryn P. Viens, eds., *Entrepreneurs: The Boston Business Community, 1700–1850*. Boston: Massachusetts Historical Society and Northeastern University Press, 1997.

Newman, Simon P. *Parades, and the Politics of the Street: Festive Culture in the Early Republic*. Philadelphia: University of Pennsylvania Press, 1997.

Nobles, Gregory H. "'Yet the Old Republicans Still Persevere': Samuel Adams, John Hancock, and the Crisis of Popular Leadership in Revolutionary Massachusetts, 1775–1790," in Ronald Hoffman and Peter J. Albert, eds., *The Transforming Hand of Revolution*. Charlottesville, VA: University Press of Virginia, 1995.

Odell, George C. *Annals of the New York Stage*. 15 vols. New York: Columbia University Press, 1927–1949.

Patterson, Stephen E. *Political Parties in Revolutionary Massachusetts*. Madison, WI: University of Wisconsin Press, 1973.

Pease, William H. and Jane H. Pease. *The Web of Progress: Private Values and Public Styles in Boston and Charleston, 1828–1843*. Athens, GA: University of Georgia Press, 1991.

Pencak, William. "In Search of the American Character: French Travelers in Eighteenth Century Pennsylvania." *Pennsylvania History* 55/1 (January 1988): 2–30.

Pencak, William and Conrad Edick Wright, eds. *New York and the Rise of American Capitalism: Economic Development and the Social and Political History of an American State, 1780–1870*. New York: New-York Historical Society, 1989.

Pernick, Martin S. "Parties, Politics, and Pestilence: Epidemic Yellow Fever in Philadelphia and the Rise of the First Party System," in *A Melancholy Scene of Devastation: The Public Response to the 1793 Philadelphia Yellow Fever Epidemic*. Philadelphia: Science History Publications, 1997.

Pollock, Thomas Clark. *The Philadelphia Theatre in the Eighteenth Century, Together with the Day Book of the Same Period*. New York: Greenwood Press, 1968.

Porter, Susan L. *With an Air Debonair: Musical Theatre in America, 1785–1815*. Washington: Smithsonian Institution Press, 1991.

Potter-McKinnon, Janice. *The Liberty We Seek: Loyalist Ideology in Colonial New York and Massachusetts*. Cambridge, MA: Harvard University Press, 1983.

The Quiet Philanthropy, 1795–1995. Massachusetts Charitable Mechanics Association, 1995.

Quinn, Arthur Hobson, ed. *Representative American Plays: From 1767 to the Present Day*. 6th edition. New York: Appleton-Century-Crofts, Inc., 1930.

Ramusson, Ethel E. "Democratic Environment: Aristocratic Aspiration." *Pennsylvania Magazine of History and Biography* 90/2 (April 1966): 155–182.

Rankin, Hugh. *The Theatre in Colonial America*. Chapel Hill, NC: University of North Carolina Press, 1965.

Ranlet, Philip. *The New York Loyalists*. Knoxville, TN: University of Tennessee Press, 1986.

Remer, Rosalind. "Old Lights and New Money: A Note on Religion, Economics, and the Social Order in 1740 Boston." *William and Mary Quarterly*, 3rd series, 47/4 (October 1990): 566–573.

Richards, Jeffrey H. *Theatre Enough: American Culture and the Metaphor of the World Stage, 1607–1789*. Durham, NC: Duke University Press, 1991.

   Mercy Otis Warren. New York: Twayne Publishers, Simon and Schuster Macmillan, 1995.

Richards, Jeffrey H., ed. *Early American Drama*. New York: Penguin Group, 1997.

Richardson, Gary A. "Plays and Playwrights, 1800–1865," in Don B. Wilmeth and Christopher Bigsby, eds., *The Cambridge History of American Theatre, Volume I: Beginnings to 1870*. Cambridge: Cambridge University Press, 1998.

Rinehart, Lucy Elizabeth. "'A Most Conspicuous Theatre': The Rise of American Theater and Drama, 1789–1829." Ph.D. dissertation, Columbia University, 1994.

   "A Nation's 'Noble Spectacle': Royall Tyler's *The Contrast* as Metatheatrical Commentary." *American Drama* 3/2 (1994): 29–52.

   "'Manly Exercises': Post-Revolutionary Performances of Authority in the Theatrical Career of William Dunlap." *Early American Literature* 36/2 (2001): 263–293.

Riordan, Liam. "'O dear, what can the matter be?': Political Culture and Popular Song in Benjamin Carr's *Federal Overture*." Unpublished paper, December 1995.

Rosswurm, Stephen. "Class Relations, Political Economy, and Society in Philadelphia," in Catherine E. Hutchins, ed., *Shaping a National Culture: The Philadelphia Experience, 1750–1800*. Winterthur, DE: Winterthur Museum, 1994.

Savage, Edward H., ed. *Boston Events: Boston for 250 Years from Blackstone to O'Brien, every notable occurrence during above period*. Boston: Tolman and White Printers, 1884.

Schudson, Michael. "Culture and Integration of National Societies." *International Social Science Journal*, 46 (1994): 63–81.

Schultz, Ronald. *The Republic of Labor: Philadelphia Artisans and the Politics of Class, 1720–1830*. New York: Oxford University Press, 1993.

Schweitzer, Mary McKinney. "The Spatial Organization of Federalist Philadelphia, 1790." *Journal of Interdisciplinary History* 24/1 (Summer 1993): 32–57.

   "The Economy of Philadelphia and Its Hinterland," in Catherine E. Hutchins, ed., *Shaping a National Culture: The Philadelphia Experience, 1750–1800*. Winterthur, DE: Winterthur Museum, 1994.

Seilhamer, George O. *History of the American Theatre: New Foundations*. Philadelphia: Globe Printing House, 1891.

Shand-Tucci, Douglas. *Built in Boston: City and Suburb, 1800–1950*. Amherst: University of Massachusetts Press, 1988.

Shaw, Peter. *American Patriots and the Rituals of Revolution*. Cambridge, MA: Harvard University Press, 1981.

Sherman, Susanne Ketchum. *Comedies Useful: Southern Theatre History, 1775–1812*, ed. Lucy B. Pilkinton. Williamsburg, VA: Celest Press, 1998.

Shiffler, Harrold C. "Religious Opposition to the Eighteenth-Century Philadelphia Stage." *Educational Theatre Journal* 14 (October 1962): 214–223.

Shils, Edward. *Center and Periphery: Essays in Macrosociology*. Chicago: University of Chicago Press, 1975.

Silverman, Kenneth. *A Cultural History of the American Revolution*. New York: Thomas Y. Crowell and Co., 1976.

Simpson, Henry. *The Lives of Eminent Philadelphians, Now Deceased*. Philadelphia: William Brotherhead, 1859.

Smith, Billy G. "Inequality in late Colonial Philadelphia: A Note on Its Nature and Growth." *William and Mary Quarterly*, 3rd series, 41/4 (October 1984): 629–645.

The *"Lower Sort": Philadelphia's Laboring People, 1750–1800*. Ithaca: Cornell University Press, 1990.

Smith, John E. *Jonathan Edwards: Puritan, Preacher, and Philosopher*. South Bend, IN: University of Notre Dame Press, 1992.

Smith, Susan Harris. *American Drama: The Bastard Art*. Cambridge: Cambridge University Press, 1997.

Spaulding, E. Wilder. *New York in the Critical Period, 1783–1789*. New York: Columbia University Press, 1932.

Stiles, Jennifer. "Import or Immigrant? The Representation of Blacks and Irish on the American Stage from 1767–1856." *Journal of American Drama and Theatre* 12/2 (Spring 2000): 38–54.

Stine, Richard D. "The Philadelphia Theater, 1682–1829: Its Growth as a Cultural Institution." Ph.D. dissertation, University of Pennsylvania, 1951.

Stoddard, Richard. "The Haymarket Theatre, Boston." *Educational Theatre Journal* 25 (March 1975): 63–70.

Stokes, Isaac N. *The Iconography of Manhattan Island, 1498–1909*. 6 vols. Union, NJ: Lawbook Exchange; Mansfield Centre, CT: Martino Fine Books, 1998.

Strand, Ginger. "The Theater and the Republic: Defining Party on Boston's Early Rival Stages," in Jeffrey H. Mason and J. Ellen Gainor, eds., *Performing America: Cultural Nationalism in American Theatre*. Ann Arbor: University of Michigan Press, 1999.

Sweeney, Kevin M. "High Style Vernacular: Lifestyles of the Colonial Elite," in Cary Carson, Ronald Hoffman, and Peter J. Albert, eds., *Of Consuming Interest: The Style of Life in the Eighteenth Century*. Charlottesville, VA: University Press of Virginia, 1994.

Tanselle, G. Thomas. *Royall Tyler*. Cambridge, MA: Harvard University Press, 1967.

Teute, Fredrika J. "Sensibility in the Forest: Elihu Hubbard Smith's *Edwin and Angelina; or The Banditti*." Paper presented at the Second Biennial Conference of the Society for Early Americanists, 2001.

Thornton, Tamara Plakins. *Cultivating Gentlemen: The Meaning of Country Life Among the Boston Elite, 1785–1860*. New Haven: Yale University Press, 1989.

Thwing, Annie Haven. *Inhabitants and Estates of the Town of Boston, 1630–1800*. Boston: New England Historic Genealogical Society, 2001.

The Crooked and Narrow Streets of Boston, 1630–1822. Boston: Marshal Jones Company, 1920.

Tinkcom, Harry Marlin. *The Republicans and Federalists in Pennsylvania, 1790–1801*. Harrisburg: Pennsylvania Historical and Museum Commission, 1950.

Travers, Len. *Celebrating the Fourth: Independence Day and the Rites of Nationalism in the Early Republic*. Amherst: University of Massachusetts Press, 1997.

Tyler, John W. "Persistence and Change within the Boston Business Community," in Conrad Edick Wright and Katheryn P. Viens, eds., *Entrepreneurs: the Boston Business Community, 1700–1850*. Boston: Massachusetts Historical Society and Northeastern University Press, 1997.

Vaughn, Jack A. *Early American Dramatists: From the Beginnings to 1900*. New York: Frederick Ungar Publishing Company, 1981.

Ver Steeg, Clarence L. *Robert Morris: Revolutionary Financier, with an Analysis of his Earlier Career*. Philadelphia: University of Pennsylvania Press, 1954.

Waldstreicher, David. *In the Midst of Perpetual Fetes: The Making of American Nationalism, 1776–1820*. Chapel Hill, NC: University of North Carolina Press, 1997.

Warner, Michael. *The Letters of the Republic: Publication and the Public Sphere in Eighteenth-Century America*. Cambridge, MA: Harvard University Press, 1990.

Warner, Jr., Sam Bass. *The Private City: Philadelphia in Three Periods of Its Growth*. Philadelphia: University of Pennsylvania Press, 1987.

Warren, Charles. "Samuel Adams and the Sans Souci Club in 1785." *Proceedings of the Massachusetts Historical Society* 60 (1927).

Jacobin or Junto, Or Early American Politics as Viewed in the Diary of Dr. Nathaniel Ames, 1758–1822. Cambridge, MA: Harvard University Press, 1931.

Watson, John. *Annals of Philadelphia and Pennsylvania*. 2 vols. Philadelphia: Leary, Stuart, and Company, 1909.

Watts, Steven. *The Republic Reborn: War and the Making of Liberal America, 1790–1820*. Baltimore: The Johns Hopkins University Press, 1987.

Werner, Robert. *Tammany Hall*. New York: Doubleday, Doran & Company, 1928.

Westcott, Thompson. *The Historic Mansions and Buildings of Philadelphia, with Some Notice of Their Owners and Occupants*. Philadelphia: Porter and Coates, 1877.

Weyler, Karen A. "A Speculating Spirit: Trade, Speculation, and Gambling in Early American Fiction." *Early American Literature* 31/3 (1996): 207–242.

Wharton, Edith. *The Age of Innocence*. Mineola, NY: Dover Publications, 1997.

Whitehill, Walter Muir. *Boston: A Topographical History*, 2nd edition. Cambridge, MA: Belknap Press of Harvard University Press, 1968.

Wiebe, Robert H. *The Opening of American Society: From the Adoption of the Constitution to the Eve of Disunion*. New York: Random House, 1984.

Wilmer, Steve. "Partisan Theatre in the Early Years of the United States." *Theatre Survey* 40/2 (1999): 1–25.

Wilmeth, Don B. *Staging the Nation: Plays from the American Theater, 1787–1909*. Boston: Bedford Books, 1998.

Wilmeth, Don B. and Christopher Bigsby, eds., *The Cambridge History of American Theatre, Volume I: Beginnings to 1870*. Cambridge: Cambridge University Press, 1998.

Wilmeth, Don B. and Tice L. Miller, eds. *The Cambridge Guide to American Theatre*. Cambridge: Cambridge University Press, 1993.

Wilson, James Grant and John Fiske, eds. *Appleton's Cyclopaedia of American Biography*. New York: Appleton and Company, 1900.

Wilson, Janet. "The Bank of North America and Pennsylvania Politics, 1781–1787." *Pennsylvania Magazine of History and Biography* 66/1 (January 1942): 3–28.

Witham, Barry, ed. *Theatre in the Colonies and United States, 1750–1915, a Documentary History*. Cambridge: Cambridge University Press, 1996.

Withington, Ann Fairfax. *Toward a More Perfect Union: Virtue and the Formation of American Republics*. New York: Oxford University Press, 1991.

Wolter, Jürgen C., ed. *The Dawning of American Drama: American Dramatic Criticism, 1746–1915*. Westport, CT: Greenwood Press, 1993.

Wood, Gordon S. *The Radicalism of the American Revolution*. New York: Alfred A. Knopf, 1992.

  The Creation of the American Republic, 1776–1787. New York: W. W. Norton and Co., 1993.

Wood, William B. *Personal Recollections of the Stage*. Philadelphia: Henry Carey Baird, 1855.

Wright, Conrad Edick. *The Transformation of Charity in Postrevolutionary New England*. Boston: Northeastern University Press, 1992.

Wright, Conrad Edick and Katheryn P. Viens, eds. *Entrepreneurs: the Boston Business Community, 1700–1850*. Boston: Massachusetts Historical Society, distributed by Northeastern University Press, 1997.

Wright, Robert E. "Thomas Willing (1731–1821): Philadelphia Financier and Forgotten Founding Father." *Pennsylvania History* 63/4 (Autumn 1996): 525–561.

  Origins of Commercial Banking in America, 1750–1800. Lanham, MD: Rowman & Littlefield, 2001.

Wyatt, Edward Avery. "John Daly Burk: Patriot, Playwright, Historian," in *Southern Sketches 7*. Charlottesville, VA: Historical Publishing Company, 1936.

Young, Alfred F. *The Democratic-Republicans of New York: The Origins, 1763–1797*. Chapel Hill, NC: University of North Carolina Press, 1967.

Young, Eleanor. *Forgotten Patriot: Robert Morris*. New York: Macmillan Company, 1950.

Young, William C. *Documents of American Theater History: Famous American Playhouses, 1716–1899*, vol. I. Chicago: American Library Association, 1973.

Index

abolition (*see also* Democratic-Republican party): 93, 94, 95
Adams, Abigail: 152
Adams, John: 11, 42, 105, 109, 151, 165
Adams, Samuel: 39, 48, 50, 56, 57, 59
adaptations (or alterations) of plays: 10–11, 85–87
"Affair of the Ferrymen" (New York): 158–159
African-Americans (Philadelphia) (*see also* abolition): 94–95, 98
Alien and Sedition Acts: 121, 150, 153, 157, 158
All in a Bustle (Milns): 148
Allen, Richard: 94
"America, Commerce, Freedom" (song): 81
American Academy of Arts and Sciences: 56
American Company (*see* Hallam-Douglass Company; Old American Company)
American Revolution
   American theatrical entertainments: 37
   British theatrical entertainments: 38–39, 43
Amory, John: 59
Ancient and Honorable Artillery Company: 107, 174 (Table 2: names of Haymarket Theatre founders with political and social affiliations)
Anderson, Alexander and John (diaries): 136, 145
André (Dunlap): 159–160 (controversy), 161
Anglican: 15, 16, 17, 32, 40
Anti-Constitutionalist (*see also* Federalist): 49
Anti-Federalist (*see also* Democratic-Republican): 54
   Boston: 173 (Table 1: names of Federal Street Theatre founders with political affiliations), 174 (Table 2: names of

Haymarket Theatre founders with political affiliations)
   New York: 179 (Table 3: names of Park Theatre founders with political, social, and financial affiliations)
   Philadelphia: 77, 101, 176 (Table 3: names of Chestnut Street Theatre founders with political, social, and financial affiliations)
anti-theatrical activity: 6, 12, 34, 47, 50
   pre-Revolutionary (*see* Presbyterians; Puritan; Quaker)
   during Revolution: 36, 37, 38–39, 40, 48
   post-war Boston: 56 (*see also* Hancock, John; Adams, Samuel; Puritan)
   post-war New York (*see also* State Constitutionalists): 43, 126
   post-war Philadelphia: (*see also* Quaker): 55
Argus (Boston): 60
artisans (*see also* mechanics): 9, 11, 29, 91, 93
Astor, John Jacob: 169
Asylum (Land) Company: 84, 154
Aurora (also known as the *General Advertiser*): 8, 74, 99, 101–102 (attacks on Theatre and Federalists), 102–103, 152
Austin, Benjamin: 59
Avowals of a Republican (White): 166

Bache, Benjamin Franklin: 74, 81, 99, 152
Bache, Sarah: 68 (letter about the Chestnut Street Theatre)
Bank of New York (The): 35, 127, 128, 129 (theater member affiliation), 130–133 (founding and history), 130 (resistance to Bank), 132 ("scriptomania"), 133, 135, 140, 141, 142 (connection to land speculation), 143 (financial difficulties), 150, 161, 179

239